GRAND STRATEGY IN THE WAR AGAINST TERRORISM

Also in this series

Non-State Threats and Future Wars
edited by Robert J. Bunker

Deterrence in the 21st Century
edited by Max E. Manwaring

Peace Operations Between War and Peace
edited by Erwin A. Schmidl

Towards Responsibility in the New World Disorder: Challenges and Lessons of Peace Operations
edited by Max G. Manwaring and John T. Fishel

Warriors in Peacetime: The Military and Democracy in Latin America
edited by Gabriel Marcella

Defence and the Media in Time of Limited War
edited by Peter R. Young

GRAND STRATEGY IN THE WAR AGAINST TERRORISM

Editors
THOMAS R. MOCKAITIS
De Paul University, Chicago

PAUL B. RICH
University of Cambridge

FRANK CASS
LONDON • PORTLAND, OR

First published in 2003 in Great Britain by
FRANK CASS AND COMPANY LIMITED
Crown House, 47 Chase Side
Southgate, London N14 5BP

and in the United States of America by
FRANK CASS
c/o ISBS, 920 NE 58th Avenue, Suite 300,
Portland, Oregon 97213-3786

Website: *www.frankcass.com*

British Library Cataloguing in Publication Data

Grand strategy in the war against terrorism
1.War on Terrorism, 2001- 2.Strategy 3.Special operations
(Military science) 4.Islam and terrorism 5.World politics,
1995-2005
I.Mockaitis, Thomas R., 1955- II.Rich, Paul B., 1950-
III.Small wars and insurgencies
363.3'2'0973

ISBN 0-7146-5313-6 (cloth)
ISBN 0-7146-8268-3 (paper)

Library of Congress Cataloging-in-Publication Data

Grand strategy in the war against terrorism / editors, Thomas R.
Mockaitis, Paul B. Rich – 1st ed.
p. cm.
Includes bibliographical references and index.
ISBN 0-7146-5313-6 (Hardback) – ISBN 0-7146-8268-3 (Paperback)
1. War on Terrorism, 2001–2. Strategy. I. Mockaitis, Thomas R.,
1955– II. Rich, Paul B., 1950– III. Title.
HV6431.G728 2003
973.931–dc22 2003016417

This group of studies first appeared in a Special Issue on 'Grand Strategy in the West Against Terrorism' of *Small Wars & Insurgencies* (ISSN 0959-2318)
14/1 (Spring 2003) published by Frank Cass

Printed in Great Britain by Antony Rowe Ltd., Chippenham, Wilts.

Contents

Preface

The title of this volume names a fervent hope rather than an actual reality. Nothing like a 'grand strategy' currently directs the war on terrorism. Since 11 September 2001, Washington has crafted some ad hoc responses to perceived terrorist threats, focusing in particular on state sponsorship. Following the successful campaign in Afghanistan, the US has moved on to Iraq with a handful of reluctant allies trailing in its wake. Meanwhile a sultry covert war grinds inexorably on, scoring small victories along the way – an arrest here, an assassination there, an occasional interdiction somewhere else. All of these moves target Al Qaeda, affiliated organizations or individuals. Not a single policy initiative addresses the root causes of terrorism.

Each of the following essays addresses an aspect of what should be a comprehensive strategy for the current war. All the authors share some key assumptions. They see terrorism as a weapon, not an end in itself. Al Qaeda and its affiliates operate in a host of countries with the tacit if not active support of at least some segment of the larger population. Each writer recognizes that while military force must be applied, it is neither the only nor even the primary means of confronting the threat.

Special forces have figured prominently in the struggle and will continue to do so because they are best equipped to do civic action and to use force in a highly focused manner. American special forces, however, have concentrated too much on their military task and not enough on their civic action role. Civic action is, in fact, 'winning hearts and minds' by a different name.

'Hearts and minds' has been trivialized without being understood. Stripped of sentiment and ideology it means nothing more than addressing the causes of unrest upon which an insurgency feeds. By addressing these causes threatened states can hope to wean moderates away from extremists and perhaps elicit cooperation that produces sound intelligence upon which military forces can act.

None of these ideas is new. Many of us have been presenting them over the past decade or longer. We have watched counterinsurgency become low-intensity conflict and then morph into operations other than war and now become 'counter-terrorism'. A rose by any other name has just as many thorns. The shape of the threat keeps changing but not its essential nature. The context in which these shadow wars must be fought has, however, changed dramatically. To use a cliché, the world has grown smaller and much more interconnected. Satellites, mobile phones, and the Internet allow for rapid communication to all parts of the globe. They have extended the reach of information and ideas and unavoidably magnified the scope and range of terror. Several of the essays in this issue deal with the crucial aspect of information warfare.

No scholarly work can ever claim to be definitive, least of all one compiled in just over a year since the event it analyzes. Research and publication are, however, part of a dialogue, an on-going conversation in which one work stimulates further study and generates new ideas. With that end in mind we offer this collection of essays in the hope that it will start or at least be part of an exchange that some day leads to a grand strategy in this war that seems likely to be with us for a long time to come.

THOMAS MOCKAITIS, Chicago, Ill.
PAUL RICH, London, June 2003

Introduction

PAUL B. RICH

The terrorist attacks of 11 September 2001and subsequent activities of Al Qaeda and its allies have given vent to considerable debate over the nature and role of international terrorism in the post-Cold War global order. Al Qaeda is one of several of examples of what some analysts see as a new form of 'new' or 'postmodern' international terrorist organisation which is neither securely linked to any one particular state patron nor especially constrained by any limits on the use of violence.[1]

Al Qaeda has proved to be a remarkable and highly adaptive international network of terrorist organisations which, since 11 September 2001, have been capable of regrouping into a series of looser organisations that have launched a series of smaller bomb attacks, of which the most spectacular to date has been the bombing in the island of Bali in October 2002.[2] Al Qaeda has shifted its focus to smaller scale operations using a large number of new recruits and has shown itself capable of responding to the US-led campaign that overthrew the Taliban regime in Afghanistan, depriving it of its major base of operations.

The surprise and ferocity of the attacks have ensured that Al Qaeda and its supposed 'leader' Osama bin Laden a status verging on the mythological in contemporary media portrayals of terrorism. Perhaps much of this is due to a general combination in many Western journalistic circles of fear and fascination. In reality it is likely, as the interior minister of Saudi Arabia, Prince Nayef, has suggested, that bin Laden is really the instrument of a much wider organisation and is only at the 'top' of Al Qaeda from the mass media's point of view.[3] A similar view has been expressed by some Western writers, including the novelist Gore Vidal who has suggested that the figure of a lone crazy man bin Laden has been chosen by a 'Bush junta' in Washington to help persuade the US public to support a war in Afghanistan.[4]

There are certainly some Scarlet Pimpernel qualities to bin Laden who appears to have the capacity to disappear and then miraculously resurface in some new region of the world. Even if bin Laden is eventually killed and Al Qaeda defeated, the organisation will in all likelihood continue to have the capacity to reproduce itself – like a magic broom – and create a whole new series of terrorist organisational networks in the Middle East and| Islamic world that will continue to threaten Western interests and security.

There are then some fantastical qualities to this otherwise grim new pattern in international terrorism. Some analysts have concluded that the September 11 attacks mark a major transformation in the nature of world politics. Fred Halliday, for example, has seen 9/11 as 'two hours that shook the world' and ranked it in historical importance with the assassination of the Archduke Franz Josef in Savajevo in 1914 or the Japanese attack on Pearl Harbor in December 1941.[5] Similarly John Lewis Gaddis has seen the September 11 crisis as destroying the brief post-Cold War order that begun in 1989 with the fall of the Berlin Wall and creating a new international order in which the geographical position and political power of the US can no longer be assumed capable of securing even its own domestic security.[6]

These assessments come in the wake of a series of bleak assessments by terrorism specialists, who have been predicting for some years the growing saliency and threat from international terrorism. Before September 11 the US Department of State's *Patterns of Global Terrorism* indicated that the number of deaths from terrorism world wide was on the increase from 233 in 1999 to 405 in 2000, while casualties rose from 706 to 791. These are of course tiny figures and can be used to justify the view that international terrorism cannot be taken seriously as a major threat to central western strategic interests. However the figures do not reveal the changing pattern of international terrorism by the late 1990s as state-sponsored terrorism by rogue regimes significantly decreased and terrorist groups were forced to search for private forms of sponsorship such as Al Qaeda.[7]

What the September 11 crisis really laid bare was general weakness in Western, and especially US, strategic thinking which still refused to take international terrorism all that seriously and was still hidebound by strategic conceptions derived from the Cold War era. As Gaddis has argued, there was a basic failure of strategic vision in the US and an inability to see how the parts of one administration's policy needed to combine into a larger and more coherent whole.[8] The reasons for this are complex, but relate in part to the evolution of strategy within the central organ of Western Cold War security, NATO, as well as the reluctance of the US to employ military force in the wake of the debacle in Vietnam in the late 1960s and early 1970s.

US strategic thinking during the Cold War was shaped by two dominant imperatives: air power and nuclear power. In both instances US strategy is highly influenced by the cost benefit analysis that underpins the logic of deterrence doctrine. Defence for the US is tightly focused on an enemy's capabilities and directed towards raising the costs for the enemies and lowering those for the US and its allies either by deterring any threatened use of force or responding with overwhelming force when aggression did occur.

This strategic mindset is ill-suited to engaging with modern global terrorism of the kind manifested by Al Qaeda. It is very difficult to raise the costs of terrorism; asymmetric warfare, by its very nature, is war waged on the cheap by people who are willing, if necessary, to die or commit suicide in pursuit of their aims. For Al Qaeda the symbolic value derived from the events of September 11 far outweighs any rational calculus of cost.[9] However it is also evident that calculation of a kind did occur in the planning of the attacks for bin Laden later said in an interview 'we calculated in advance the number of casualties from the enemy, who would be killed based on the position of the tower. We calculated that the floors that would be hit would be three or four.'[10] However this suggests that cost-benefit calculus for terrorists is limited to *means* rather than *ends* whereas for conventional Western strategy the calculus links means *with* ends.

Since the end of the Cold War there has been a slow shift in US strategic thinking away from the gradual projection of military force (as had occurred unsuccessfully in the Vietnamese case) towards a doctrine of decisive force to ensure compellance from recalcitrant regimes. In the process, the conventional distinctions between the political and the military as well as the operational levels between strategic and tactical began to dissolve. Modern warfare took on a fourfold complexion of tactical, operational, strategic and political.

This doctrine – widely known as the Powell Doctrine after the then General Colin Powell's successful employment of it in the 1991 Gulf War against Iraq – was a reflection of the use of new military technologies that included precision strike weapons that could make the projection of force both more decisive and more credible.[11] It was to be confirmed again in Bosnia and Kosovo in the 1990s, though had not been used with any serious purpose against international terrorism before September 11 with the notable exception of the rather disastrous use of cruise missiles against Al Qaeda installations in Afghanistan and Sudan in the wake of the East African embassy bombings in August 1998.[12]

Grand Strategy

It is clear that Western strategic thinking is at an impasse in the wake of September 11 and this collection seeks to contribute to the debate over the nature and course of Western 'grand strategy' in response to the terrorist challenge presented by Al Qaeda and its extremist Islamic allies and supporters. Grand strategy is a contested concept and can have a variety of different meanings. It is rather poorly understood among scholars of International Relations, though on a wider plane there are signs that it is increasingly intruding into public debate.[13] In a conventional nineteenth century sense it is closely linked to a state's ability to project power and force in international relations and is the overall strategy that informs and underpins this.

This conception of grand strategy is still very visible in strategic studies and is reflected, for instance, in the work of the US strategic theorist Edward Luttwak. Luttwak has defined grand strategy in terms of encapsulating 'the highest level of interaction between any parties capable of using unregulated force against one another'.[14] This covers clearly a wide field of interaction between states, international bodies and private organisations in so far as these intrude into major strategic fields dominated by the ability to project military force. However it obviously does not cover all the field of international politics. Relations between states may for long periods not be governed by the dictates of grand strategy. For instance, the relations between the US and Qatar and the other Gulf states throughout the post-war period were not dictated by grand strategy. In the aftermath of the revolution in Iran in 1979, however, this rapidly changed and may again be confirmed if the US chooses to invade Iraq.

This conventional definition of grand strategy has begun to be questioned by academic analysts who have sought to widen its area of compass from narrow military force projection towards a wide range of human activities. These include international institutions, non-governmental bodies, private business and multinational corporations which in many cases play a more significant role in international politics than many states. This has been the approach for instance of the Grand Strategy Project at Yale University in the late 1990s involving such figures as John Ikenberry and Michael Doyle.[15] Ikenberry has in turn initiated a wide debate in the US on the nature of its grand strategy in the post-Cold War context, pointing out that since the 1940s the US has had in effect two grand strategies: one heavily realist in orientation organised around deterrence, containment and the maintenance of a global balance of power and a second one that is broadly liberal in orientation and directed towards the reconstruction of the world economy.

The first grand strategy is mainly concerned with a balance of global military power and is concerned with the adequate projection by the US of military force to secure its long term security. The second on the other hand has a rather wider definition of what 'security' really is and is orientated towards working through the Bretton Woods institutions such as the World Bank and the World Trade Organization (WTO) – successor of the General Agreement on Tariffs and Trade (GATT) that were set up after the Second World War to stabilise the global economy. It was the second of these grand strategies that generally prevailed under the two Clinton administrations in the 1990s at a time when there was no really coherent US military grand strategy rather a series of ad hoc reactions to individual crises such as Somalia, Bosnia and Kosovo.

The two grand strategies stem from different intellectual traditions, though this did not prevent them from more co-existing during the Cold War. They became in effect two component parts of something like an overall US strategy towards the Eastern bloc and underpinned what Ikenberry has seen as two 'historical bargains' that the US struck with its European and Asian allies: one a security bargain in which the US afforded its allies security protection and access to American markets and technology and a second 'liberal bargain' in which these same allies agreed to accept US leadership or hegemony and operate within an agreed politico-economic system.[16]

This grand strategy was beginning to unravel in the immediate aftermath of the Cold War in the 1990s. It has taken the crisis of September 11 to crystallise the broader strategic dilemma the US now faces as it seeks to forge a new global strategy against terrorism The emergence of the US as the sole superpower in a unipolar global order has made Washington less willing to strike the same sort of strategic bargains that it made during the Cold War. The overwhelming superiority of the US compared to its other allies encourages it towards a unilateralist strategy of going it alone. Such a new grand strategy is likely to be far less concerned with international stability as America seeks to isolate and if need be dismantle 'rogue states' such as North Korea and Iraq which it sees as threats to world peace.[17]

Neither of the two grand strategies that saw the US through the Cold War are likely to have the same importance in the post-Cold War period, though a debate rages in Washington over just how much use they may still have. If the central reality is one of global apocalyptic violence then both may need to be seriously downgraded as the US faces up to the prospect of waging global war. There are, though, clearly huge dangers in what Ikenberry calls a new 'neo imperial grand strategy' based on the US unilateralism. 'America's well meaning imperial strategy', he writes 'could undermine the principled multilateral agreements, institutional infrastructure, and cooperative spirit needed for the long-term success of non-proliferation goals.'[18]

The US faces the prospect indeed of 'imperial overstretch' if it seeks to take on by itself a global war against terror without bringing its allies on board as well. If it is to be involved in peacekeeping and state or 'nation building' in failed or weak states which have been breeding grounds for terrorist and insurgent groups then it may find that the older grand strategies still have some relevance. It may still be able to use a limited form of deterrence strategy against states that harbour terrorists while, similarly, it will need the support of global economic institutions to rebuild failed states. So it is not by any means the case that the post-Cold War world is totally different to the one before it.

This raises the question whether a grand strategy against global terrorism might be factored into existing grand strategy rather than define something wholly new and different. It is this question which is now being debated in the wake of the September 11 attacks.[19] Some critics see the US administration's 'war on terror' as really hiding a wider imperial 'grand strategy' that is aiming to overthrow the Iraq regime of Saddam Hussein and gain control of the oil reserves of the Middle East.[20] On the other hand postmodernist writers such as James Der Derian see the whole idea of a grand strategy as an illusion promoted by a military lobby keen to see an increase in arms expenditure.[21]

The concept of grand strategy is thus clearly a considerably contested one and there are different avenues down which it may go. For some analysts it is linked, in the post-Cold War era, to a revival of academic interests in geopolitics, which had long been unfashionable in the post-war years due to its close linkage in the early 1940s with Nazi strategic doctrine. John Lewis Gaddis has suggested that the seismic shift in international politics following the collapse of the Soviet Union provides an opportunity for focusing on geopolitics centred on metaphors derived from geology rather than game theory.[22]

International terrorism, however, is highly adaptive and based on networks that are global in reach. While it may, as in the case of Al Qaeda, make use of particular countries as base areas – Sudan in the early 1990s followed by Afghanistan after 1995 – it has also developed terrorist cells in Europe, Africa, the US and South East Asia. Any grand strategy against this form of international terrorism clearly has to be global in nature. It can no longer assume any dominant state patronage as in the case of older international terrorist movements such as the late Abu Nidal that depended at various stages from support from Syria and Iraq. To this extent, the centrality of Iraq in the current Bush administration's 'war on terror' indicates two separate strands of 'grand strategy' in US strategic thinking – one that is global against Al Qaeda and a second and rather separate one against the Iraqi regime and the threat from its capacity to manufacture weapons of mass destruction. Efforts by some pundits to try and link the two by asserting that Iraq has in some form provided support and backing to Al Qaeda remain very unconvincing with little or no evidence to substantiate this rather far-fetched thesis.[23]

To this extent, then, geopolitics have no immediate and direct linkage to any 'war on terror' against Al Qaeda and other similar international terrorist movements that do not operate in any distinct geographical region. However, at another level, geopolitics may be said to intrude into the debate on counter-terrorist strategy since one of the main aims of any such strategy is a proactive effort to undermine the organisation's use of the Islamic religion to bolster and legitimise its aims. Here we enter the difficult arena of inter-cultural or cross 'civilisational' interaction which will be discussed more fully in the third section of this introduction. Any such dialogue will be concerned to address what Richard Falk has termed the 'geopolitics of exclusion' since within the Islamic world there is a widespread feeling from even moderate Islamic believers that Western media portrayals of Islam are biased and that the Islamic world is still portrayed through an orientalist gloss in the West that views it as culturally inferior. Achieving what Falk terms a 'normative adjustment' may be a protracted and long-term process but is arguably crucial to the ultimate success of any Western 'war on terror'.[24]

Before we discuss the complexities of such an inter-civilisational dialogue to prevent the current conflict degenerating into a civilisational war, it is first necessary to examine the nature of the current international terrorist threat.

The Nature and Significance of Contemporary Terrorism

During the Cold War debate on terrorism tended to be dominated by the wider phenomenon of insurgency and guerrilla warfare. This was frequently located in the colonial context as nationalist and ethnic movements mobilised against European colonial rule and often fell under the rubric of 'revolutionary war' or *guerre revolutionnaire* since it appeared to be the latest phase of a type of warfare that stretched back to the French Revolution.[25] In its heyday from the mid-1940s to the mid-1960s it was often difficult to distinguish 'terrorism' from 'guerrilla insurgency' since the latter employed terrorist methods to mobilise populations against colonial regimes (as the National Liberation Front did against the French colonial regime in Algeria in the 1950s).[26]

Other movements such as the Provisional IRA in Northern Ireland came from a background of resistance to British rule where guerrilla insurgency had largely failed to take off (with the possible exception of border regions like South Armagh) and resorted to terrorist methods as the central means of waging war against the British state and forcing its eventual withdrawal from the island of Ireland. In Palestine the brief attempt at developing a guerrilla insurgency against the Israeli state in the aftermath of the 1967 Arab–Israeli war soon proved to be a disaster, thus turning groups such as the Popular Front of the Liberation of Palestine (PFLP) into terrorism.[27]

Finally, by the late 1960s terrorist movements in Europe such as the Baader Meinhof group in Germany and the Red Brigades in Italy developed among relatively affluent and bored middle class youth, though in the process forge links with terrorist movements in the developing world such as the PFLP in Palestine.

Seen in this context, terrorism during much of the Cold War period was really a substitute for guerrilla warfare and often a weapon of the politically weak. For the most part it managed to claim few real successes: It failed on its own to defeat the British in Northern Ireland or remove the French from Algeria. Where it did have any sort of major political impact it was mainly in an authoritarian direction, helping to secure the collapse of democratic regimes in Uruguay, Turkey and Argentina and their replacement by military dictatorships.[28] When seen in this context, it might be concluded that the most successful examples of terrorism employed for clear strategic objectives come less from terrorist groupings from below but at the state level, as power is used, as an effective terrorist device to quell potential opposition or subversion.[29]

It is thus not altogether surprising that analysts generally agree that there is no really distinctive 'terrorism' paradigm – its ideological roots seemed generally to stem from the traditions of European anarchism and nihilism and it offered no really genuine paradigm of revolution by which it could displace Western models of liberal democracy.[30] Seen in this light terrorism at the state level appeared to offer no longer term political success to dissident or marginalised groups and, at best, offered only one means available to attract international attention to their cause, which in the end had to be attained by political means.

International terrorism, on the other hand, has been a relatively recent development in the history of terrorism and has its first major roots in Palestinian resistance to Israeli rule in the West Bank and Gaza Strip.[31] In its first phase it developed among a predominantly secular political intelligentsia that despaired of orthodox methods of insurgency in defeating the immense power of the Israel Defense Forces (IDF). The patterns established by this first phase of international terrorism in the late 1960s and early 1970s were to be copied and emulated by a younger generation of more religiously-inspired terrorists a decade or so later following the Iranian Revolution in 1979. As Bruce Hoffman has pointed out, in 1968 there were virtually no religiously-inspired terrorist movements as such while by the mid-1990s they amounted to some one third of all international terrorist movements.[32]

Religiously-inspired terrorist movements are generally more likely to move towards a more fanatical and uncompromising political ideology than their secular counterparts. They tend to work on the assumption that their actions are divinely sanctioned and are thus dedicated to employing what they see as sacred violence against enemies who they see as quintessentially evil. Some may have short-term objectives such as the release of political prisoners or the removal of armies of occupation (whether this be the IDF from the West Bank or the US military from Saudi Arabia). However most tend to be heavily orientated towards longer term objectives where terrorist actions become part of a global strategy of *jihad* against what is perceived to be an evil and corrupt West and its satellite states in the Middle East and South East Asia, a phenomenon that Mark Juergensmeyer has termed 'cosmic war'.[33]

While it is true that some secular terrorist movements in the past such as the Tamil Tigers in Sri Lanka and the Kurdistan Workers' Party (PKK) in Turkey have employed suicide bombings, generally it is religiously-inspired terrorist movements that have resorted to this tactic. The contemporary phase of suicide bombing in the Middle East stems from the Hizballah movement since 1982 among the Shiite population in Southern Lebanon during the Lebanese civil war. From there it spread to the Palestinians, a group of whom formed the al-Aqsa Martyrs Brigades in late 2000 and adopted suicide bombing as a tactic in contrast to the mass casualty attacks by Hamas and Islamic Jihad. Suicide bombing has the advantage of being relatively cheap as a tactic since the cost of each bomb is around $150 and draws considerable international media attention to the conflict. At the same time it is an effective response given the relative lack of success in smuggling in large scale weapons onto the West Bank and also confirms the apparent Islamic commitment of the movement's adherence to martyrdom.[34]

Suicide bombing was of course a tactic that Al Qaeda took one dramatic stage further with the September 11 bombings, ensuring a major dramatic impact on global public opinion. It takes martyrdom to a new and rather 'purer' level than the suicide bombing on the West Bank or South Lebanon since the collective suicide of the 19 plane hijackers on September 11 was purely in the cause of a global Islamic *jihad* rather than more immediate political demands of local ethnic or nationalist movements. However it is likely that the basic impulses behind the suicide terrorism of Al Qaeda remain the same as they were in other movements, namely that it is largely an individual decision and there is little or no evidence to suggest that the influence of a charismatic religious or political leader is sufficient by itself to drive a person to commit terrorist suicide.[35]

If this is now the strategy of movements such as Al Qaeda it was not one that the West took especially seriously in its early phases. In the 1980s during the last period of the Cold War radical Islamist movements were often viewed in the West as allies in the overthrow of communist regimes. Following the Soviet military intervention into Afghanistan at the end of 1979 Islamist movements in Afghanistan received extensive Western support in their military campaign to secure a Soviet military withdrawal. The 1980s in fact became a highpoint in Islamism as radical Islamist movements sought a revolutionary transformation in Algeria and Egypt; the turning point only came following the collapse of the Berlin Wall in 1989 and the Soviet withdrawal from Afghanistan earlier the same year. By the early 1990s radical Islamism was pushed onto the defensive as Egypt mounted a major crackdown on its Islamist opposition. In 1992 the Algerian government suspended elections in which the radial Front Islamique de Salut (FIS) looked set to gain political power through electoral means unleashing a violent civil war.[36]

The apparent ability of Middle Eastern states to contain radical Islamist movements led many observers to believe that the main phase of Islamism was now over as none of the movements (to Western analysts at least) appeared to offer any serious solutions to the economic and social problems of Middle Eastern societies or to their young, mainly male Islamist adherents.[37] This assessment however has proved to somewhat premature as Islamic terrorism has entered a new phase. The strategic implications of this will now be considered in the following section.

International Terrorism and Civilisational War?

For some pundits and higher range journalists the current crisis surrounding Al Qaeda epitomises the thesis of Samuel Huntington that the basis of post-Cold War global conflict is rooted in civilisational conflict. Well before September 11 they suggested that certain cultures and subcultures are key breeding grounds for terrorism with Islamic cultures being one notable example.[38] Huntington's work was notable for upgrading this debate from the level of simple cultural comparisons into a more sophisticated analysis of post-Cold War global politics in which the former clash of global political ideologies had now been replaced by clashing civilisations. This approach was by no means entirely new in International Relations since work on civilisational rivalry and conflict stretched back to Arnold Toynbee and his multi-volume *Study of History,* which had enjoyed considerable popularity from the late 1940s to early 1960s before being heavily attacked by professional historians.[39]

Huntington, however, managed to renew the debate on civilisations at an opportune time at the close of the Cold War since he appeared to provide not only an analysis of contemporary conflicts but also a method of predicting future forms of conflict. The old ideological rivalry between Western capitalism and Eastern bloc communism was now replaced by eight competing civilisations: Western, Japanese, Confucian, Hindu, Islamic, Slavic-Orthodox, Latin American and – 'possibly' – African. Huntington sees a trend in each of these towards a 'civilisational consciousness' that will eventually lead to future wars being increasingly fought along civilisational 'fault lines', which implies a return of geopolitics to the centre of the study of international politics.[40] While the West is currently on top, there is a growing possibility that other civilisations will be able to develop in time the capacity to challenge this dominance.

Herein lies the appeal of this thesis to many outside the West, despite the fact that it has been strongly attacked by Western radicals for its failure to embrace any systematic analysis of global economic disparities or for its gross simplification in the way that cultural identities are formed.[41] It is notable in this instance that the radical Islamic exponents of an Islamic civilisational challenge to the West such as the Egyptian cleric Sayyid Qutb appealed to the same romantic conservative interpretation of civilisational heritage as those such as Huntington and Toynbee (in his earlier phase) in the West.[42]

In one sense it is possible to see Huntington's thesis as hearkening back to the past and imprinting nineteenth century political and cultural divides on twenty-first century global politics. His thesis fails to engage with any of the complexities of contemporary ethnic and sub-state conflicts which often occur within the same civilisational complex. Similarly, his 'civilisations' really appear to be describing a variety of possible super states in the making, leading in turn to a renewal of balance of power politics in the future as US unipolar dominance is eventually successfully challenged.[43]

However, another reading of Huntington indicates that his work can point to a rather grimmer future than that of nineteenth-century European Bismarckian balance of power politics writ large. Although he did not discuss the dimension of international terrorism (which at this time was not considered of major strategic magnitude) when this is factored in we do begin to see the possibility of a new strategic end state of civilisational war. This is not a concept that is very familiar in contemporary International Relations debate, though in military terms it perhaps most closely resembles the concept of 'total war' in the era of secular industrialised warfare. Thinking through its possible implications for global politics is rather like 'thinking the unthinkable' was during the Cold War and mapping the possible implications of a breakdown in the nuclear balance of terror.

'Civilisational war' is really the ultimate long-term aim of Al Qaeda if it manages to secure a strong enough centre of strategic gravity in the Islamic world. This presumes a series of revolutionary overthrows of key Islamic states such as Pakistan, Saudi Arabia and Indonesia and the loss in these states of any sort of effective Western political influence. This might not seem an immediate prospect but it needs to be seen within a longer term process of progressive economic marginalisation of large parts of the Islamic world while at the same time experiencing high population growth rates. In 1980, for instance, Muslims constituted 18 per cent of the world's population while by 2025 this is projected to rise to 30 per cent. At the same time, in the Middle East, North Africa and Pakistan large numbers of

Muslims are effectively disengaging from the global economy. Middle East countries are growing at two thirds the rate of developing countries leading to the dismal prospect of huge numbers of young unemployed Muslims coming of age over the next 20 years with little hope of buying into the lifestyles of the developed West.[44]

Crucial to the success of a global *jihad* the new revolutionary Islamic regimes would then deploy against the Western world weapons of mass destruction, including in particular nuclear weapons, which would give such a radical Islamic alliance significant political and strategic leverage with the West. In turn, alliances could be built with other non-Western regimes such as China, North Korea (assuming no reunification with South Korea takes place) and perhaps some other radically-inclined regimes in Sub-Saharan Africa.

It is possible therefore to conceptualise civilisational war in different forms. The more 'moderate' form just outlined might lead to a revival of a Cold War type stand-off between the West and an Islamic-led global alliance with terrorist and insurgent movements being financed and supported by both sides in a series of proxy wars in peripheral states. A more revolutionary or crusader form, on the other hand, would be one driven by radical Islamists eager to wage a full-scale *jihad* against the West involving spectacular terrorist attacks and large-scale Western military responses. This though would be a form of crusading warfare beyond the bounds of contemporary nationalism in which the goals would be predominantly religious and linked to the ideal of a revival of the Islamic caliphate.[45] While extremely unlikely, this latter model would clearly be a grim prospect with warfare and military action taking place with large casualties and considerable savagery on both sides.

'Civilisational war' is a remote political prospect at present since it depends upon a major revolutionary transformation in the state system in the Islamic world. Something on these lines may well start unravelling though if there is a revolutionary overthrow of the weak and narrowly-based Saudi state.[46] However it is a concept that needs to be understood as part of a longer term strategy of radical Islamic terrorist movements.

It is also of course possible that these movements may themselves implode in sectional and ethnic rivalry. The failure of internationalist models of political mobilisation in the Westphalian state system suggests that in time radical Islamic insurgents will be integrated into state structures so nullifying the romantic hopes of bin Laden and the Al Qaeda leadership for a revival of the Islamic caliphate. In this sense then there is considerable uncertainty among analysts over the durability of the present strategic threat posed by Al Qaeda to Western interests.

Whatever the case the potential threat of civilisational war should make this a major dimension in the formulation of Western grand strategy which needs to consider not only military responses but a host of economic, political and cultural dimensions as well. An inter-civilisational 'dialogue' involving religious and educational leaders might provide a basis for this sort of strategy to develop since this is clearly a far more wide-ranging issue than simply winning 'hearts and minds' in the traditional idiom of counterinsurgency. The UN has been especially keen to promote the notion of an inter-civilisational 'dialogue' and from 31 July – 3 August 2001 held a conference on this at Kyoto in Japan. The conference stressed the importance of promoting tolerance and respect for other civilisations and cultures and dialogue as an 'ongoing process in which the participants not only show a willingness to exchange information by sharing their own thoughts and listening to others, but also the openness to transform their own world views by integrating other perspectives into their own ways of thinking'.[47]

While at one level these aims are laudable they are highly removed from the embittered and empassioned power bases of international terrorist movements. As this collection seeks to show, the emerging pattern of 'new' global terrorism raises the prospect that, unless it is progressively contained by a concerted Western response, there will emerge over the next couple of decades a progressive radicalisation of Islamic religious mythology and symbolism to a point where it could threaten global political stability.

The Outline of this Special Issue

This collection seeks to address some of these themes. In the first contribution Tom Mockaitis examines the nature of the contemporary international threat against the West from radical Islamic organisations such as Al Qaeda. He stresses that in many respects Al Qaeda resembles more one of insurgency rather than a purely 'terrorist' *per se* and this means that any successful counterinsurgency strategy will, as in the past, have to pay great respect to winning 'hearts and minds' as well as military victories. This does not mean that there is not a strongly religious dimension to Al Qaeda and bin Laden's goals, but this is all the more reason for Western strategy to place great emphasis upon a careful diplomatic strategy towards moderate Middle Eastern states, whose support is crucial for any successful global counterinsurgency.

A similar position emerges in the next contribution by Paul Rich which examines Al Qaeda's structure and organisation in some detail. Considerable stress is placed in this on the leadership role of bin Laden and the manner in which he managed to gain a dominant figurehead position in the Islamic world in the 1990s as the earlier radical Islamic impulse from Iran began to wane. The essay also looks at the longer term global strategy of the organisation and looks at the argument over whether it is largely a terrorist or insurgent organisation. It argues that it is really both with a multifunctional strategy that seeks to appeal to different constituencies throughout the Islamic world. Currently some analysts stress the way that Al Qaeda is seeking to penetrate the Islamic societies of South East Asia, though the essay also warns that in many ways the softer states of Sub-Saharan Africa can also be viewed as potentially important base areas for its operations.

In the third contribution Warren Chin develops a penetrating assessment of Operation 'Enduring Freedom' in Afghanistan. It looks at the relatively easy defeat of the Taliban regime though is cautious about any premature conclusions over America's ability to fight unconventional warfare. America's relatively easy victory was really facilitated by the distribution of power in Afghanistan and the recognition by key warlords that the US entry into the country changed the correlation of forces and that it was thus in their self-interest to back the American-led operation. In some respects this repeats earlier phases of foreign intervention in Afghanistan stretching back to the nineteenth century.

However, the Afghan state is highly decentralised and there has not been in reality a complete US victory in the country since the war against the Taliban remnants continues. The country indeed presents a major challenge to US grand strategy since the Bush administration has resisted pressures to expand the peacekeeping forces in the country or ISAF (International Security Assistance Force) from its current level of 5,000. Afghan economic and political rehabilitation continues on a rather slow and protracted basis, though it can be argued that there are limits to what the country can realistically absorb productively in the terms of foreign aid and investment. However it is unlikely, Chin argues, that an Afghan army strong enough to challenge the power of the warlords will emerge within at least five years if not much longer.

Overall, Operation 'Enduring Freedom' remained a flawed strategy with its over reliance on military technology. Chin warns that continuing reliance on this as opposed to a serious long-term political commitment to deploy ground forces to flush out terrorist base areas risks in the long term greater instability in the international system as it fails to engage with terrorist movements and indeed provides the right environment for them to flourish through what he terms, after Carlos Marighela, a 'militarised situation'.

Additional problems emerge too in the case of the deployment of special forces against international terrorist and insurgent networks. The fourth contribution by Anna Simons and David Tucker looks particularly at US Special Forces while the next study by Alastair Finlan concentrates on British Special Forces. Both essays in a sense are exercises in demystification since the increasing emphasis in political debate on the role of special forces in combating contemporary terrorism runs the risk of promising more than it can deliver. In both the US and British cases special forces remain small elite groups with a fairly intense internal pecking order centred on alleged expertise and prestige. They tend to be distrusted by conventional military bureaucracies and their deployment depends upon regular conventional backup and precise timing as well as a lot of luck.

It is also evident that when special forces are placed in an advisory role (as US Special Operations Forces) were with local military leaders in Afghanistan) there is the risk that they will develop a strong mutual empathy with those they are advising. This leads in turn to trust being placed in allies who may not in the event perform as expected – a phenomenon that appears to have occurred in Afghanistan and partly explains the failure of Operation 'Anaconda'. It is likely that special forces will be best employed in small local engagements as well as in a guiding role, as they were with the Northern Alliance before the invasion that overthrew the Taliban regime. It is unlikely, as Finlan's essay warns, that special forces can be used in a multiplicity of operations over a far flung range of countries since this will risk severely overstretching them. To this extent then it cannot be presumed that special forces will have all that pivotal role in the 'war against terror' as has sometimes been simplistically presumed.

The sixth study by Ghada Hashem Talhami moves on to look at the role of academics in the spread of myths concerning the nature of Islamic and its supposed 'threat' to the West in the post-Cold War era. Talhami looks at the work of Samuel Huntington in the spread of ideas concerning a clash of civilisations and argues that this has had the effect of moralising US foreign policy in a manner that was largely unforeseen at the end of the Cold War. Talhami wonders whether this is not part of a more deep-rooted American obsession with evil, stretching back to the original puritan tradition of the English settlers and embodied in powerful epics such as Herman Melville's *Moby Dick* (1851).[48] It may be though that 'this phenomenon is a necessary adjunct to the conduct of foreign policy in a populist democracy'. Whatever the case, there clearly has been a remoralisation of US foreign policy in a manner that has not be seen since the early Cold War. The danger of this is that it risks playing precisely into the hands of Al Qaeda indicating to large sections of opinion throughout the Muslim world that there is now a new Western crusade against Islam. The US, as a consequence, risks going to war based upon a misconception of their 'enemy'.

At first it might be thought that a similar theme of misperception emerges in the case of Russian attitudes towards terrorism. However, as Stephen Blank argues in the seventh contribution, the Russian response to terrorism has been largely dictated by a military concern to maintain the cohesion of what remains of its former empire rather than a wider strategic concern to engage with international terrorism. The brutal military incursion into Chechnya, he argues, has largely destroyed the political power base of any 'moderate' Chechen leadership that might seek to undertake negotiations with the Putin regime in Moscow. This thus raises the dangers of the counterinsurgent war there escaping any sort of political definition and becoming sheer violence for its own sake.

The Russian government has been largely forced to acquiesce too in the growing US role in Central Asia, though from a Western viewpoint the Russians remain very problematic allies in any grand strategy against terrorism. Moscow's strategy of brutal military domination contrasts markedly with the 'liberal imperialism' of the Bush administration in the US. However, as Blank shows in the latter part of his study, Russia plays a key part in a wider alliance with China centred on the Shanghai 6 or Shanghai Forum. The revamping of this in 2001 in Uzbekistan reflected growing disillusion with the capacities of the Commonwealth of Independent States (CIS) (covering the former Soviet Union) to act as an effective regional security organisation in Central Asia. Not only could this lead to the involvement of Chinese troops in formal military exercises with the Russians, but might also lead to the Russians supporting the Chinese in any future war by China to regain Taiwan.

So overall, diplomatic developments in Central Asia do not point to any simple Russian integration into a coherent grand strategy against terrorism. As Blank points out, Russian policy resembles in many respects a Matrioshka doll so that the more you look the less there is, certainly the less there is that makes uniform sense from a Western perspective. Clearly the real test of Russian diplomatic credibility is whether it can initiate some major reforms of its domestic institutions dealing with its national security to ensure that its foreign policy is driven more by diplomatic rather than military concerns.

The following two studies, contribution eight by Philip Towle and nine by Susan Carruthers, examine recent media and film representations of insurgency and terrorism. This is a dimension that terrorism and insurgency analysts are beginning to take increasingly seriously since the emergence of global terrorism is, to a large degree, a reflection of the growth of a globalised mass media. Terrorist movements have traditionally depended upon the mass media to both report and highlight the impact of the various terror attacks that they make on civilian populations, Indeed this search for media publicity is precisely the central force that drives them forwards. However, as Philip Towle points out in his study, terrorism is still subject to the same strategic axioms as any other military initiative. If it overplays its hand and makes too great an impact on its intended victim then this can result in a massive media backlash, uniting the media against them and so securing for governments a free hand in defining their political and military responses.

Towle suggests that this has really been the case with Al Qaeda with the September 11 attacks. Neither the Twin Towers, nor even the Pentagon, were really centres of gravity and merely ended up mobilising both national and international outrage. Indeed, the attacks can be seen as uniting important segments of elite opinion across the world in a manner that Al Qaeda almost certainly imagined to be impossible. This has consequently empowered governments to act in unforeseen ways to attack international terrorist networks. Towle's essay does not look at the manipulation of the media by Al Qaeda itself with a series of press releases to *Al Jazeera* television and stage managed video interviews with bin Laden. The impact of these on global Islamic opinion remains to be fully assessed since it undoubtedly feeds into a wider global media battle for Islamic opinion. However, his study clearly points to the media being one of the key centres of gravity in any international 'war on terror'.

In the ninth contribution Susan Carruthers takes this theme rather further by examining the current mood in Hollywood through two recent films that deal with US military engagement with insurgents, *Black Hawk Down* (2001) and *We Were Soldiers* (2002). Both films can be seen as reflecting a more hawkish and militaristic outlook in Hollywood following a spate of anti-Vietnam War films, such as Francis Ford Coppola's *Apocalypse Now* (1979).

Black Hawk Down, directed by the British film director Ridley Scott, provides detailed account of the disastrous firefight of US Rangers in Mogadishu in 1993 leading to the loss of some 19 US lives and an estimated 1,000 Somalis. In many respects the film appeals back to an older tradition of military heroism, captured in films such as *Zulu* (1964) in which beleaguered Western military units fight their way out of apparently hopeless situations against terrific odds. Though the Clinton administration decided in the aftermath of the Mogadishu episode to pull out of Somalia (and also refused to intervene in Rwanda the following year to prevent a disastrous genocide) the film presents the episode as what Carruthers terms an 'ennobling, redemptive portrait of soldiers at war'. To this extent the film, according to Carruthers, provides a 'made-to-order mood music for the "war on terror"'.

Similarly the film *We Were Soldiers*, directed by Randall Wallace, reconstructs a battle in Ia Drang valley in Vietnam in an early stage of the Vietnam War in November 1965. The soldiers in question are no less than the 1st Battalion, 7th Cavalry – Custer's old regiment. Like the Rangers in Mogadishu they too are in a situation where they are facing great odds but save themselves from total defeat at the cost of 234 casualties.

Carruthers suggests that both films really avoid any serious questioning of the proportionality of means to ends and end up simply valorising obeying orders, acting heroically and saving one's life. It is doing one's duty that is good. This shifts the focus considerably away from the earlier critical engagement in Hollywood with war, though the two films are different in the way they portray the enemy. The Somalis in *Black Hawk Down* never really emerge beyond archaic stereotypes of frenzied warriors while *We Were Soldiers* marks a serious departure in US Vietnam war movies by developing a fairly sophisticated depiction of the Vietnamese and the logic of their military decision-making.

However, in a more general sense, Carruthers concludes, both films mark an attempt by the movie industry to prepare US opinion for a more active military engagement with enemies abroad with the restoration of older themes of heroism and duty. There is moreover some evidence to suggest that the theme in both films of beleaguered US soldiers fighting their way out against a heavily armed enemy is one that has made its way into battlefield reporting. In the case of the battle in the Shah-I-Kor Valley in Operation 'Anaconda' in Afghanistan for instance one report saw the operation as one 'where the enemy had nothing to lose and US soldiers had to fight for their lives'.[49]

The last contribution by Kevin O'Brien focuses on another key dimension in the 'war on terror', that of information warfare. This is by no means a new phenomenon post September 11 and the 'asymmetric' threat from Al Qaeda may still ultimately rest on the use of chemical or biological attacks in the West. However, O'Brien stresses the growing use by terrorist of cyberspace to plan their operations. Likewise, counter-terrorist operations in turn are increasingly going to be structured around Information Operations in order to mobilise sufficient intelligence information in order to neutralise terrorist networks.

This dimension of contemporary grand strategy has hitherto been rather under-emphasised in recent debate since the Al Qaeda network has so far desisted from attempting any sort of cyber attacks on Western information systems, though this is probably not beyond their capabilities. In future terrorist network are likely to be increasingly attracted to multi-dimensional strategies that combine overt terror attacks on Western targets along with attempts to cripple Western information systems. The general nature of this threat has so far led, O'Brien points out, to a series of initiatives by individual states, businesses and NGOs to improve the security of the global information environment – though how successful these really are remains to be seen.

Terrorist groupings may for the present be averse to cyber attacks since they do not appear to provide the same kind of immediate media publicity that more conventional attacks usually generate. However, a more sophisticated generation of computer literate terrorist may emerge in the next 10–15 years who may be far more attracted to trying to wage information war against the West. In this sense then cyber war may well become an increasingly salient dimension to the construction of Western grand strategy against terrorism.

NOTES

1. Steven Simon and Daniel Benjamin, 'America and the New Terrorism', *Survival* 42/1 (Spring 2000) pp.59–75; S. Simon and D. Benjamin, 'America and the New Terrorism: An Exchange', *Survival* 42/2 (Summer 2000) pp.156–72.
2. 'An Ever Shifting Web', *The Economist* (19 Oct. 2002).
3. *Pravda* (12 Oct. 2001).
4. Gore Vidal, 'The Enemy Within', *The Observer* (London, 27 Oct. 2002).
5. Fred Halliday, *Two Hours that Shook the World (*London: Saqi Books 2002) p.31.
6. John L. Gaddis, 'And Now This: Lessons From the Old Era for the New One' in Paul Kennedy *et al.*, *The Age of Terror* (Oxford: The Perseus Press for the Yale Center for the Study of Globalisation 2001) p.6.
7. Raphael F. Perl, 'Terrorism, the Future and U.S. Foreign Policy', *CRS Issue Brief for Congress* (13 Sept. 2001).
8. See Gaddis (note 6) p.17.
9. Audrey Kurth Cronin, 'Rethinking American Strategy in the Age of Terrorism', *Survival* 44/2 (Summer 2002) p.130.
10. 'Transcript of Usama Bin Laden Video Tape' (13 Dec. 2001), <www.fasorg/irp/world/para/ubl-video.htm> p.3.
11. For details of this doctrinal shift see General Wesley K. Clark, *Waging Modern War* (Oxford: Public Affairs 2002) pp.5–11.
12. For details of these bombings and their impact see Peter L. Bergen, *Holy War: Inside the Secret World of Osama bin Laden* (London: Phoenix Paperbacks 2002) pp.122–9.
13. In part this neglect of grand strategy is a result of the manner in which strategic studies developed during the post-1945 era under the rubric of a Cold War realism that took the existing state system more or less for granted. 'Strategy' as such did not appear very relevant in an era of bipolar superpower dominance of the international system and in International Relations the classical realist paradigm made way by the 1980s towards a more structurally-orientated neo-realism that emphasised the structural underpinnings to international order. This removed the element of voluntarism in political decision making and appeared to make conflict a resultant of structural determinants inherent to the international system.
14. Edward Luttwak, *Strategy: The Logic of War and Peace* (Cambridge: Harvard UP 1987) p.180.
15. 'The Grand Strategy Project: Project Description and Background', <www.yale.edu/iss/projects_gs-desc.htm>.
16. G. John Ikenberry, 'America's Imperial Ambition', *Foreign Affairs* (Sept./Oct. 2002) p.48.
17. Ibid. p.55.
18. Ibid. p.56.
19. Barry R. Posen, 'The Struggle Against Terrorism: Grand Strategy, Strategy and Tactics', *International Security* 26/3 (Winter 2001/02) pp.39–55.
20. Eric Margolis, 'War on Terror Masks Bush's Grand Strategy', *The Toronto* (10 March 2002). See also Anthony Sampson, 'West's Greed for Oil Fuels Saddam Fever', *The Observer* (11 Aug. 2002).
21. James Der Derian, 'The Illusion of Grand Strategy', *The New York Times* (25 May 2001).
22. John L. Gaddis, 'Living in Candlestick Park', *The Atlantic Monthly* (April 1999). For a more detailed study of geopolitical thought in the West see Geoffrey Parker, *Western Geopolitical Thought in the Twentieth Century* (London and Sydney: Croom Helm 1985).
23. See in particular Laurie Mylroie, *Study of Revenge: Saddam Hussein's Unfinished War Against America* (Washington DC: The AEI Press 2000) placing Saddam Hussein behind the

terrorist attacks in the US including the bombing of the World Trade Center in 1993 and the September 11 attacks.

24. Richard Falk, 'False Universalism and the Geopolitics of Exclusion: The Case of Islam', *Third World Quarterly* 18/1 (1997) pp.7–23.
25. John Shy and Thomas W. Collier, 'Revolutionary War' in Peter Paret (ed.) *Makers of Modern Strategy: From Machiavelli to the Nuclear Age* (Princeton UP 1986) pp.815–62.
26. Ariel Merrari, 'Terrorism as a Strategy of Insurgency', *Terrorism and Political Violence* 11/2 (Summer 1999) pp.1–38.
27. Ely Karmon, 'Fatah and the Popular Front for the Liberation of Palestine' (25 Nov. 2000), <www.ict.org.il/articlesdet>.
28. Gerard Chaliand, *Terrorism: From Popular Struggle to Media Spectacle* (London: Saqi Books 1987) p.110.
29. Paul Wilkinson, 'The Strategic Implications of Terrorism' in M.L. Sondhi (ed.) *Terrorism and Political Violence* (New Delhi: Har-anand Publications for the Indian Council for Social Science Research 2000).
30. Though one analyst suggested in the 1970s that European terrorism might perhaps develop into a revolutionary paradigm. See H. Edward Price, 'The Strategy and Tactics of Revolutionary Terrorism', *Comparative Studies in Society and History* 19/1 (Jan. 1977) pp.52–65.
31. Bruce Hoffman, *Inside Terrorism* (London: Gollancz 1998) p.68.
32. Bruce Hoffman, *Holy Terror: The Implications of Terrorism Motivated by a Religious Imperative* (Santa Monica, CA: RAND 1993) pp.1–2.
33. Mark Juergensmeyer, *Terror in the Mind of God* (Berkeley: Univ. of California Press 2002) p.9.
34. Yael Shaher, 'The al-Aqsa Martyrs Brigades', *ICT* (24 March 2002) <www.ict.org.il/articles>.
35. Ariel Merari, 'The Readiness to Kill and Die: Suicidal Terrorism in the Middle East' in Walter Reich (ed.) *Origins of Terrorism* (Cambridge:Cambridge UP 1990) p.207.
36. Walter Lacquer, 'A Failure of Intelligence', *The Atlantic Monthly* (March 2002).
37. Olivier Roy, *The Failure of Political Islam* (London: I.B. Tauris 1994).
38. Conor Cruise O'Brien, 'Thinking About Terrorism', *The Atlantic Monthly* (June 1986).
39. For a discussion of this earlier debate see Paul B. Rich, 'Civilizations in European and World History: A Reappraisal of the Ideas of Arnold Toynbee, Fernand Braudel and Marshall Hodgson', *The European Legacy* 5/3 (2000) pp.341–52.
40. Samuel Huntington, 'The Clash of Civilisations', *Foreign Affairs* 72/3 (Summer 1993) pp.21–49.
41. See in particular Fred Halliday, *Islam and the Myth of Confrontation: Religion and Politics in the Middle East*, (London: I.B. Tauris 1996).
42. Peter Partner, *God of Battles: Holy Wars of Christianity and Islam* (London: HarperCollins 1997) p.307.
43. A point made by Richard E. Rubinstein and Jarle Crocker, 'Challenging Huntington', *Foreign Policy* 96 (Fall 1994) pp.113–28.
44. Steven Simon and Benjamin Daniel, 'The Terror', *Survival* 43/4 (Winter 2001) p.13.
45. 'In modern terms holy war is most likely to be invoked when religious fervour and radical nationalism converge', Partner (note 42) p.310.
46. Said K. Aburish, *The Rise, Corruption and Coming Fall of the House of Saud* (London: Bloomsbury 1995).
47. United Nations University, International Conference on the Dialogue of Civilizations, 31 July – 3 Aug. 2001 Tokyo and Kyoto, *Conference Report*, p.3.
48. Similar questions were asked at the time of the US engagement in Vietnam (such as Norman Mailer's 1967 novel *Why Are We in Vietnam*?).
49. Michael Elliott, 'We Put the Capital "M" in Miracle', *Time* (18 March 2002).

Winning Hearts and Minds in the 'War on Terrorism'

THOMAS R. MOCKAITIS

Terrorists belong to organizations with a recognizable structure. These organizations have goals beyond reeking havoc on their enemies. They require safe havens in which to train and plan operations. States or elements within them provide these havens by allowing clandestine organizations to blend with the general population, tacitly if not actively supporting them. Since they often mount operations from within the target state, terrorist cells require support networks within those countries as well. These characteristics describe not a new phenomenon but a very old one: The US and its allies face an insurgency, albeit on an international rather than a local scale. The nature of the conflict points the way to its resolution: a counterinsurgency campaign on a global scale.

Insurgency and counterinsurgency have been the subject of extensive study in the half-century following the Second World War. While some analysts consider this type of conflict a Cold War phenomenon, others have argued its persistence into the contemporary world.[1] The principles of counterinsurgency are as valid for today's war on terrorism as they were when practitioners worked them out against Communist insurgents 50 years ago.[2]

Unfortunately, then as now the formula for defeating insurgents is far easier to state than to apply. Intelligence remains the key to victory. The wisdom of General Sir Frank Kitson, who has had more experience in counterinsurgency than any living soldier, has lost none of its edge. Defeating insurgents or terrorists 'consists very largely in finding them'.[3] Garnering accurate and timely information requires winning the trust of the general population who support the insurgents, tacitly or actively. Trust and cooperation depend in turn on recognizing and as far as possible addressing the real needs and the legitimate grievances on which the insurgency feeds. Good intelligence allows the security forces (military, paramilitary, and police) to use force against the terrorists in a limited and focused manner so as not to further alienate the general population.[4]

This strategy has generally been described as 'winning hearts and minds'. A hearts-and-minds strategy is as essential to defeating Al Qaeda today as it was to rooting out Communist *guerrillas* in Malaya 50 years ago.

The current threat differs from earlier insurgencies primarily in scope and complexity. Previously insurgents operated in a local arena; now they act on a global stage. Once they relied on word of mouth and print media to spread their message; now they have access to the Internet and global airwaves. The car bomb used to be the primary 'weapon of mass destruction'; now it has given way to the jetliner, the anthrax spore, and the radiological bomb. Previously the most deadly insurgents operated in support of a national or ethnic cause. They may have developed a global reach, but they had a geographic center of gravity. The Irish Republican Army (IRA) struck targets in London and murdered British soldiers in Germany, but Northern Ireland remained its primary base of operations. The Palestine Liberation Organization (PLO) hijacked airliners, but it always had a known headquarters that Israel could strike (Jordan, Lebanon, Tripoli). Al Qaeda, on the other hand, has a broader agenda, enjoys the support of perhaps half a dozen friendly states and has supporters in many others.

Today's insurgents or terrorists are also better funded than their predecessors. Osama bin Laden's personal fortune is well known. His organization receives additional money from state sponsors and until recently controlled a lucrative opium trade out of Afghanistan.

Finally, the insurgents of yesterday used terror to achieve maximum effect with minimum loss of life. They struck a balance between spreading fear for a calculated purpose and creating widespread revulsion at their acts. Today's perpetrators exercise no such restraint; they seem determined to take as many lives as possible in their attacks.[5]

These differences of degree and complexity must not obscure the similarity between insurgencies past and present. Al Qaeda has definite goals. It needs the active support of a few states and the tacit support of many people who share its sense of grievance even if they do not applaud its methods. Despite appearances to the contrary, bin Laden uses terror in a calculated way to achieve a particular effect.

Al Qaeda also has a discernable organization, albeit a complex and decentralized one, and a loose command structure. All of these elements make the organization vulnerable if they can be understood and exploited. Understanding depends on intelligence, which can best be gathered from erstwhile supporters. Supporters will defect only if they believe that they have more to gain from the opponents of Al Qaeda than they do from the organization.

Counter-terrorists stand an even better chance of weaning away the soft support surrounding the hardcore insurgents. People generally support an insurgency out of a shared sense of wrong or frustration at not having their basic needs met. The coalition opposing the insurgency must recognize that it feeds on grievances widely felt in the Arab and larger Muslim worlds. Not all of these grievances can be laid at the doorstep of the United States, but US foreign policy in the Middle East has angered many. Addressing the causes of unrest will not persuade bin Laden and his most ardent supporters to cease their operations, but it might convince at least some individuals in the communities in which he operates to cooperate with authorities.

The 'war' on terrorism must be based on a sound hearts-and-minds strategy conducted like the terror campaign itself on a global scale. Reasonable adjustments to US policy in the Middle East and the larger Islamic world may produce enough cooperation to increase intelligence on Al Qaeda. A protracted struggle with few dramatic victories requires a similar effort to persuade the American public and the Western alliance of the continued need for the struggle. A hearts-and-minds strategy requires a clear understanding of the nature of Al Qaeda and its affiliates, their goals, and the sources of unrest on which they feed.

The Nature of Terrorism

Consideration of this hearts-and-minds campaign must begin with some clarification of what terrorism is and the role it plays in Al Qaeda's larger struggle. Unfortunately, terrorism has become such a diverse phenomenon that either it disappears under a host of precise definitions or it is covered by too broad an umbrella. Experts have offered more than a hundred definitions of terrorism.[6] The US Department of Defense has adopted a one such definition:

> The calculated use of unlawful violence or the threat of unlawful violence to inculcate fear; intended to coerce or to intimidate governments or societies in the pursuit of goals that are generally political, religious, or ideological.[7]

This definition captures the essential elements of unlawful, politically motivated violence but leaves out the equally important symbolism. Terrorism has variously been described as 'drama', 'theater', and 'propaganda of the deed'.[8] However useful definitions may be for purposes of academic discourse, they obscure important distinctions among terrorists essential to combating them. Security forces must know precisely what kind of terrorist activity they face.

Most analysts identify several types of terrorism. Nationalist insurgencies make use of terror as a weapon as do the governments seeking to repress them. The current Intifada in Palestine/Israel and the struggle for Northern Ireland illustrate these two types of terrorism. Drug dealers may use terror to intimidate rivals, the government, or anyone else who threatens their lucrative trade. Nationalist and narco-terrorists may conduct transitional operations, but they retain a decidedly local focus. A host of purely domestic terrorists from the Unabomber to Pro-life extremists who murder doctors at abortion clinics have goals so narrow or so diffuse as to render them what one expert calls 'nuisance terrorists'.[9] Attacks by such groups or individuals can be quite deadly as the 1995 Oklahoma City bombing demonstrates, but they pose no serious threat to an organized state and can best be treated as criminal activity. The bomber of the Alfred P. Murrah Federal building, Timothy McVeigh, was loosely affiliated with the Christian Patriot militia movement that seeks to replace heterogeneous America with a White, 'Aryan', 'Christian' nation.[10]

A host of Marxist inspired insurgencies rocked Europe and Latin America in the 1970s and 1980s. Some like the Italian Red Brigade or the German Baader-Meinhof group belong in the nuisance category; others like the Salvadoran Fabrundo Marti National Liberation Front (FMLN) or the Nicaraguan Sandinistas were genuine liberation movements, although they were not above using terror to achieve their goals.

Al Qaeda does not fit neatly into any category, a fact that has led many observers to describe it as a 'new' form of terrorism. The organization, which means 'the Base' in Arabic, has forged links with several other terrorist groups. While it deals in narcotics, it sees them merely as a source of revenue to fund its operations. It has an international agenda but also seeks to overthrow specific governments such as those of Egypt and Saudi Arabia. Religious, political, and ideological goals motivate Al Qaeda. The organization enjoys the sponsorship of several states, has a global financial network, and cells in many countries. This complexity suggests that for purposes of countering it, Al Qaeda should be thought of as an insurgency rather than a purely terrorist organization.

Al Qaeda

Osama bin Laden's motivation and ultimate goal are profoundly religious. A Saudi by birth, he is part of a larger Islamic movement known as the *Salafiyya* (venerable forefathers). This movement considers much of contemporary Islam as corrupted by idolatry and seeks to replace secular Muslim governments with Islamic ones governed by *shari'a* law. As the term 'forefathers' suggests, they see themselves facing the same challenge as did the Prophet Muhammed in his day: to rid the *umma* (Muslim community) of idolaters.[11]

The religious nature of Al Qaeda must not obscure the sharply focused portion of its agenda and highly rational approach to achieving it. Nothing could be more dangerous than to dismiss bin Laden as yet another religious fanatic pursuing a hopelessly millenarian dream. Unfortunately, some analyses group him with Christian fundamentalist terrorists such as Timothy McVeigh.[12] The two saw the world in Manichean terms, chose highly symbolic targets, and had no regard for who or how many they killed. McVeigh's Christian patriotism, however, has adopted broad, virtually unattainable apocalyptic goals. Bin Laden has a much more specific agenda, although his long-term vision may be equally apocalyptic, and has set about attaining it in a very methodical way. The pragmatic nature of at least some of these goals makes Al Qaeda vulnerable to a hearts-and-minds campaign.

Fortunately, bin Laden has been quite clear about his grievances against the US and his agenda for the Muslim world. A *Fatwa,* or religious proclamation, issued by bin Laden and the leaders of five other terrorist groups in February 1998 outlined three justifications for attacking America and Americans: First, the presence of US troops on the sacred soil of Saudi Arabia; second, US policy towards Iraq, and third, US support for the State of Israel.[13] The first cause concerns bin Laden the most, but he certainly makes use of the others. Americans stunned by the 9/11 attacks would do well to remember that Al Qaeda remains most concerned about events in the Islamic world. They hate America precisely because of US support for the 'heretical' regimes of Saudi Arabia and Egypt. They have made tactical use of both the Israel/Palestine imbroglio and the Iraq embargo but primarily to create a sense of solidarity with the rest of the Muslim world.

Organization and Methods

Al Qaeda has succeeded where most terrorist organizations have failed in keeping its organization and even its activities hidden from the intelligence organizations of the most powerful nations for a relatively long time. The US State Department's *Patterns of Global Terrorism, 1997* does not even include Al Qaeda in its list of terrorist groups.[14] Although now suspected in earlier incidents, bin Laden's organization announced itself in dramatic fashion with the near simultaneous bombings of the US embassies in Nairobi, Kenya and Dar es Salaam, Tanzania in August 1998. Two years later it struck again with a suicide bombing of the USS *Cole* in Aden harbor. Despite these attacks and bin Laden's rabid hatred of the US, September 11 found America totally unprepared for the diabolical but brilliantly executed attacks on the World Trade Center and the Pentagon.

Even today precise intelligence on Al Qaeda remains difficult to obtain. Bin Laden has adopted the communist cell system of organization. Terrorist cells of perhaps a dozen or fewer operatives live and work as ordinary citizens in some 60 countries. Only the leader of each cell knows anyone at the next level of command, and he may know only one individual. Capturing a cell thus yields little useful information on the larger organization. Several cells may operate within a single country and be totally ignorant of each other's specific missions and only generally informed about the larger strategy. Even individual cell members might be ignorant as to the full extent of an operation. Some of the 9/11 hijackers may not have been told they were on a suicide mission until the planes had actually been seized.

Once in place Al Qaeda cells may require little direction from their superiors, although prior to 9/11 and perhaps even now routine communication would have been easy to hide among the billions of e-mails that travel through cyberspace or the equally numerous cellphone calls that circle the globe without wires. 'Sleeper' cells deployed years ahead of an operation may be instructed to act on a certain date or when opportunity presents itself. Until the cell becomes operational, its members live and work as normal residents, scrupulously obeying the law and avoiding any behavior that would bring them to the attention of authorities. The 9/11 hijackers avoided any public behavior or appearance that would have identified them as Muslim, even going so far as to drink alcohol and frequent strip clubs.

A complex global network that weaves in and out of the legal financial system supports terrorist cells around the world. Al Qaeda draws funds from legitimate business ventures and Islamic charities (whose contributors may or may not know their contributions support terrorism), from personal fortunes of people like bin Laden, and from state sponsorship.[15] An international effort resulted in freezing $112 million in terrorist assets by August 2002.[16] However, experts and government officials agree that these assets represent a fraction of funds available for terrorism. The international effort has hampered Al Qaeda but not paralyzed it. Compared to counter-terrorism, terrorism costs very little, particularly in countries where cells can count on indigenous support. The perpetrators of the Bali nightclub bombing needed few resources to pull off their devastating attack in October 2002 and probably could rely upon a sympathetic element in Indonesia's Muslim community to feed, house, and hide them.

While the outline of Al Qaeda's organization has become clear, its extent remains hard to determine. Arrests of terrorist suspects in more than 90 countries reveal the global extent of its network.[17] Estimates of terrorist numbers run into several thousand hardcore activists with a much larger cushion of soft support and an almost bottomless well of potential recruits. These estimates can be extrapolated from estimated numbers of Mujahedin who fought the Soviets in Afghanistan and who form the base of bin Laden's support: '5,000 Saudis, 3,000 Yemenis, 2,800 Algerians, 2,000 Egyptians, 400 Tunisians, 350 Iraqis, 200 Libyans and dozens of Jordanians'.[18] A few thousand terrorists or insurgents may not seem like much next to the might of the US military and its NATO allies, but it is sobering to remember that the so-called Provisional Irish Republican Army has done enormous damage with only a few hundred active members.

Terrorist Operations

Despite the oft-repeated claims of pundits that a 'new terrorism' strides the globe, Al Qaeda operations resemble those of similar organizations over the last century. Like all such organizations it seeks high profile, symbolic targets selected for their dramatic effect. The World Trade Center and Pentagon represent respectively American economic and military power. The embassies in East Africa and the USS *Cole* symbolize the ability to project that power abroad. However, in the mass media age, terrorism need not choose such high profile targets to be effective. Journalism, particularly television, has the power to magnify the significance of any incident.[19] Once the terrorists establish credibility, even limited violence will draw considerable attention, especially given the 'if-it-bleeds-it-leads' mentality of contemporary journalism.

Besides going after symbolic targets, terrorist or insurgents will also select critical infrastructure, the sinews of trade, commerce, and ordinary life. The more complex a society, the more vulnerable it is to attack. Beyond the tremendous loss of life and extensive damage to property, the 9/11 hijackers grounded the civilian air fleet, shut down Wall Street, and cost the US economy billions of dollars in lost revenue. Power stations, bridges, dams, tunnels, rail and communications grids, and a host of other potential targets have the capacity to paralyze vast areas of the country. To take a single example, the entire East–West rail network depends on a single turnstile located in Cincinnati, Ohio to reroute trains.[20] The reliance of vast areas of the public and private sector on computer technology and the Internet has been a source of endless anxiety among those assessing threats to the US. Attacks against the economic sinews of the homeland have created such concern that in 1997 President Clinton established a Commission on Critical Infrastructure Protection.

In addition to highly symbolic sites, terrorists will also select targets of opportunity. The early 2003 killing of a US serviceman in Kuwait provides a case in point. The shift to seemingly random targets of opportunity occurs when a society under attack 'hardens' the high profile targets terrorist prefer. This phenomenon has caused some analysts to describe target hardening as 'target displacement'.[21] US installations and even individual Americans, regardless of whether or not they work for the government, can no longer take their security for granted, particularly when traveling abroad. Bin Laden's *Fatwa* proclaimed the sacred duty to kill any and all Americans indiscriminately. Al Qaeda and its affiliates have proven their ability and determination to carry out this diabolical order.

Both the indiscriminate nature of the killing and its extent mark a departure from established terrorist practice. Previously insurgents or states making use of terror needed to be concerned about domestic and international opinion; religiously motivated terrorists, ironically, exercise no such restraint.[22] As one commentator aptly observed, contemporary terrorists have 'modified Sun Tzu's edict from "kill one person, frighten a thousand" to "kill a thousand, frighten a million"'.[23]

The increasing lethality of terrorism had become the subject of widespread discussion even before 9/11. Most terrorism experts, however, expected biological, chemical, or nuclear weapons to cause mass casualties. Virtually everyone seriously underestimated US vulnerability to a well-planned conventional attack. Still, weapons of mass destruction remain the biggest security concern for threatened states. The 1995 release of sarin nerve gas on the Tokyo subway by the Aum Shinrikyo cult killed 12 people and injured 5,000, but the attack had the potential to kill 20,000.[24] This incident and the 2002 use of a nerve agent by Russian troops ending a hostage situation in a Moscow theater, which killed almost 200 of the hostages, provide sobering reminders of just how deadly a chemical attack can be.

Biological agents such as anthrax or smallpox pose an even greater threat, as do nuclear weapons. Experts envision two nuclear terrorism scenarios: detonation of a nuclear bomb and, far more likely, spreading of radioactive material via a conventional explosion (a radiological or 'dirty' bomb). Al Qaeda has made a concerted effort to get nuclear, chemical, and biological weapons, and at least some of its state sponsors certainly have them.

Meeting the Threat: Counter-Terrorism or Counterinsurgency?

The scope and magnitude of the terrorist threat make countering it a daunting task. The US has already taken significant steps to defend the homeland, including heightened security at airports. Sobering assessments of the vulnerability of our vast and complex society, however, make abundantly clear the futility of a purely defensive posture. Inspecting one fully loaded container on an 18-wheeler truck would take five customs agents three hours; the 11.5 million trucks entering the US in 2000 received a cursory inspection at best.[25] This realization no doubt led the late Sir Robert Thompson to dislike the prefix 'counter', because it surrendered the initiative to the terrorists.[26]

Al Qaeda can only be defeated by a comprehensive offensive strategy. Such a strategy must combine conventional with unconventional operations and the highly focused use of force. Focus in turn depends on precise intelligence, which can only be acquired from local informants. These informants will only talk if they believe they have a compelling reason to do so. Persuading them that they have such a reason to cooperate is essential.

Contemporary and historical experience make clear the impossibility of persuading hardcore Al Qaeda members to give up their cause. Suicide bombers promised a place in paradise will hardly be amenable to other inducements. They can only be apprehended, killed, or rendered ineffective by making it impossible for them to come out of hiding or communicate with anyone. However, the soft cushion of supporters essential to any insurgent or terrorist group might be persuaded to cooperate or at least to desist in supporting Al Qaeda. Providing an incentive for such cooperation requires taking a sobering look at US policy toward the Middle East. No matter how extreme Al Qaeda's agenda may seem, legitimate grievances cause many in the region to at least tacitly support bin Laden.

Discerning the nature of those grievances and as far as possible addressing them constitutes what during the Cold War came to be called 'winning the hearts and minds of the people'. In communist inspired wars of national liberation a hearts-and-minds campaign often consisted of providing the basic amenities of community life (running water, basic health care), a grant of land, and eventual independence, though political rights were usually rather far down the list.[27]

The scope and complexity of the Al Qaeda threat requires a more complex approach. The Western alliance led by the US must assist countries such as the Philippines to combat indigenous insurgencies backed by Al Qaeda. The conquered nation of Afghanistan needs to be rebuilt as a demonstration of the benefits of opposing terrorism as well as of the costs of supporting it. Each geographic context requires a different hearts-and-minds campaign. Another such campaign needs to be waged in allied states and here at home. Educated voters in the US and Europe need to be convinced that the measures taken to combat terrorism are reasonable and proportional to the threat and not merely a pretext for promoting a partisan agenda. Finally, the moderate majority in key Arab states must be persuaded to support the war or to at least stop supporting Al Qaeda. This last task will be the most difficult to achieve since it requires some significant changes in US foreign policy.

Al Qaeda's Goals

The West has concentrated too much, perhaps intentionally, on bin Laden's apocalyptic rhetoric at the expense of ignoring his more specific agenda. 'These events [American aggression and Al Qaida terrorism] have divided the whole world into two sides', he proclaimed in the aftermath of 9/11, 'The side of believers and the side of infidels... Every Muslim has to rush to make his religion victorious.'[28] Although bin Laden does believe in a Manichean struggle between good, represented by his brand of Islam, and evil, which includes all non-believers, he has more limited short-term objectives. Despite the devastating attacks on the US, bin Laden remains focused on the Islamic and more specifically the Arab world. Like others in the Islamist movement he has long sought to replace secular regimes with conservative Islamic states governed by strict shariah law. The US has become a target largely because of its support for these regimes, although bin Laden's hatred of Western secularism, which now pervades the world via the airwaves and the Internet, cannot be discounted. Al Qaeda has singled out the governments of Egypt and Saudi Arabia for special attention, but those in Pakistan, Indonesia, and even Iraq can hardly feel secure.

Egypt gave birth to a Muslim terrorist group that predates Al Qaeda but has since come under its wing: Islamic Jihad. This group carried out the murder of President Anwar Sadat in 1981, apparently with the blessing of the blind cleric, Sheik Omar Abdurrahman. Exiled to the US, the Sheik inspired the 1993 World Trade Center bombing masterminded by Ramzi Yusuf in the hope that ending American support for Sadat's successor Hosni Mubarak would topple his secular government.[29] Egypt faces a persistent threat from Islamic extremist terrorism. In 1997 these terrorists murdered 40 Japanese tourists at Luxor, threatening the country's vital tourism industry. After Israel and Saudi Arabia, Egypt has been America's closest ally in the region since the signing of the 1979 Camp David Accords.

Not surprisingly, 15 of the 19, 9/11 hijackers were Saudis. Saudi Arabia is the birthplace of Islam and of Osama bin Laden. Schooled in the militant Wahhabi sect, bin Laden came to view the Saudi monarchy as deviating from the true path of Islam and corrupted by contact with the US.[30] The Al Qaeda leader was incensed by the presence of American troops on the soil 'where the feet of the Prophet had trod', especially when they remained long after the 1991 Gulf War had ended. Like Abdel Rahman, bin Laden concluded that the 'Great Satan' posed an even greater threat than the apostate regimes.

While bin Laden had no love for the Iraqi dictator Saddam Hussein, he seems to embraced the Arab adage that 'the enemy of my enemy is my friend'. He also has ties to militants in several states where the government at least opposes him. Muslim insurgents in the Philippines, the terrorists who bombed the nightclub in Bali, Indonesia, and the Palestinian group Hamas all have ties to Al Qaeda. So apparently does the government of Yemen and at least some of the factions in Somalia. Muslim terrorists involved in the Kashmir struggle look to bin Laden, as does a significant portion of the Pakistani population. His millenarian dream is to draw the entire Muslim world into a single state or federation for the Manichean struggle with the West.

Fashioning a Hearts-and-Minds Campaign

Defeating Al Qaeda requires not only understanding its agenda, but, as far as possible, addressing the causes of discontent upon which extremism feeds. Critics of this approach will undoubtedly object to 'giving in to terrorism'. A host of historic examples, however, suggest that any sophisticated insurgency or terrorist movement requires the tacit support of a population that aids it out of some sense of grievance. Addressing institutionalized religious, social, and economic discrimination did not produce the peace accords in Northern Ireland, but they almost certainly would not have been signed without some improvement in the lives of the majority of Catholics.

A hearts-and-minds campaign will not substitute for homeland security or offensive military action; all three must form part of a comprehensive strategy. Hearts-and-minds can, however, help to separate moderates from extremists, the first step in getting intelligence on terrorist whereabouts and intentions. Such a campaign should be based on two considerations: avoiding any action likely to drive moderates and extremists together, and taking positive steps to separate moderates from extremists.

Do No Harm

In combating terrorism, threatened states should follow the ancient adage that guides physicians: at the very least, do no harm. Every action should be weighed to consider whether it would make the situation better or worse. Tactical gains should not be made at the expense of strategic goals. Separating moderates from extremists must always remain the over-riding consideration of counter-terrorist strategy.

The invasion of Iraq illustrates how some actions can do more harm than good. Launched ostensibly to remove Saddam Hussein so that he could not provide Al Qaeda with weapons of mass destruction, Operation 'Iraqi Freedom' has definitely soured. Coalition forces may have come as liberators, but they are now seen as conquerors. While few in the Arab world had any love for Saddam, most resent the high-handed manner in which the US engineered his removal without international approval. They rightly point out that Washington demanded Iraqi compliance with all UN resolutions while winking at Israel defiance of the same organization. This resentment has inspired Mujahidin from all over the Middle East to join their Iraqi brothers in the current querrilla war against the coalition.[31] Persistent threats against Syria and Iran threats risk widening the conflict and seem to validate Al Qaeda's claim that the war on terrorism is really a war on Islam.'[32]

President Bush's crusade has also damaged relations with America's Arab allies, most of whom had reason to fear both Saddam and bin Laden. The Saudis had refused to allow the US to use bases on their soil for the invasion of Iraq. The Saudi monarchy clearly feared terrorist retaliation. These fears proved well founded when suicide bombers killed 34 people in Riyadh in May 2003.

A More Balanced Foreign Policy

Avoidance of actions with negative repercussions will not be sufficient to change the mood of simmering hostility towards America that permeates much of the Muslim world. The US must take positive steps to improve its image in the Middle East and South Asia. This change need not be complete surrender to terrorist demands, some of which cannot be met in any event. However, certain practical policy shifts would go a long way towards alleviating human suffering and perhaps improving US relations with public opinion in the region.

Once again the example of US policy towards Iraq comes immediately to mind. The regimen of sanctions, in place for 12 years, did nothing to weaken Saddam's grip on power. Embargos never make dictators uncomfortable. If anything, they cause people to support even an unpopular regime. Ordinary Iraqis blame the US not Saddam for the suffering brought on by sanctions. Precise numbers as to the untold deaths caused directly or indirectly by the destruction of critical infrastructure during the 1991 Gulf War and by denial of most foodstuffs and medicines ever since. Conservative estimates run in excess of 400,000 from 1991–98 alone, most of them children under the age of five who died of readily treatable diseases. [33]

A September 2000 letter to the Security Council President from Human Rights Watch noted that 800,000 children in Iraq were malnourished.[34] The most recent UNICEF report reveals that although hunger among children had declined by more than half from 1996 to 2002, 'there are still close to one million children under the age of five suffering from chronic malnutrition in Iraq today – that's nearly a quarter of all children of that age'.[35] The suffering of the Iraqi people has fueled anti-American sentiment and provided grist for Al Qaeda's propaganda mill. This sentiment persists in the seething resentment of the allied occupation of Iraq.

The Iraqi embargo and subsequent invasion also angered other Arabs, largely because America's closest regional ally, Israel, suffers no consequences for flaunting numerous UN resolutions and international agreements. Few US policies anger Muslims more than the one-sided approach of the US in resolving the Israel–Palestine conflict. Palestinian suffering has never figured prominently in bin Laden's ideology, but it remains central to some of the organizations under the Al Qaeda umbrella. The plight of the Palestinians creates widespread sympathy among moderate Arabs who would otherwise not support terrorism. The centrality of this single issue in the domestic politics of so many neighboring Arab states could be seen in the refusal of many to discuss Iraq with either Secretary of State Colin L. Powell or Vice President Richard B. Cheney until Washington did more to end the violence in Palestine–Israel. Democrats and Republicans alike have steadfastly refused to pursue a more balanced policy towards the belligerents. Ironically, the US could exercise enormous leverage on the parties since it bankrolls them both. Although resolution of the Palestinian–Israeli crisis would not produce immediate or widespread support for the US war on terrorism, it would undoubtedly make cooperation with moderate Arab states much easier.

The US might also use its leverage with those Arab states to greater advantage. Next to Israel Egypt receives the largest share of foreign aid in the Middle East. Perhaps requiring that more of that aid go towards internal development and relief of poverty might alleviate the suffering upon which extremism feeds. Even prosperous Saudi Arabia has some accountability to the US. The oil rich country does not need monetary assistance, but, as the 1991 Gulf War demonstrated, it cannot defend itself. US military aid and defense guarantees might be made conditional on the monarchy's cracking down on extremism and doing more to stem the flow of money from wealthy Saudis to Al Qaeda.

Nation-Building

A president who campaigned on a promise not to engage in nation-building finds himself stuck with a belly full of it and faces more in the near future. Failed states remain a persistent problem in the post-Cold War world. 'The need for post conflict peace-building' followed intervention in Bosnia, Kosovo, Afghanistan and now Iraq. Anxious not to repeat the mistake of the 1980s, when American aid evaporated following the Soviet withdrawal form Afghanistan, and the Taliban filled the vacuum, the Western alliance has committed itself to a lengthy occupation and development of the country. Invading Iraq has provided the same dilemma. With no viable alternative to Saddam in a country divided into a Kurdish North, a Shiite South, and a Sunni Arab center, the US and the few allies that join it have no choice but to occupy the country for the foreseeable future. The same challenge will follow interventions in Somalia, Yemen, or indeed any place that terrorists operate. How the anti-terrorist coalition handles such occupation and development can have a vital impact on winning hearts and minds and, therefore, on the outcome of the war on terrorism.

Al Qaeda like more traditional insurgent groups feeds on discontent. The organization requires very few active members so long as it enjoys widespread tacit support, a sympathetic sea in which the extremist fish can swim (to use the Maoist metaphor). Removing the causes of discontent can help to create an environment far less conducive to terrorist operations. In the context of most failed states, a hearts-and-minds campaign consists of meeting basic human needs. People who do not have enough food, clean drinking water, and basic health care will probably be little concerned with political rights. Improving their quality of life might even wean them from extremist political ideology. Under the right circumstances, enough of them might be persuaded to provide background information on terrorist cells. In such impoverished places suitable outlays of cash might go a long way in inducing cooperation.

Hardcore terrorists will not be persuaded to give up the cause, no matter how generous the inducements. September 11 forced a re-evaluation of the terrorist profile. Most of the hijackers were well educated and from middle-class backgrounds. Infiltrating Al Qaeda will prove extremely difficult if not impossible. However desirable, infiltration is not essential to producing operational intelligence. Carefully analyzed and assembled, information from the population in which the terrorists hide can produce such intelligence. Counterinsurgency expert and retired British general Frank Kitson described this process as turning 'background information into contact information'.[36]

Friends and Allies

Hearts and minds have to be won in friendly states as well as in hostile ones. Since the Western alliance consists of popular democracies, domestic opinion in each member state must be persuaded not only as to the justness of the war on terrorism as a whole, but to the rightness of each action within it. In the immediate aftermath of 9/11 the US enjoyed sympathy and widespread support from every NATO ally and most affiliated states. This support lasted through the war in Afghanistan and resulted in substantial material assistance, especially during the current occupation. As in Kosovo, the NATO allies have been content to let the US provide strategic lift and firepower while they supply peacekeepers.

European support dwindled as war with Iraq approached. Britain alone of the NATO allies has supported the US unconditionally, largely for reasons unrelated to the war on terror. The UK desires to keep NATO an Atlantic alliance with a Washington–London axis rather than see it become a European defense force with a Paris–Berlin axis. France and Germany have been most vocal in their opposition to adventurism in the Persian Gulf. Chancellor Gerhard Schröder campaigned (and may have won) on the promise that Germany would not follow the US blindly into war with Iraq. The Russian Federation supported the Afghan war to the point of allowing the US to use former Soviet bases in neighboring Uzbekistan, but it too opposed war with Iraq. Not surprisingly these nations had been critical of the embargo even before 9/11. Indeed, France and Russia had lucrative trade arrangements with Baghdad.

While the US has encouraged, cajoled, and pressured some allies into supporting a war, it could do so only by agreeing (however reluctantly) to work through the UN. In drafting a Security Council Resolution on Iraq, France, Russia, and China insisted on language that would require Washington to seek further Council approval for military action in the event that Baghdad failed to cooperate with arms inspections or did not disclose its weapons of mass destruction.[37] The Bush administration had wanted the resolution to contain a tripwire clause allowing it to attack Iraq immediately in the event of a breach of the UN agreement. The US never got its enabling resolution and so forged its own 'coalition of the willing', which looks more like a coalition of the coerced. In a protracted war against terrorism, American unilateralism will prove unsustainable.

Hearts and Minds at Home

Maintaining popular support for a comprehensive war spanning the globe and lasting years requires a hearts-and-minds campaign at home as well as abroad. In the immediate aftermath of 9/11, few Americans had to be convinced of the need for immediate and robust action against Al Qaeda. Fortunately, Afghanistan provided an unambiguous target that could be struck quickly and with relative impunity. As memory of 9/11 wanes, however, sustaining enthusiasm for a protracted war that produces few dramatic victories may be problematic. The most significant successes prevent terrorist incidents from happening in the first place. The cumulative effect of small, unseen victories, most occurring in the sordid underworld of covert operations, will ultimately win the war. Such victories do not, however, generate popular support nor provide political capital. This realization may have prompted the administration to shift its emphasis to a conventional war against Iraq. Such a move may, however, have disastrous consequences in the long run.

As with the overseas hearts-and-minds campaign, the first imperative at home must be to 'do no harm'. Unfortunately, the temptation to exploit for political purposes the uncritical support given the White House in the current crises may prove irresistible. Potential policy failures fall roughly into a few categories. The government may be tempted to opt for highly dramatic but largely ineffective (and perhaps counterproductive) actions. The party in power may also use the war on terrorism to push its own agenda. Finally, in their zeal to arrest terrorist suspects, law enforcement organizations may target innocent citizens who belong to the 'wrong' ethnic group. Such action will not elicit the cooperation of these citizens, who probably have the background knowledge and language skills to help authorities catch the real terrorists. The past year has seen unhealthy developments in all three categories.

As I have already noted, war with Iraq served an immediate need for clearly visible and highly dramatic action to combat terrorism. Invading and occupying the country has had no appreciable effect on Al Qaeda, as recent bombings illustrate. Washington has produced no compelling evidence (indeed little evidence at all) of a link between Iraq and bin Laden. Since his organization has developed and perpetrated its most dramatic acts while the Iraqi embargo and 'no-fly zones' have been in effect, it is hard to imagine that Saddam has smuggled much aid to anyone. The attacks against an Israeli-owned resort and an El Al airliner at Mombasa in late November 2002 and the May 2003 bombings in Saudi Arabia and Morocco underscore the fact that Al Qaeda has no single geographic center of gravity and plenty of sponsors willing to fund it.

The Iraq War will, at best, have no effect on the war against terrorism; at worst, it could exacerbate an already bad situation. Virtually all Arab states and most of the European allies opposed the war. Unilateralism could drive Arab moderates into the arms of the extremists. Iraq may yet implode in the wake of the American-led invasion, creating yet another failed state that has to be occupied and governed. The Turks remain concerned about the effect of Kurdish autonomy. War with Saddam has also had immediate implications for Iran, Syria, the Gulf States – in fact, the entire region. Under such circumstances, it is difficult to escape the conclusion that domestic political considerations and a desire to control Iraqi oil motivated the war.

Public opinion and political calculations may be behind another administration initiative: the new Department of Homeland Security created in January 2003. Proposed under the auspices of facilitating cooperation between disparate federal departments and agencies that have at least some security function, this bureaucratic megalith may actually hamper counter-terrorism operations, especially if it adopts the top-down, micro-management approach so characteristic of American corporate culture. The key to combating terrorism is decentralization not centralization. Local agencies and organizations must have the freedom to act on hot intelligence immediately without asking up the chain of command for permission to respond.

The same decentralization should be included in reform of both the FBI and CIA, two organizations strangely left outside of the new office. Like the 'duck and cover' campaign of the 1950s, however, the new Cabinet department creates a sense of security, albeit if only from the grandiloquence of its title.[38]

Of all the inappropriate actions taken since 9/11, the serious and steady erosion of civil liberties in the name of 'national security' remains the most alarming. US citizens and innocent residents guilty of no more than immigration violations have been detained without trial, and in some cases without even being charged, denied legal council and even held incommunicado. Reminiscent of the incarceration of Eugene V. Debbs on the grounds that his constitutionally protected free speech represented a 'clear and present danger' during the First World War or internment of Japanese Americans during the Second World War, these acts treat the entire Muslim-American community as inherently suspect. This policy is as unwise as it is unethical. The same Muslim community being harassed has the language skills and regional knowledge Washington so desperately needs in the war on terrorism.

Conclusion

Historical evidence and contemporary experience suggest that terrorism is a weapon and not an end in itself. The current struggle should, therefore, be seen as a counterinsurgency campaign against an organization with very specific regional objectives based upon a larger ideological goal. Such an organization can only be defeated with precise intelligence that allows for the highly focused and limited use of force. This intelligence can only come from the larger communities in which the insurgent terrorists operate. Members of these communities must be encouraged rather than coerced to cooperate in the struggle. They will be motivated to do so only if they see such action as substantially and materially bettering their lives. Addressing the urgent needs and legitimate grievances of such a population can provide such motivation. There is no substitute for an effective hearts-and-minds campaign.

NOTES

1. Volumes have been written on insurgency and counterinsurgency. I have argued for the applicability of counterinsurgency methods to a variety of conflicts in *British Counterinsurgency in the Post-Imperial Era* (Manchester: Manchester UP 1995); and *Peace Operations and Intrastate Conflict: The Sword or the Olive Branch?* (Westport, CT: Praeger 1999).
2. See for example, Robert Thompson, *Defeating Communist Insurgency: Experiences from Malaya and Vietnam* (London: Chatto & Windus 1966) and Douglas S. Blaufarb, *The Counterinsurgency Era* (NY: Free Press 1977).
3. Frank Kitson, *Low-Intensity Operations: Subversion, Insurgency and Peacekeeping* (London: Faber 1971) p.65.
4. For a detailed discussion of this approach see Thomas R. Mockaitis, *British Counterinsurgency, 1919–60* (London: Macmillan 1990).
5. Bruce Hoffman, *Inside Terrorism* (NY: Columbia UP 1998) pp.189–90.
6. Walter Laqueur, *The New Terrorism: Fanaticism and the Arms of Mass Destruction* (NY: Oxford UP 1999) p.5.
7. *Department of Defense Dictionary of Military and Associated Terms, Joint Publication 1-02*

(Washington DC: Department of Defense 2002) p.443.
8. The phrase was coined by Carlo Piscane in 1857. Cited in Hoffman (note 5) p.17.
9. Laquer (note 6) p.4.
10. For a discussion of the Christian Patriot movement see Hoffman (note 5) pp.105–20.
11. Discussion of religious character of Al Qaeda based on Michael Scott Doran, 'Somebody Else's Civil War: Ideology, Rage, and the Assault on America', in James Hodge Jr and Gidoen Rose (eds.) *How Did this Happen? Terrorism and the New War* (NY: Public Affairs 2001) pp.31–52.
12. See, for example, Bruce Hoffman, 'Chapter 4: Religion and Terrorism', in Hoffman (note 5) pp.87–129.
13. Cited in Christopher Harmon, *Terrorism Today* (London and Portland, OR: Frank Cass 2000) p.189.
14. See <http://www.state.gov/www/global /terorism/1997Report>.
15. For a detailed discussion of Al Qaeda's financing see William F. Wecshler, 'Strangling the Hydra: Targeting Al Qaeda's Finances', in Hodge and Rose (note 11) pp.129–44.
16. Rensselaer Lee and Raphael Perl, *Terrorism, the Future, and U.S. Foreign Policy, Issue Brief for Congress* (Washington DC: Congressional Research Service 18 Oct. 2002), received through CRS Web, p.CRS-2.
17. Ibid.
18. Richard Engel, 'Inside Al-Qaeda: A Window into the World of Militant Islam and the Afghan Alumni', *Jane's Defence Weekly* (28 Sept. 2001) p.4 < .
19. Laquer (note 6) p.44.
20. Robert Steele, 'Takedown: Targets, Tools, and Technocracy', in Lloyd Matthews (ed.) *Challenging the United States Symmetrically and Asymmetrically: Can America be Defeated* (Carlisle, PA: US Army War College Strategic Studies Institute 1998) p.125.
21. Stephen Sloan, 'Terrorism and Asymmetry', in ibid. p.185.
22. Hoffman (note 5) p.95.
23. Stephen Sloan (note 21) pp.180–81. Sloan published his remarks before 9/11.
24. Nadine Gurr and Benjamin Cole, *The New Face of Terrorism: Threats from Weapons of Mass Destruction* (New York: I.B. Tauris 2000) p.283.
25. Stephen Flynn, 'The Unguarded Homeland: A Study in Benign Neglect', in Hodge and Rose (note 11) p.187.
26. Robert Thompson, *Defeating Communist Insurgency: Experiences from Malaya and Vietnam* (London: Chatto and Windus 1966).
27. See Mockaitis, *British Counterinsurgency* (note 4).
28. Text of bin Laden's taped remarks, Associated Press, APTV-10-07-01.
29. Fouad Ajami, 'The Uneasy Imperium: Pax Americana in the Middle East', in Hodge and Rose (note 11) p.16.
30. F. Gregory Gause III, 'The Kingdom in the Middle: Saudi Arabia's Double Game', in Hodge and Rose (note 11) p.112.
31. Loosely translated, 'holy warriors', the term *mujahidin* has been applied to the foreign fighters who helped drive the Soviets from Afghanistan. These fighters became the backbone of Osama bin Laden's organization.
32. See US Response: Bush Warns Iran, Syria on Terrorism,' NTI: Global Security Newswire, 22 July 2003, <www.nti.org/d_newswire/issues/2003/7/22/ls.html>.
33. Anglican Observer Office at the UN *et al.*, in association with *Save the Children,* 'Iraq Sanctions: Humanitarian Implications and Options for the Future' (6 Aug. 2002) <www.globalpolicy.org/security/sanction/iraq1/2002/paper.htm#5>.
34. Hanny Megally, Executive Director Middle East and North Africa Division, Human Rights Watch, letter to His Excellency M. Moctar Ouane, Permanent UN Representative of the Republic of Mali, President of the Security Council (20 Sept. 2000) <www.hrw.org/press/2000/09/ouaneltr.htm>.
35. Carel de Rooy, Head of UNICEF Iraq, quoted in, 'Malnutrition down by half among Iraqi children' (21 Nov. 2002) <www.unicef.org/>
36. Frank Kitson, *Bunch of Five* (London: Faber 1977) pp.296, 298.
37. Security Council Resolution on Situation between Iraq and Kuwait, UN document, S/RES/1441 (2002), 8 Nov. 2002.
38. See unpublished essay by Thomas R. Mockaitis and Eugene Robkin, 'Duck and Cover', (unpublished) 22 Nov. 2002.

Al Qaeda and the Radical Islamic Challenge to Western Strategy

PAUL RICH

The 11 September 2001 global crisis prompted by the attacks on the World Trade Center and the Pentagon raises major questions concerning the nature and trajectory of terrorism in the post-Cold War global order. Hitherto, terrorism has been largely debated by analysts at the level of nation states. Terrorist and insurgent movements have also been largely anchored in nationalist and ethnic power bases even when they have sought to mobilise a trans-national ideological appeal on religious or class grounds. There have been a few exceptions to this pattern such as the alliance between the German Baader-Meinhof group and the Japanese Red Army Faction, but even such international alliances as this did not, until at least the 1980s, presage anything like a global terrorist network necessitating a global strategic response.

Counter-terrorist strategies have thus been largely formulated at the nation state level.[1] During the Cold War from the late 1940s to the early 1980s, the debate on terrorism was heavily influenced in the West over political ideology given that many of the insurgent formations were dominated by a Marxist programme of 'national liberation' and a global war against 'Western imperialism'. Counter-terrorist responses by Western states such as Britain, France and the US was largely at the nation state level. While there was widespread swapping of intelligence information between states, nothing like a common global or international response to terrorism emerged given the basic ideological divisions of the Cold War.

Most democratic states have thus resisted the internationalisation of insurgent issues, evidenced by the considerable opposition in Britain to UN or US involvement in Northern Ireland. One of the strongest regional response to terrorism has been that of the European Union in the form of moves to establish a common data base among EU members of known members of terrorist organisations and moves to establish a common EU-wide police force. However, even this still remains in relatively early stages of development and it is not clear how it will work with continuing EU expansion.

Given this largely national response to terrorism – together with some developing regionally-based initiatives like those of the European Union –

the activities of the Al Qaeda terror network present the possibility of terrorism entering for the first time the arena of global strategy. Rohan Gunaratna for instance has argued that 'the global fight against Al Qaeda will be the defining conflict of the early twenty-first century' involving an international collaboration of security, intelligence, law enforcement authorities and national militaries.[2] If this is the case, then it suggests that one of the main strategic implication of the September 11 crisis lies in a shift in the centre of gravity of terrorism from the nation state to a global level. This in turn necessitates a global strategic response by Western states to what is seen as a major attack on their core values. However, the new phase of global terrorism appears to be hydra-headed since there are in fact multiple centres of gravity making any anti-terrorist strategy protracted, complex and without a clearly defined strategic end state.

This study examines these issues and is organised into three sections. The first section discusses the nature of Al Qaeda's challenge to conventional strategy. The second section looks at Al Qaeda in terms of the debate over whether there is now a distinctly 'new' form of terrorism operating in global politics; the third section assesses the capacity of the movement to reorganise itself after the defeat of the Taliban regime in Afghanistan while the final section examines the evolving structure of the Al Qaeda organisation in the wake of the defeat of the Taliban and its continuing capacity to challenge global order, especially in the Middle East and South East Asia.

The Challenge to Conventional Strategy

One immediate response to the terrorist attacks of September 11 was a conventional perception that they in some sense marked a new or possibly postmodern 'Pearl Harbor' in that this was a direct attack on American soil. This sort of perception indicates the paucity of serious strategic discussion on terrorism and its impact at the global level. The main strategic debate that had gone on immediately prior to the attacks was focused on the National Missile Defense system and strategic defence against possible missile attacks by 'rogue states' such as North Korea, Libya, Iraq or Iran. Strategic thinking for the most part remained cast in a strongly realist mind set that emphasised interactions between states, though some analysts of terrorism did point to the growing significance of a religiously-motivated 'new terrorism' that was increasingly moving away from older forms of hierarchical organisation towards decentralised groupings linked through the Internet and email and capable of achieving a high degree of anonymity.[3]

This general lack of a coherent strategic framework through which to understand contemporary terrorist organisations reflects a more general sense of uncertainty in strategic thinking in the post-Cold War period. In its conventional Clauswitzean sense strategy refers to the use of military means to achieve political ends employing as far as possible rational schemes to achieve objectives, whether this be through actual military combat or the threat of it. This conception of strategy has always worked best in societies where there was no particularly sharp distinction between the military and civilian policy makers. In classical empires such as Greece and Rome as well as medieval states in Europe political rulers were often the head of the army in any case. This pattern continued throughout the nineteenth century and into the twentieth century as the Nazi regime in Germany largely sought to fulfil Hitler's grand strategy for a new European order (until impending military defeat led to a desperate attempt at a coup in July 1944 to reintroduce some sense of rationality into German military strategy facing annihilation on three fronts).

After 1945 grand strategy became increasingly dominated by the threat of nuclear conflict. Global military conflict between the superpowers was now inherently irrational since it threatened 'mutual and assured destruction'. Strategic thinking now turned to the logic of deterrence and the threat of military escalation. It was only possible in this context to employ limited military power below commonly understood thresholds as the US and later the Soviet Union discovered to their cost in Vietnam and Afghanistan. Grand strategy pivoted around the projection of military power appeared increasingly outmoded and more suited to the era of Napoleon and Bismarck than to a modern global order in which even large nation states appeared beholden to modern international financial institutions and the support of close allies.

There was, perhaps, one notable exception to this shift away from grand strategy during the Cold War in the efforts of Richard Nixon and his National Security Advisor Henry Kissinger, a strong admirer of the diplomacy of Metternich after the Napoleonic wars, to forge a new tripolar world in the 1970s by bringing Communist China back into the international mainstream. This effort though proved rather short-lived as détente with Moscow collapsed in the wake of the 1979 Soviet invasion of Afghanistan into a 'new Cold War' that ultimately proved to be one of the factors bringing about the very collapse of the Soviet regime in 1991.

The end of the Cold War and US hegemony of the global system has thus, somewhat paradoxically, left the United States without any clear grand strategy. Throughout the post-war period the US tended to rely upon a rather ill-defined 'soft power' to buttress its global domination marked by superior cultural, intellectual and media resources. It is this 'soft power' which has now come under challenge by the September 11 crisis forcing in the process a new debate over global strategy for both the US and the West. In the first instance this debate is directed against the immediate challenge in the form of the Al Qaeda and other terrorist networks. However, if the war becomes a long one, then there is likely to be an inevitable momentum within this debate leading towards a far more profound strategic re-examination of western global power and influence and the possible alliance choices in pursuit of a new pattern of global stability.

Al Qaeda and 'New' Terrorism

The September 11 crisis has forced Western democratic states to start developing a new global counter-terrorist strategy that embraces many of the features that military analysts have for some years now been debating in the form of 'post modern warfare' or 'new war'. Much of this new warfare has occurred in fractured or 'failed' states such as Somalia, Sierra Leone and Afghanistan and is signified by the apparent randomness of much of the violence which often appears to take on a logic of its own. The groupings involved in such conflicts can be diverse ranging from ethnic and 'tribal' groupings to large scale gangs formed out of dispossessed youth under the control of a series of local 'warlords' or strongmen.[4]

Terrorism has also been seen by some analysts to have evolved into a new form in the post-Cold War era as the role and significance of political ideology has declined in international politics. Mark Juergensmeyer has described this 'new terrorism' as appearing 'pointless', since it, 'does not lead directly to any strategic goal, and it seems exotic since it is frequently couched in the visionary rhetoric of religion. It is the anti order of the new world order of the twenty-first century.'[5] Terrorism is in this sense a new form of public performance which seeks to rouse both a general audience world wide as well as a specific audience of committed followers. Religious terrorism has the additional feature of being part of a wider project of what Juergensmeyer has termed 'cosmic war' which employs images of warfare on a grand scale as part of a process of collective psychological empowerment by followers believing that they are ordained by God to wage war against evil. War in thus becomes 'not only the context for violence but also the excuse for it'.[6]

These insights are undoubtedly useful in understanding a movement such as Al Qaeda, and indeed comparing it to other similar religious extremist groups. There are nevertheless dangers in developing the resulting thesis that all such groups classified as engaged in cosmic war are by definition resistant to any form of diplomatic dialogue. The implication of this line of reasoning is that the West has to engage in some form of permanent war on terror which precludes any form of dialogue or diplomacy. This stands in sharp opposition to evidence throughout the Middle East where many Islamist movements in states such as Algeria,

Egypt, Turkey and Morocco have engaged in extensive dialogue with the state. In some instances movements resort to terrorism since they see no other way of prosecuting their goals. Later they may draw back from terrorism activities if opportunities are opened up for dialogue with national governments. This appears for the most part unlikely in the case of Al Qaeda, though some of the insurgent movements it has allied itself to may in time seek such alternative channels of political dialogue.

Al Qaeda reflects the fragmentation and globalisation of radical Islamic insurgent movements in the course of the late 1980s and 1990s. Many of these movements have moved out from simple domestic conflict into the global arena. In part this has been due to a decline in the number of states willing and able to 'sponsor' terrorist movements in the post-Cold War era such as Libya, Iraq, North Korea, Cuba and Syria. It has also reflected a pattern of increasing mobility of terrorist volunteers by the 1980s and 1990s. In the wake of the successful insurgency against the Soviet occupation of Afghanistan in the 1980s, many Arab and Muslim volunteers came to Afghanistan to support Mujahidin resistance. After the Soviet withdrawal in 1989 they were followed by a further wave of recruits supporting the Taliban. By the mid-1990s Afghanistan was one of the most obvious locations for bin Laden to centre his Al Qaeda organisation once it became obvious that the government of Sudan, where he had been based following his departure from Saudi Arabia in 1991, was no longer capable of shielding him.

This mobility of the recruits to Al Qaeda is largely due to the marginalisation of many Islamic radical movements by several Middle Eastern regimes during the late 1980s and 1990s. Al Qaeda's development in the 1990s occurred at a time when many analysts were beginning to point to an apparent peaking of radical Islamism in the Middle East as states embarked on ruthless campaigns of repression and infiltration. In Algeria the Islamic movement became split between the Front Islamique de Salut (FIS) and the more terrorist inclined Groupe Islamique Armée (GIA) during a bitter civil war following the suspension of elections in early 1992 that the FIS looked set to win.

Similarly in Egypt a militant upsurge of Islamic violence in the early 1990s by the al-Jamaa and Jihad was met by repression such that by 1995 the government claimed that it had contained the violence, though this did not prevent further attacks on Western tourists at Luxor and Cairo that killed over 100 Western and Egyptians. In 1996 the Egyptian government announced an Upper Egypt development plan (involving 25 per cent contribution from the government and rest from private sources) in order to meet some of the grievances of the Islamic militants. Widespread distrust appeared still to exist in Upper Egypt towards the government and the police, although in July 1997 the jailed leaders of both the Egyptian insurgent groups declared a unilateral ceasefire.[7] This was probably embarrassing to bin Laden since he had assigned the Gama al-Islamiyya a key operating position inside Al Qaeda.[8]

Some of the uprooted followers of these movements have drifted to Al Qaeda, sometimes coming from 'peripheral' *jihads* such as Bosnia, Kashmir or Chechnya. They have brought a variety of military and organisational skills. Bin Laden's military chief in Afghanistan, for instance, was the Egyptian dissident Muhammad Atef, a former police officer with considerable knowledge of Egyptian intelligence techniques.[9] Additionally, Al Qaeda has recruited full time international terrorist drifters such as Sheik Omar Abdurrahman and Ramzi Yusuf who tried to blow up the World Trade Center in 1993. Following this operation bin Laden sent Ramzi to the Philippines since he was in effect a terrorist nomad who could be sent to more or less any part of the Islamic world.

It appeared to many of these radicals that the upsurge of radical Islamism which had begun with the Iranian Revolution of 1979 was now running out of steam. Following the death of the Ayatollah Khomeini in 1989 the Iranian regime seemed to be moving progressively towards a more pragmatic accommodation with the West. In many Middle Eastern societies Islamists appeared to have abandoned strategies of armed confrontation with the state in favour of a more long-term programme of infiltration of the society's institutions and imposing in the process increasingly tight restrictions on what books or newspapers they can read, what programmes they can see on television or at the cinema or what clothes they may wear. In some instances this strategy appears to be working as in Egypt and indicates a general advancement in Islamist political influence throughout the Arab world.[10] However, such a gradualist strategy does not necessarily accord with a campaign of global *jihad* against the West.

The decline in Islamist political radicalism was starkly exemplified in 1997 when the Iranian President Mohammed Khatami wrote to President Hosni Mubarak of Egypt condemning the Luxor killings as inhumane and cowardly.[11] There were signs too that some Islamic insurgent movements were getting bogged down in sectarian and ethnic divisions which hampered their political effectiveness. Apart from the continuing divisions between the FIS and GIA in Algeria, there were mounting divisions between Sunni and Shia Muslims in Pakistan while Hizballah in Lebanon also underwent a split. In Afghanistan the victory of the Taliban regime in 1996 did not end intra-Islamic dissension but if anything severely heightened it. The regime rested largely on southern Pashtun support and went on a violent offensive against ethnic minorities such as Uzbeks and

Tajiks as well as the Shiite Hazaras, who became victims of a bloodbath in Mazar-i-Sharif in 1998 (in which between 5,000 and 6,000 were massacred) when the Taliban finally retook the city after being expelled the previous year.[12] These internal Shia–Sunni tensions within Afghanistan threatened to get out of control following the murder by the Taliban of 11 Iranian diplomats in Mazar in July 1998 and Iran came to the brink of war with its neighbour.[13]

Bin Laden's mobilisation of Al Qaeda during the 1990s reinvigorated calls for global *jihad* and seize the initiative from other radical Islamic groups such as the floundering Shiite mullahs in Iran. There was no longer any serious claim within Iran to establish a theocratic state based on the doctrine of supreme law giver of *velayat-ifaqih* and the regime appeared to many to be slowly moving towards an accommodation with the West. By contrast, bin Laden based his appeal on a rather different set of myths rooted in the idea of waging *jihad* against the West in order to remove the modern nation state system from the Muslim world and resurrect the Muslim caliphate (which was ended after the First World War). Ayatollah Khomeini's charismatic appeal was always rather limited given his strongly Shiite messianic message and he failed to galvanise the majority of the Sunni community despite the fact that it actually comprises around 90 per cent of all Muslims.

Bin Laden has had considerable success in appealing to Muslims of whatever background, Sunni or Shiite, with a message that stresses the need to restore the values of an Islamic golden age before it was humbled before Christians and Jews. Although bin Laden's background is one steeped in the Wahhabism of Saudi Arabia, there is little to suggest that he has sought to mobilise a specifically Sunni radicalism in opposition to that of the Shiites.[14] Much of bin Laden's thinking was shaped by the teaching of the Palestinian Abdullah Azzam while he was a student in Saudi Arabia. Azzam basically melded together the Arabic and Wahhabist forms of Islam with those of the Deobandi versions from Pakistan. Azzam was in turn strongly influenced by the teachings of the Egyptian writer Sayyid Qutb who was executed by President Nasser in 1966. Qutb rejected the idea that Western ideas of modernity, including civil society, the nation state and free expression could be reconciled with Islam and urged the overthrow of the state system in the Middle East.[15] Here in essence are the roots of Al Qaeda's ideology of global *jihad* against the West

Bin Laden's programme goes beyond simple opposition to Israel and calls for a Palestinian state by demanding the removal of US forces from Saudi Arabia and indeed a revolutionary overthrow of the Saudi and Pakistani regimes which he sees as apostates from Islam. Al Qaeda has become the fountainhead for Islamic revolutionary movements around the world and calls for a multitude of holy wars against Western interests. Bin Laden champions the restoration of the Islamic caliphate as a focus for a world wide Islamic cultural renewal against corrupting Western influences, though he has stated that the only way to do this is by force. In February 1998 he announced from Afghanistan the creation of the 'World Islamic Front for Jihad against Jews and Crusaders' which declared its intention to attack Americans and American allies anywhere in the world.[16]

Bin Laden's message amounts to a radical Islamic grand strategy seeking both to unify Muslims internationally and to wage global war against western and especially American interests. This project might be seen by many in the West as hopelessly utopian as it seeks to remove the entire edifice of the Westphalian state system that has been imposed on the Middle East and South East Asia since at least the nineteenth century. It emerges from a cultural tradition though in which Islam was forged very much through what Michael Scott Doran terms a 'triumph of the will' as Muhammad and his followers in the seventh century started a movement that brought down empires.[17] It is felt that this can be repeated again in the wake of the defeat of the Soviet Union in Afghanistan in the 1980s.

Some analysts have focused strongly on bin Laden's iconographic status as a symbol of Islamic willingness to stand up to the United States. However it would be wrong to overly stress the figure of the man as opposed to the ideas behind Al Qaeda – this leads quite naturally to the Western media then portraying him as a latter day Ian Fleming villain with grandiose designs for world domination. It is the idea of global Islamic *jihad* which have drawn such strong support among some quarters in the Islamic world combined with the fact that bin Laden seeks the revolutionary overthrow of corrupt Middle East regimes that are seen to be conniving with the West.[18] Al Qaeda's call for a revolutionary Islamic internationalism comes in the wake previous secular internationalism movements, most notably that of the Third Communist International after the Bolshevik Revolution in Russia in 1917 that soon fell prey to the cynical promotion of Soviet state interests under Stalin from the late 1920s onwards.[19]

There is a strongly internationalist quality to the Al Qaeda organisation which has managed to recruit among the disaffected *umma* right across the Islamic world. John Mackinlay has suggested that bin Laden is really a 'global insurgent' since he has taken the model of nationally-based insurgent movements and applied it at the global level since 'he does not rely on population to sustain him, his targets lie beyond his centre of gravity but are still within the reach of his operational organisation'.[20]

Clearly Al Qaeda has developed a complex international network that represents the most significant terrorist movement in global politics yet seen. It is one that has taken many observers, schooled in the precepts of realism and the centrality of sovereign state interests, somewhat by surprise. In part this was due to the general weakness of Arab political organisation and the absence of a strong state tradition in the Middle East, which has traditionally been viewed by Western analysts as being centrally located on tribe and clan. Al Qaeda has compounded these stereotypes by adapting some aspects of the Leninist model of democratic centralism and forging a tightly organised cell structure instilled with precepts of self-sacrifice, reverence for leadership and fierce ideological loyalty.[21]

The model may well set a new pattern for international terrorist movements in the twenty-first century, though much will depend too on Al Qaeda's capacity to interlock with local insurgency movements. Islamists have displayed a remarkable creativity in their mobilising ideologies that can relate to local conditions and Al Qaeda may in time face similar problems of the international communist movement in the early twentieth century as it sought to mobilise an internationalist revolutionary ideology at the global level that still related to the widely differing conditions at the local level.[22]

Al Qaeda's record in Sudan and Afghanistan suggests that it has taken on some of the features of sovereignty when it acquired access to import and export licensing, travel documents and the protection of its members from any action by the host government. Steven Simon and Daniel Benjamin have even suggested that Al Qaeda acts as a 'quasi virtual state' since in Afghanistan it enforced rules, controlled territory and maintained armed forces.[23] Whether these quasi sovereign features will continue now that the organisation has lost any cohesive territorial base remains to be seen; it is clear though that the loss of its control over parts of Afghanistan has been a setback, even if this fails to prevent it mounting further spectacular terrorist attacks. Nevertheless there still remains a basic strategic problem for Western defence planners when formulating strategies against a movement such as this. Al Qaeda has no one single centre of gravity but multiple ones. It is this flexibility that makes it one of the most important examples of asymmetric warfare in the twenty-first century.

Al Qaeda and the Rise and Fall of the Taliban

Al Qaeda's network certainly secured one central objective in the form of massive international shock and surprise with the September 11 bombings. The network is a loosely organised one and – as some analysts have been noting for years – resembles in some respects modern business organisations with its decentralised structure of authority and reliance upon local level initiative for the formulation of new 'projects'. Peter Bergen has seen Al Qaeda as a form of multinational holding company with a core management group holding partial or complete interests in various other 'companies'.[24] This extreme organisational flexibility certainly helped it to regroup following the reversal it suffered after the US-led invasion of Afghanistan following the September 11 attacks.

Al Qaeda's capacity to do this was partly aided by the strategy employed by the US-led coalition that removed the Taliban regime from power in Kabul. Operation 'Enduring Freedom' was at best only a limited success as it revealed major failings in US strategic thinking. The operation was put together in great haste by the Bush administration in order to appease US domestic opinion and reassure it that something was being done to avenge the destruction of the Twin Towers. This meant that no really long-term strategy was developed towards developing a stable post-Taliban regime. The US-led coalition dropped some 12,000 bombs and missiles and spent some $3.8 billion in the first three months of the war to remove the Taliban. It killed some 3,000 enemy soldiers and captured a further 7,000. It failed though to capture most of the Al Qaeda leadership that had been active in Afghanistan before September 11. US strategy was primarily directed towards attempting to split the less dogmatic sections of the Taliban from the hardliners by killing key figures such as Mullah Omah and Defence Minister Obeidullah Khan and Justice Minister Mullah Nooruddin Turabi. It was hoped that this would then enable coalition to be forged between an amenable 'rump Taliban' and other Pashtun elements assembled by Pakistan leading to a unity government under the former king Zahir Shah.

There was a large degree of fantasy behind this project since much depended upon successfully eliminating the hardline Taliban figures and successfully bringing the other Taliban sections on board. It is hard to see how they would have easily accepted the authority of the elderly king who had been in exile for the last three decades. Moreover although Zahir Shah is formally descended from the Mohamedzay Pashtun clan, he has been alienated from Pashtun cultural traditions having been educated in Persian and French.[25]

In the event the Taliban collapsed much sooner than expected in the face of a protracted bombing campaign and the US eventually ended up installing a narrowly-based regime in Kabul centred around Hamid Karzai.[26] Karzai is a rather untypical figure in current Afghan politics. An intellectual and committed Westerniser he is chief of the Pashtun Popalzai tribe centred on the city of Kandahar. He initially tried to work with the Taliban, hoping for a posting as ambassador to the UN. In 1998 he began to organise against the regime and the following year took over his tribe's chieftainship. In the wake of the September 11 attacks he began organising a militia to foment an anti-Taliban movement inside Afghanistan. At this point the US ambassador Wendy Chamberlain ignored him, though he was taken rather more seriously by the British government. Inside the Bush administration the question of whether to support Karzai prompted some heated debate as Colin Powell was reluctant to come out in his support if this meant antagonising the Pakistani Inter-Services Intelligence which up to this point was opposed to him given that most of his support came from within the non-Pashtun Northern Alliance.[27]

In the event, Washington only finally came out in support of Karzai some four weeks into the war against the Taliban. By this stage it was clear that Karzai enjoyed the support of many of the modernisers in the Northern Alliance coalition such as Dr Abdullah Abdullah, General Mohammed Qasim Fahim and Younis Qanooni. The collapse of the Taliban led to Karzai heading a new interim administration established under UN auspices in Bonn on 6 December 2001 that was to rule for six months, though it was also clear that to many tribal leaders Karzai was heavily dependent on US support. The new administration proved very quickly to be very weak and unable to transcend major divisions between the 'United Front' (consisting of the Northern Alliance plus the Uzbek faction of General Abdul Rashid Dostum) and the 'Rome Group' centred around the former king Zahir Shah.[28]

This weakness of the post-Taliban administration of Afghanistan has played to a considerable extent into the hands of Al Qaeda. Throughout December a major strategic opportunity to flush out most of the remaining 3,000–4,000 'foreign militants' was lost as the US continued to rely heavily on warlord allies in the south of the country. It was during this period that bin Laden himself escaped from the country over one of the many mountain routes into Pakistan and Al Qaeda began to refocus its activities towards South East Asia.

So how successful has been the US-led campaign in Afghanistan in the aftermath of the September 11 attacks? In many respects the removal of the Taliban regime succeeded in hitting only one of the centres of gravity of the organisation. Right from the start of the planning for the Afghanistan invasion the US has been faced with the basic problem of defining exactly who its enemy was and its ultimate strategic aim. Afghanistan has undoubtedly been a useful base for Al Qaeda operations, though it was by no means the only terrain on which it could operate. There are numerous other locations where terrorist training could take place. Being closely linked to any one particular rogue state such as Sudan and then Afghanistan has proved financially quite costly for Al Qaeda – by the time it moved to Afghanistan it was short of funds having lost an estimated $150 million in Sudan. The terrorist operations it did launch out of Afghanistan were notable for their relative cheapness and dependent upon committed men who required relatively few funds.[29]

In any case Al Qaeda has managed to penetrate most societies in the world where there are sizeable Muslim communities and in the process established 'the most complex, robust and resilient money-generating and money-moving network yet seen'.[30] Al Qaeda creamed off profits from providing goods and service to many Muslim communities around the world as well as engaging in a variety of activities including money laundering, drug trafficking and black marketeering. It has even engaged in illegal trading in precious stones such as diamonds from West Africa, striking deals that were reputed to be worth $20 million in the months before September 11.[31]

Al Qaeda has also established bank accounts round the world as a means of disguising its funds which in many cases it has received from private individuals or Islamic welfare organisations. Tracking these links down will in many cases take years and will depend upon heightened international cooperation. This form of global terrorism has affected the global economy and transformed the geopolitical nature in which terrorism can be viewed.[32]

Even though Afghanistan is likely to remain in a highly fragmented state for the next decade or more – with the possibility even of some form of revival in Taliban support – it is unlikely that Al Qaeda will seek to make the country its central base of operations once more. The continuing Western military involvement in the territory ensures that it would be a difficult terrain to re-enter. There are strong signs that Al Qaeda has once more relocated, this time towards South East Asia as well as other possible terrains such as Chechnya and Kashmir. The geopolitical significance of this will thus be examined in the last section of this essay.

A Shift Towards South East Asia?

The Bali bombing on 12 October 2002 suggests that in the months since the defeat of the Taliban regime in Afghanistan Al Qaeda has begun a process or refocusing its strategy and altering its main axis of operations to South East Asia. One analyst, Kumar Ramakrishna, has likened this strategy to that of General Vo Nguyen Giap in Vietnam who, in the early stages of the Vietnam War at least, avoided direct military confrontation with the US military since he knew he could never win such a confrontation. Indeed such an indirect strategy was premised around the notion that the US centre of gravity was less its fielded military force but domestic US public opinion which lost faith in prosecuting the war.[33] The central difference at this point though is that while Giap saw US public opinion as capable of being moved towards outright opposition to the war in Vietnam bin Laden has stated that they are enemies of his global *jihad*.

In any case, Al Qaeda's links with South East Asia were by no means entirely new since bin Laden had been instrumental in sending Ramzi Yusuf to the Philippines in the wake of the bombing of the World Trade Center in

1993. In Manila Ramzi planned with two others to assassinate Pope John Paul II in January 1995 while on a visit to the Philippines. A fire in his flat forced him to flee and he was eventually betrayed in Pakistan and extradited to the US where he was sentenced in 1997 to 240 years in prison.

Over the subsequent years Al Qaeda has managed to forge a series of links with Islamic insurgent groups in the region such as Kumpulan Militan Malaysia (KMM) and the Jemaah Islamiyyah (JI), which operates in Singapore, Malaysia, Indonesia and the Philippines. In addition there are reported links with Filipino radical groups such as Abu Sayyaf and the Moro Liberation Front (MLF) as well as the Indonesia group Laskar Jihad, which is involved in a violent conflict with Christians in Poso in Central Sulawesi.

In the Philippines Al Qaeda established Islamic welfare organisations such as the International Islamic Relief Organisation (IIRO) and Mercy International. These organisations were initially run by Arabs but then Filipinos progressively took over as the Arabs came to be linked to terrorist networks. The anti-terrorist campaign being waged by the Filipino government and military also prompted Al Qaeda to penetrate the business and commercial sectors and there was a rapid growth in companies with Al Qaeda links, partly due to a lack of international interest in the region until the East African embassy bombings in 1998.

There was also a lack of support during the 1990s in the West for Filipino intelligence operations, though throughout the 1990s the growth of the MLF threatened Filipino political stability as it sought to undermine the peace accord that had been negotiated between President Fidel Ramos and the Moro National Liberation Front (MNLF) in 1996.[34] A more militant wing of the MNLF eventually split away under the leadership of Professor Abdul Rasul Sayyaf and has engaged in anti-Christian terrorist activities in pursuit of an independent Muslim state in the Southern Philippines. One of the main financial backers of Abu Sayyaf has been reputedly Muhammed Jamal al-Khalifa, who married bin Laden's sister.[35] This group is widely believed to have close links to Al Qaeda and to have engaged in widespread terrorist activities including the kidnapping of Western tourists. This has done much to damage the tourist economy of the Philippines.

In the case of Indonesia, Al Qaeda was hampered during the 1990s by the repressive military regime and tended to work with Indonesian Islamists in exile in Malaysia. However from the early 1990s it began to establish a pan-Islamic network by infiltrating Jemaah Islamiyyah and the Indonesian-based Islamic Group (IG). The existence of a regional network however remained a secret until it was uncovered by the Internal Security Department (ISD) of Singapore, leading to a series of arrests in January

2002. The training of the JI recruits had taken place at Negri Sembilan in Malaysia before they were sent on to Afghanistan for tougher training by Al Qaeda.[36]

The Bali bombing of October 2002 can thus be seen within a wider context of a well organised and persistent strategy of infiltration of the South East Asian region by Al Qaeda with the objective of establishing a coherent regional terrorist network that transcends state boundaries. The bombing was planned by operatives from JI led by Imam Samudra (who has been trained in Afghanistan) and was targeted against western presence in South East Asia, especially Australian tourists.

The long-term implications of this strategy are profound. Islam was introduced into the region by traders and has traditionally accommodated itself to other religious traditions such as Buddhism, Hinduism and Christianity. For the most part the Islamic tradition in South East Asia has been tolerant and has avoided the strains of Islamic radicalism that have been prevalent in the Middle East. The impact of the 1979 Iranian revolution was relatively marginal and tended to drive the Islam of the region into culturally conservative channels rather than overt political radicalism.[37]

However in the Philippines radical Islam in the southern part of the country has been able to present itself as a response to a dominant Catholicism shaped by the Spanish crusading colonisers and deeply influenced by the assimilating values of the conquistadors. Islam in this context is strongly linked to the promotion of separate ethnic and cultural identity in locations such as that of the Moros in the southern islands of the Philippines who have retained their own distinct language in the face of Christian settlement in the islands. Paradoxically the Islamic identity of this region was heightened by CIA recruitment of Muslims from this part of the Philippines to engage in insurgent war against Soviet occupation of Afghanistan in the 1980s.[38]

Al Qaeda seeks to transform this situation in South East Asia by mobilising the young, predominantly male *umma* in the region behind its call for global *jihad*. It then links them to wider patterns of terrorism and insurgency in Afghanistan and the Middle East. Court evidence has revealed that Al Qaeda operatives have used Malaysia as a base for operations such as the bombing for the USS *Cole* in Yemen while Kuala Lumpur was, along with Hamburg, the major base for the September 11 attacks.[39]

The stress of South East Asia, however, may detract from other locations such as Sub-Saharan Africa where Al Qaeda has shown itself capable of working with considerable effect, as evidenced by the 1998 embassy bombings in East Africa and the blowing up of the Paradise hotel in Mombasa in November 2002. Africa has a large and growing Muslim population, though in many cases they are heavily embroiled in the local politics of their respective countries. African states are also weak and in some cases, such as Somalia and Sierra Leone, have effectively collapsed.

There is evidence that bin Laden views the continent as a good recruiting ground for new terrorist recruits and a relatively safe place to plan operations and construct bombs. It is also a terrain where it really might be possible to dissolve weak post-colonial state structures and integrate them into a grander political edifice that would fit into his grand design of a new Islamic caliphate. The career of one of his operatives, Emad Abdel wahid Ahmed Alwan, otherwise known as Abu Mohammed, illustrates that such a strategy may be developing. Abu Mohammed went to Africa from Afghanistan in June 2001 with the objective of uniting Islamic groups in Egypt, Algeria, Sudan as well as Sub-Saharan Africa under the overall aegis of Al Qaeda. In early 2002 Abu Mohammed reached Algeria where he tried to contact Hassan Hattab leader of the radical Islamist Groupe Salafiste Pour Prediction et Combat (GSPC) with the aim of getting him to attack targets with international rather than local significance in return for Al Qaeda funds. Hattab appears not to have been interested and Abu Mohammed then went on to contact other movements in Sub-Saharan Africa before finally being killed by Algerian security forces in November 2002.[40]

The African case suggests that Al Qaeda has a range of different options open to it now that it has moved from Afghanistan. However there are also signs that in doing this the movement risks becoming overstretched and vulnerable to increasing Western intelligence penetration as it embarks on such as massive project as global *jihad*.

The Longer Term

In the longer term the major challenge presented by Al Qaeda is that it may develop the capability to mount a major strategic attack on the West involving weapons of mass destruction (WMD). September 11 was a major symbolic attack which was highly successful in terms of securing a high level of terror and panic in large sections of the Western media. The actual destruction it wrought was not as much as Al Qaeda apparently intended since bin Laden hoped for many more thousands of American casualties. It certainly demonstrated American's strategic vulnerability to this kind of attack and this could impact eventually even on its military capabilities. The use of WMD in one or more major American cities would have a significant impact on its military personnel who would be overstretched in maintaining law and order and rescuing victims. Likewise it is not inconceivable that spectacular attacks may be mounted on American or Western military installations, bases or ships (the crash landing of a plane onto an aircraft carrier for instance). Such attacks would in all eventuality push the West onto the strategic defensive.

Al Qaeda was not completely closed to Western intelligence penetration prior to September 11 as subsequent trial evidence has made clear. However the organisation was able to benefit from what some critics have seen as a marked weakness by Western intelligence agencies such as the CIA to take any risks with its agents, who for the most part failed to 'go native' in states such as Afghanistan.[41] However, the mobilisation of Western intelligence capacities subsequent to September 11 strongly suggests that Al Qaeda is far less likely in the future to repeat the success of its Hamburg-based cell in attacking New York and Washington without any prior intelligence warning. This does not of course mean that the odds are entirely in the West's favour . If Al Qaeda can continue to form new cells as old ones are broken up the probability is that it must sooner or later strike lucky with another major target.

The strategic challenge for the West is thus a very difficult one. It has in the longer term to mount a strategy that can in the end undermine Al Qaeda's ideological appeal to disaffected Islamic groups throughout the Muslim world.[42] By any standards this can be considered a daunting task. However it is probably true to say that Al Qaeda, like all other terrorist groups, will have some sort of finite lifespan. Most terrorist groups either fail, dissolve from within or evolve into other forms of political organisation even if they leave a legacy of terrorist involvement behind them. What exactly the life-span of a rather novel form of international terrorist organisation such as Al Qaeda is impossible to predict.

To this extent the challenge facing the West is to evolve a sophisticated multifaceted strategy of combating global terrorism involving the freezing of terrorist assets and bank accounts, the successful intelligence penetration of terrorist networks and the careful targeting of particular terrorist targets with decisive military force, including smart weaponry. If kept to a generally low level of military engagement this strategy is increasingly likely to produce results so long as it avoids what is seen as a direct engagement with the Muslim world and an attack on its core values. To do otherwise risks producing a massive political reaction in the Islamic world with a major long-term threat to Western strategic interests in the region.

NOTES

1. Some analysts saw the Western examples of terrorism in the late 1960s and 1970s as more a case of the spread of violence through contagion as terrorist aims, methods and ideology were borrowed from the Third World. See Manus I. Midlarsky, Martha Crenshaw and Fumihiko Yoshida, 'Why Violence Spreads', *International Studies Quarterly* 24/2 (June 1980) pp.262–98.
2. Rohan Gunaratna, *Inside Al Qaeda: Global Network of Terror* (London: Hurst 2002) p.221.
3. See for instance Ian O. Lester *et al.*, *Countering the New Terrorism* (Santa Monica, CA: RAND 1999).
4. See the collection Paul B. Rich (ed.) *Warlords in International Relations* (Basingstoke, UK: The Macmillan Press 2000).
5. Mark Juergensmeyer, 'Understanding the New Terrorism' in Bruce Hoffman *Inside Terrorism* (NY: Columbia UP 1998)
6. Mark Juergensmeyer, *Terror in the Mind of God* (Berkeley: Univ. of California Press 2001) p.149.
7. Fawaz A. Gerges, 'The Decline of Revolutionary Islam in Algeria and Egypt', *Survival* 41/1 (Spring 1999) pp.113–25; Jeffrey A. Nedoroscik, 'Extremist Groups in Egypt', *Terrorism and Political Violence* 14/2 (Summer 2002) p.71.
8. Yoram Schweitzer, 'Osama bin Laden and the Egyptian Terrorist Groups'.
9. It was Atef who reputedly set up the organisational networks behind the East Africa embassy bombings in 1998. 'Al Qaeda's Egyptian Leaders', <www.stratfor.com>; Olivier Roy, 'The Radicalization of Sunni Conservative Fundamentalism', <www.isim.nl/newsletter/2/geenral/2.html>.
10. John R. Cooley, *Unholy Wars: Afghanistan, America and International Terrorism* (London: Pluto Press 2000) p.262.
11. Ibid. p.117.
12. Ahmed Rashid, *Taliban: Islam, Oil and the New Great Game in Central Asia* (London and NY: I.B. Tauris 2001) p.74.
13. Cooley, *Unholy Wars* (note 10) pp.204–5. The Taliban claimed the Iranians were not diplomats but intelligence agents. The Iranians were angry that the Taliban's actions threatened its growing rapprochement with the Clinton administration in the US.
14. As suggested for instance by Roy (note 9).
15. Robert Marquand, 'The Tenets of Terror', *Christian Science Monitor* (18 Oct. 2001).
16. Peter L. Bergen, *Holy War: Inside the Secret World of Osama bin Laden* (London: Phoenix 2002), p.39; Reuel Marc Gerecht, 'The Gospel According to Osama Bin Laden', *The Atlantic Monthly* (Jan. 2002).
17. Michael Scott Doran, 'Somebody Else's Civil War', *Foreign Affairs* (Jan./Feb. 2000) p.27.
18. Roland Jacquard, *In the Name of Osama Bin Laden* (Durham, NC, and London: Duke UP 2002) p.111.
19. For details of this phenomenon and its impact on international relations see Fred Halliday, *Revolution and World Politics: The Rise and Fall of the Sixth Great Power* (Basingstoke, UK: Macmillan 1999) pp.103–10.
20. John Mackinlay, 'Global Insurgent', *The World Today* 51/11 (Nov. 2001).
21. Gunaratna (note 2) p.222.
22. Doran (note 17) p.37.
23. Steven Simon and Daniel Benjamin, 'The Terror', *Survival* 43/4 (Winter 2000) p.10.
24. Bergen *Holy War* p.32 (note 16); Yael Shamar, 'Osama bin Laden: Marketing Terrorism' <www.ict.org.il/articles>, (22 Aug.1998).
25. Nyier Abdou, 'My enemy's enemy', *Al Ahram* 8 (14 Nov. 2001).
26. Carl Conetta, *Strange Victory: A Critical Appraisal of Operation Enduring Freedom and the Afghanistan War* (Washington DC: Project on Defense Alternatives Monograph #6, 30 Jan. 2002) p.5.
27. Ahmed Rashid, 'Hamid Karzai from Lightweight to Heavyweight in Afghan Politics', *Eurasia Insight* (10 Dec. 2001).
28. Amin Saikal, 'Afghanistan after the Loya Jirga', *Survival* 44/3 (Autumn 2002) p.50.

29. Peter Bergen, 'The Bin Laden Trial: What Did We Learn?', *Conflict and Terrorism* 24 (2001) p.430.
30. Gunaratna (note 2) p.61.
31. Amelia Hill, 'Bin Laden's $20m African "blood money" Deals', *The Observer* (20 Oct. 2002).
32. Yael Shahar, 'Tracing Bin Laden's Money'<www.ict.org.il>.
33. Kumar Ramakrishna, 'An "Indirect" Strategy for Trumping Al-Qaeda in Southeast Asia', <www.ndu/inss/symposia/Pacific2002/ramakrishnapaper.htm>.
34. Gunaratna (note 2) p.183.
35. Cooley (note 10) pp.255–6.
36. ibid. p.186.
37. Ramakrishna (note 33) p.6.
38. Cooley (note 10) p.250.
39. Gunaratna (note 2) p.194.
40. Jason Burke *et al.*, 'Terror that Haunts Africa', *The Observer* (1 Dec. 2002).
41. Reuel Marc Gerecht, 'The Counterterrorist Myth', *The Atlantic* (July/Aug. 2001); and 'The Necessity of Fear', *The Atlantic* (28 Dec. 2001).
42. Gunaratna (note 2) p.238.

Operation 'Enduring Freedom': A Victory for a Conventional Force Fighting an Unconventional War

WARREN CHIN

A persistent view in both academic and military circles concerns the effectiveness of conventional military power fighting unconventional wars.[1] The failure of counter insurgency campaigns by the Europeans in their former colonies, the US in Vietnam and Somalia, the Soviets in Afghanistan and more recently in Chechnya suggests that conventional military forces are ineffective when fighting unconventional wars. Interestingly, this problem is also apparent within the context of conventional forces of Third World states; a good example of this being the failure of the Vietnamese army in its war in Cambodia in the 1980s, all of which suggests that this failure is due to some intrinsic weakness of conventional military power.

The apparent success of the US military campaign Operation 'Enduring Freedom' (OEF) against the Taliban government of Afghanistan and Osama bin Laden's 'terrorist organisation',[2] Al Qaeda, presents a new perspective that challenges this orthodox view because, on paper at least, the conventional force fought a successful campaign against an unconventional opponent. Indeed, although it is acknowledged that significant problems remain to be confronted, OEF is seen as providing proof that the ongoing 'transformation' of the American military means that it can operate effectively in all the spectrums of conflict.[3] Thus, according to Air Force General Richard B. Myers, Chairman of the American Joint Chiefs of Staff, while recognising the need for a multifaceted strategy to defeat the threat of global terrorism, in the military realm the most effective way of addressing the threat was through greater investment in C4ISTAR technologies.[4]

However, what if the victory achieved by the US was a chimera? This essay explores this possibility. As such it begins by questioning why conventional military power has performed so poorly in unconventional wars in general. It then focuses specifically on why the Taliban collapsed so spectacularly and assesses whether the US will realise its political objectives through the use of force in Afghanistan and the wider campaign against Al Qaeda. Given the speed with which the Taliban regime was defeated a discussion of failure might seem rather at odds with the reality on the ground.

However, appearances can be deceptive. A good illustration of this was the Soviet invasion of Afghanistan in 1979, which was extremely successful in its early phases but was eventually defeated by the Mujahidin.

The Challenge of Conventional Forces Fighting Unconventional Wars

The pursuit of decisive victory has proved an elusive goal in modern times. Even within the context of conventional inter-state war a notable trend has been the declining frequency with which this goal has been achieved.[5] Sir Michael Howard believes three conditions apply if victory is to be achieved in war today.

First, operational victories must be gained so that the opponent is incapable of either physical or moral resistance.

Second, the defeated power must be deprived of all sources of outside support in reversing the military verdict.

Third, and most important, a government must be found in the defeated country to take on the responsibility of imposing the peace terms on its population. As such, it is vital that the victor's settlement should take into account 'the interests, and the honour of the defeated peoples'.[6]

Of importance are those political factors that obstruct conventional forces from achieving victory in unconventional wars. Quite often the political object or reason for the war makes compromise impossible and this will affect the achievement of Howard's third condition for victory in modern war: the ability of the major military power to offer a meaningful political solution. Thus, in the case of France its wars to preserve its empire in Indochina and Algeria failed in part because Paris was unable to offer the local populace the one thing they wanted: political independence. As a result, governance relied increasingly on direct military coercion to control the populace, which in the case of Algeria degenerated into state terror.[7] Similar problems confronted the US in Vietnam and the Soviet Union in Afghanistan.

There is, however, a further dimension to the political object of the war which focuses on the asymmetry of interests of the belligerents involved. Quite often the conventional forces reasons for fighting are not as powerful as those of its less well-armed opponent and consequently there is a threshold, usually measured in terms of casualties, above which the government of the conventional force is unwilling to continue prosecuting the war. Once this threshold has been reached political and societal demoralisation sets in and the major power is defeated. Frequently, the strategy of the weaker opponent is predicated on creating a bloody, attritional and protracted conflict.[8]

The problem of asymmetry of interests has been particularly acute within the context of the post-Cold War world. As Sir Lawrence Freedman explains, in the current international system there are no major military threats to the interests of major powers like the US. Instead, war is something that erupts on the periphery of the world stage, primarily in the Third World. However, the major military powers are becoming increasingly involved in these wars because of a combination of motives based on moral revulsion on the part of their electorates, and fears that the conflict could escalate and become a much wider war. Consequently, the US became involved in conflicts like Somalia and Bosnia where it had no real interests. The strategic importance of this commitment was that conventional military power remained vulnerable to the opponent's efforts to manipulate American public support for such operations.[9]

This view is contested by Ivan Arreguin-Toft, who points out that even though a major power's interest in a particular conflict might be limited, this may not be perceived as such by its government and military at the time of the conflict.[10] Thus, in Vietnam, although it was clear that the outcome of the war would make no real difference to the material interests of the US, there were other issues at stake that made the war extremely significant in terms of prestige, power, and checking the influence of the Soviet Union and China.[11] Why then does the recent record of wars between strong and weak powers show a net gain to the underdog?[12] Arreguin-Toft's argument is that since World War II, two dominant strategies emerged in different parts of the world system.

The first he terms *blitzkrieg*, that is, conventional war, which originated in Europe during World War II and became the dominant model of war for both Western and Eastern blocs during the Cold War.

The second is *guerrilla* warfare, namely unconventional war, which arose primarily in the Third World. It is, he believes, the interaction between these two different strategies that has frequently resulted in the failure of conventional forces in unconventional wars.[13] The solution therefore is to select the appropriate strategy, but why is conventional or *Blitzkrieg* war an inferior method of responding to *guerrilla* war?

In operational and tactical terms the contrasting organisation and methods used in conventional and unconventional wars provide an important explanation as to why conventional forces have performed badly in unconventional wars. Conventional wars are military operations conducted between land, sea and air forces, which are designed to concentrate the maximum level of force against an opponent's armed forces. Wars are won through the execution of successive battles that seek to annihilate the enemy's forces. It is by defeating the enemy's armed forces in battle that both military and consequently strategic victory is achieved. Examples of such wars include the two world wars of the twentieth century.

Unconventional wars are characterised by a conscious decision made by a state or sub-state group to rely on an unorthodox range of means to achieve their aims. Such actions include urban and *guerrilla* warfare, and terrorism. As such there is no immediately identifiable force and no set piece battles. From the perspective of the conventional force, fighting an unconventional war is a frustrating experience simply because there is no clear delineation between front and rear areas, it is unclear who the enemy is and there are no major battles. As a result, it is difficult, if not impossible to know where to concentrate all available firepower and consequently how to defeat the opponent. It is this style of war that is so prevalent today. Of the 110 wars that took place between 1989 and 1999, only seven were classic inter-state conflicts; the rest were civil wars primarily involving unconventional forces.[14]

The Transformation of the US Military

Arreguin-Toft's analysis suggests that governments and military organisations are capable of making rational choices concerning their mode of operation. In reality, it is not clear that they are so detached and objective in their thinking. A military organisation that is trained and equipped to fight in a certain manner will find it difficult to adjust its doctrine, organisation and equipment so that it can conduct different types of operations. It is perhaps this inertia that explains why the major military powers have retained their conventional forces when the experience of wars over the last 50 years indicates the need for change.

The American military does not have a good track record in fighting unconventional wars. Such is the scale of this failure that one observer commented that a pronounced characteristic of unconventional war was that it usually entailed the defeat of the US military in such conflicts.[15] Ironically, the political and military reaction of the US to this poor performance has been to maintain its commitment to high-technology conventional war. Thus, the introduction of the Weinberger Doctrine in the 1980s was a political declaration that the US preferred to fight a particular style of war that conformed to the basic maxims of conventional war.[16]

The American armed forces also resisted external pressure to reform so that they were better equipped to operate within unconventional conflict environments. Although organisational and doctrinal changes were imposed on them in the 1980s, the US military remained firmly committed to fighting conventional war.[17] This bias has continued even though technological, economic and social changes have resulted in the proliferation of unconventional wars, or what Metz has described as 'postmodern' wars in the post-Cold War era.[18] Evidence of this conservatism within the US military can be seen in its failure to embrace the new opportunities presented by the current information revolution.[19] Consequently, in the view of the American military, twenty-first-century war will merely be an evolution of late twentieth-century war. It was feared that the United States' conventional forces would not be able to deal with the emergence of new enemies possessing new capabilities.[20]

More recently Cohen has commented on the innate conservatism of the current strategy of 'Transformation' that is being developed in the latest American defence review.[21] Even now spending plans for conventional battle accounts for 75 per cent of the defence budget.[22]

Other observers have also commented on how the values and norms of American society have given the military establishment a natural predisposition towards fighting conventional war. In essence conventional war is the American way of war.[23] For example, Bowyer Bell argues that:

> America can impose the American way of war upon any conflict no matter how unconventional... Wars are won by the big battalions, by weapons and morale and by generals with luck, won by the application of skill and the weight of metal.[24]

Change within the American military establishment has been conceived so as to ensure that wars, even unconventional wars, are fought on American terms, that is, as though they were conventional wars. Of critical importance to the realisation of this goal has been the investment made by the US in battle-winning technologies which have resurrected the prospect of decisive victory, even in a messy environment of what one analyst described as today's 'mud wars'.[25]

Operation 'Enduring Freedom' (OEF)

OEF represents a good case study to evaluate how successfully American conventional military power has been in imposing its template of war fighting on the environment of unconventional war. The idea that OEF represents a watershed in war might be dismissed because, on paper at least, it was an incredibly one-sided conflict. Afghanistan was a failed state,[26] by 2001 Afghanistan had been locked in a civil war for over 23 years. It had no real system of government, little in the way of an organised bureaucracy, no permanent armed forces, and an economy that generated a gross national product of little more than $5 billion, most of which was raised via smuggling and the drug trade.[27] How could the Taliban government resist the power of the United States' military? As one journalist commented: 'It was very much like an elephant stamping on an ant.'[28]

However, material superiority is no guarantee of victory in war and the Soviet Union's experiences in Afghanistan provided a salutary warning of the dangers of fighting in Afghanistan. The Soviets could never have anticipated how costly this war was going to be when they seized Kabul in 1979. At the height of Soviet involvement in 1986 more than 115,000 troops with the support of 40,000 Afghan government troops and 70,000 paramilitary forces proved unable to control the activities of 70,000 lightly armed Mujahidin *guerrillas*. Soviet casualties over the ten years were over 13,500 killed in action and between 35,000 and 37,000 wounded.[29] In spite of their best efforts the Soviets failed to destroy the Mujahidin or achieve their aim of preserving the Marxist government in power.

Soviet withdrawal in 1989 did not bring the war to an end largely because the Soviets continued to supply the communist government in Afghanistan. Hopes of peace after the collapse of the Soviet Union in 1991 were also quickly dashed because any semblance of national unity had been destroyed by 13 years of civil war; the war empowered particular ethnic minorities that opposed the recreation of a state dominated by the Pashtun majority – traditionally the dominant ethnic group in Afghan politics. Equally important was the willingness of other regional powers to support the various warring factions within Afghanistan as a way of achieving their own aims. It was partly through such intervention by Pakistan and Saudi Arabia that the Taliban came to power in 1996.[30]

The identification of Osama bin Laden and Al Qaeda as the culprits behind the attacks against the World Trade Center and the Pentagon drew the US into this extremely complex civil war. Under normal circumstances both the ongoing war and the current state of Afghanistan would have been sufficient to deter any form of US intervention in this conflict. Thus, plans formulated under the Clinton administration to attack Al Qaeda in Afghanistan and remove Osama bin Laden were shelved both by Clinton and initially the Bush administration.[31]

The objectives of the campaign, as stated by President Bush, were as follows: the destruction of terrorist training camps and associated infrastructure within Afghanistan, the capture of Al Qaeda's leadership and the ending of all terrorist activity within Afghanistan. Added to this was the goal of bringing about the downfall of the Taliban and the creation of a new government capable of providing peace and stability.[32]

In an unconventional war there were significant obstacles standing in the way of the Americans achieving these goals. In political terms it was not clear that killing Osama bin Laden was going to make a significant difference in terms of reducing the terrorist threat posed by Al Qaeda. Related to this were the fundamental social and political conditions in the Middle East that legitimised the actions of Al Qaeda in eyes of ordinary

Arabs. The Arab–Israeli dispute, the suffering of ordinary Iraqis under the UN sanctions regime and the deployment of US forces to Saudi Arabia reinforce the impression that the Arab and the Islamic world are under attack from 'US imperialism', and yet politically the Bush administration is not in a position to offer compromise on any of these issues.

It was also clear that domestic support for war in Afghanistan could not be taken for granted. Thus, although the polls showed strong domestic support for the war (the *Washington Post* in October 2001 found that 94 per cent of people interviewed said they supported the US-led military action),[33] this support was not unconditional. Polls taken in November 2001 indicated that, while the majority of Americans did not object to the commitment of ground forces to operations in Afghanistan, they were anxious that the government might become locked into a protracted war and that US forces might incur significant casualties. Only 52 per cent of the sample said they would still support the war if it became a long struggle in which US casualties were significant.[34]

Moreover, irrespective of surveys of public opinion, the Pentagon's plans were affected by the perception of a fickle public and hence were conscious of the need to fight a short war and keep casualties to an absolute minimum. The political sensitivities surrounding the use of force can be seen from the cautious way in which the Pentagon committed ground forces to the war and the tactics used in operations.[35] Similarly there was no support for the commitment of US troops to the long-term goal of national reconstruction within Afghanistan.

In operational and tactical terms achieving a quick victory was not going to be easy. Geographical constraints reinforced the limits imposed by concerns over casualties and militated against the deployment of a large ground force. Because Afghanistan is a landlocked country, sustaining a ground force operating at the end of a long supply chain via the sea or air was extremely difficult and imposed a ceiling on the numbers of troops operating in theatre. Equally important was the problem of fighting a war in mountainous terrain. Some of the mountain ranges were so high that helicopters, the principal means of manoeuvring forces within the country, experienced extreme flying problems at these altitudes and it was feared that this might result in units becoming isolated and being destroyed.[36]

The nature of the terrain even proved restrictive to light infantry forces.[37] For example, the 10th Mountain Division and the 101st Air Assault Division were forced to leave their artillery in the US because of concerns over how deployable these weapons would be in the mountainous terrain of Afghanistan.[38]

Operating within existing political and geographical constraints meant either waiting and building the necessary infrastructure to sustain large-scale military operations (it took the US two years to construct such an infrastructure to support its operations during the Vietnam War between 1965 and 1967) or relying heavily on technology to achieve the rapid and decisive application of military power. Technology provided an important force multiplier by speeding up both the planning and decision-making cycle of the campaign and allowed the headquarters to run the operation from its base in Tampa Florida, which was 7,000 miles from the battlefields in Afghanistan. Through the use of satellites and data links with unmanned aerial vehicles the headquarters could see the smallest tactical action on the ground in real time.[39]

Equally important, the extensive use of information systems and precision guided munitions (PGMs) made it unnecessary to deploy large forces to support the campaign. Here was clear evidence of the trend described by the Tofflers as the de-massification of war in which, instead of relying on shear mass to destroy the enemy, technology allowed the use of much smaller but more accurate forces.[40] The small scale of the air campaign is clear when compared to 'Desert Storm'. In the case of the latter, the average sortie rate was 3,000 per day. In contrast, in OEF the number of sorties was less than a tenth of this figure and averaged at 200 sorties per day. According to General Tommy R. Franks, commander of CENTCOM, the 200 sorties hit the same number of targets struck by the much larger sortie rate achieved during 'Desert Storm'.[41] In 'Desert Storm' ten aircraft were needed to destroy a single target, in contrast, during OEF, a single aircraft was used to destroy two targets.[42] Increases in precision compensated for the relatively slow rate of aerial attacks. In total PGMs accounted for 70 per cent of the total munitions used in the air campaign during OEF, compared to 30 per cent in Kosovo and 10 per cent in the 1991 Gulf War.[43]

The accuracy of aerial strikes also made it unnecessary to deploy a large ground force. Instead, a small number of special forces were committed to Afghanistan 12 days after the start of the war and, at the height of the war, there were no more than 4,000 US personnel actually deployed within Afghanistan.[44] This relatively small force, which often numbered no more than a few hundred men on the ground at any time, provided targeting information for air strikes to destroy Taliban and Al Qaeda forces. Apparently this synergy between ground forces and air power helped bring about the collapse of the Taliban regime and played a key role in destroying Al Qaeda's infrastructure within Afghanistan.

In a sense, OEF represents the realisation of Luttwak's post heroic military policy, which encouraged the US government to invest in hi-tech stand-off weapons as a means of limiting the possibility of casualties;[45] by December only seven US personnel had been killed and only one of those was caused by the enemy.

However, this dependence on technology, caused in part by the nature of American strategic culture as well as the political imperatives of the war, created significant problems within the political and military domain of the actual campaign. A good illustration of the problems created by this dependency was the air war launched against the Taliban. The earliest stages of 'Enduring Freedom' were characterised by a distinct lack of success in this domain.

In fact, by the end of October there was an increasing sense of dissatisfaction at the lack of progress being made. Journalists began to speak of a stalemate or possible quagmire emerging in Afghanistan, the Taliban were described as being a formidable enemy and the Northern Alliance as lacking the will or the means to defeat the Taliban.[46] Increasingly people began to speculate on the inevitability of a large-scale commitment of US and European forces to remove the Taliban.[47]

The ineffectiveness of the air campaign was caused in part by the imposition of an operational plan designed to defeat a state possessing a recognisable economic and political infrastructure that could be targeted and destroyed. The initial strategy employed was essentially a variation of a theme first used in the Gulf (1991) and then Kosovo (1999): destroy the enemy's air defence capability, attack and destroy the Taliban command and control infrastructure, the Taliban's military forces and those of Al Qaeda, and then hope the regime gave into the demands of the US. Such a plan of operation reflected the basic tenets of current USAF doctrine on the use of air power to achieve strategic effect. This template of operations ignores psychological and moral aspects of the opponent, because these are too difficult to assess, instead it views the enemy as a material system that can be damaged through precision strikes.[48]

But after 23 years of civil war Afghanistan possessed no such structures or targets. As a result, the bombing campaign made little sense and had little or no military effect. Supposed command and control centres located near population centres were bombed and, although PGMs were used, civilian casualties were still caused. So far casualty estimates vary wildly from between 400 to 5,000 Afghan civilians killed as a result of US air strikes.[49]

If it is found that more Afghans died as a result of US bombing than were killed in the attacks against the US on September 11, then this raises profound questions regarding the justness of the American war. An additional problem concerns the impact of such attacks on the hearts and minds of the Afghan people. By the summer of 2002, some Afghans were accusing the US of being no different from the Soviet Union's occupying forces.[50]

Ground operations were also affected by an over reliance on technology. For example, within the first two days of Operation 'Anaconda', which was a three week campaign to mop up the last remnants of Al Qaeda, US special forces were ambushed and trapped by elements of Al Qaeda in the Sha-I-Kot Valley. Intelligence and surveillance systems failed to identify the presence of enemy forces near the landing zone of the force that was ambushed. Apparently, at the height of the battle over 100 US troops fought 800 Al Qaeda fighters. Seven American soldiers were killed, the largest loss suffered on single day since Somalia in 1993.[51]

This intelligence failure happened in spite of American domination of the battle space. Although the US claimed that over 600 Al Qaeda fighters were killed in the operation only a small number of bodies were recovered and it is believed that the vast majority of the Al Qaeda force escaped across the border to Pakistan.[52] Apparently, this failure could have been prevented if more American ground troops had participated in the operation.[53]

The Military and Political Weaknesses of the Taliban

Other analysts explain the defeat of the Taliban in terms of the incompetence of the regime. For example, Connetta argues that the Taliban were something of a 'paper tiger'. The Taliban military machine consisted of a 'hardcore' of between 2,000 and 3,000 personnel, a further 8,000 supporters who joined after 1995 and between 8,000 and 12,000 foreign volunteers. In addition, support from other warlords and different tribal groups provided a further 25,000 soldiers, but the loyalty of this last group was suspect.[54] As a result, the Taliban relied too heavily on its small cadre of military leaders and troops to retain control of the country.

The Taliban also made the tactical mistake of allowing their forces to be caught in open ground where air power was used effectively. Had they remained in the towns and cities they might have been able to negate the effect of air power, cause the US to inflict innocent civilian casualties and, more importantly, inflict casualties on US forces.[55] However, once the air campaign shifted its focus away from targeting the enemy's infrastructure to bombing its forces in the frontline, the rate of attrition resulted in the exhaustion of the Taliban's military hardcore, and the Northern Alliance was able to take advantage of the Taliban's weakened state.

A puzzling aspect of the Taliban's military strategy was that they did not seek to counter America's high-tech *Blitzkrieg* with their own variant of protracted *guerrilla* war. The prevailing view appears to be that this was not a viable option open to the Taliban because their political incompetence and religious dogmatism alienated the majority of the people. Thus, the rapid collapse of their position throughout the country was caused by their inability to create a viable society or state apparatus through which to govern or develop policies that were likely to win the hearts and minds of most Afghan people.

According to Goodson, the Taliban were first and foremost a military rather than a political movement and the senior members of the government divided their time between fighting the war and trying to run the country. They had no policy for reconstruction, education, public health etc. Instead they relied on external organisations to provide such measures. Kabul and Herat were without electricity for several years and water throughout the country was unsafe to drink.[56]

Apparently in their efforts to secure control over the country the Taliban's actions also helped to exacerbate ethnic tensions within Afghanistan. For example, it is claimed that during their 1998 offensive against Mazari-i-Sharif, the Taliban killed over 8,000 minority detainees. There were also concerns that the Taliban were contemplating the genocide of the Hazari Shias.[57]

In addition, there were rumours of dissent and opposition within the Taliban movement itself. The Taliban was composed of a mixed bag of different Pashtun tribes, religious moderates and hardliners, and Pakistani volunteers. It is suspected that even if they defeated the Northern Alliance the Taliban coalition could not have remained intact. As Rashid points out, the potential for such a split occurred in 1998 when Kalqi members of the Taliban were arrested for plotting a coup. Virtually all those arrested came from the eastern provinces of Konar, Laghman and Nagarhar.[58] Consequently, once the US and the Northern Alliance ground offensive began both the population and the local warlords changed sides at the first opportunity.

The problem with viewing the Taliban as being politically and militarily incompetent is that it fails to explain why the movement was able to conquer virtually the entire country in only two years (1996–98). Reference is made to the help provided by the Saudis and the Pakistani military, however, military might did not help the Soviets in their efforts to gain control of the country and their support for the regime of Najibullah did not prevent the collapse of this faction in 1992. Similarly, the Northern Alliance had been a recipient of military aid from Russia and other Central Asian states.

It is important to recognise that the Taliban's religious programme actually appealed to a wide cross section of Afghan society and that religion represented an important source of power.[59] Although nearly all the warring factions in Afghanistan tried to seize the flag of Islam to legitimise their pursuit of power, their actions, especially after the fall of the Soviet-backed Najibullah regime in 1992, served to discredit them in the eyes of many ordinary Afghans. In contrast, the Taliban movement emerged as a direct counter to the abuses of warlord government. Their credibility was enhanced further because so much of its membership was drawn from religious schools in both Afghanistan and Pakistan, and because their actions demonstrated a strong commitment to a version of Islam that, although anti-modernist, tapped into the core beliefs and values of many ordinary Afghan people.[60] In essence, the Taliban offered a war weary population the opportunity of living within a stable and secure society that operated within a legitimate moral framework.

Why then did the regime collapse so spectacularly? It is not satisfactory to claim that the root cause of their collapse was the incompetence of the government. A more cogent explanation might be found by examining the distribution of political power within the Afghan state and the mechanisms that were available for government to exert control over the country. In *The Prince* Machiavelli examines the question why some regimes are easier to defeat and conquer than others. In his view, the answer to this question can be found by examining the make up of political power within the state. Machiavelli made a distinction between two different types of regime. The first was characterised by a marked concentration of power, usually in the hands of a single head of state. In the second regime type, power was decentralised and the head of state was forced to negotiate the extent of his control with competing powers within the state in a political relationship that was confederate in nature. Not surprisingly, it is the second regime that is the easiest to defeat because there is considerably more potential for internal squabbling, civil war and external intervention.[61]

Afghanistan is a perfect illustration of a state where the distribution of power is based within a confederate framework. Even the geography of the country militates against centralised control because of the difficulty of moving from one part of the country to another. The problems of centralising power were compounded by the failure of the Durrani tribe's efforts to build a viable nation-state and the consequent collapse of the country into civil war from 1978 onwards, which resulted in the proliferation of new groups bidding for power.

Under these circumstances, although the Taliban were able to exploit the latent legitimising power of Islam to justify their pre-eminence within the state, the government also depended on the consent of rival political and military groups operating within Afghanistan. In essence support for the Taliban had always been conditional and was based on rational calculation of self-interest by other ruling groups. Viewed in this way the collapse of the Taliban was caused more by the recognition by Afghanistan's local powers that the entry of the Americans changed the correlation of forces within the country and that self-interest dictated that the wisest course of action was to abandon the Taliban.

This analysis of the Taliban's fall from power is important. First, it explains why the adoption of a Maoist style of protracted *guerrilla* war was not an option for the Taliban. Ultimately this depended on all the factions perceiving a common threat and being willing to operate as a loose military coalition as they had done during the Soviet intervention. Second, the way in which the regime collapsed also brings into question the long-term value of the US military victory. If the defeat of the Taliban was the product of political self-interest rather than moral revulsion on the part of the people, then who is to say that the correlation of forces will not change once again and help bring about the resurrection of the Taliban?

Also of interest is another of Machiavelli's observations about these two regime types. He points out that while the centralised state is more difficult to defeat, once its armed forces have been vanquished and its government removed, the power of the state collapses and the conquest of the country is relatively easy. In contrast, conquest of the decentralised confederate regime is more difficult because there are many independent sources of power that are capable of resisting a victor's conquest and control of a country.[62]

This is precisely the challenge confronting the Americans at the present time within Afghanistan. It is becoming increasingly clear that military victory has not resulted in the termination of the war within Afghanistan and that there is considerable frustration within the Bush administration at the failure of OEF to produce more tangible results. Thus, in August 2002 Donald Rumsfeld was looking at new ways to reinvigorate the campaign against the Taliban and Al Qaeda.[63] By the end of August there were even reports from diplomatic sources within Kabul that Mullah Omar had returned to his old base in Kandahar.[64]

The problem of translating a military victory into strategic success has become more complicated because of the dependence of the US government on the Northern Alliance. This meant that it was forced to compromise on the government created by the Bonn Conference, which met to decide on an interim government in December 2001. As a result, both the interim administration, which ran the country for six months and the new government created as a result of the Loya Jirga in June 2002, lack legitimacy because of the continuing domination of the warlords and the over representation of the Tajiks within the government.[65]

The US has also been reluctant to embrace some of the other challenges imposed when fighting an unconventional war, and this has complicated the problems of securing control of a politically fragmented state. Victory in unconventional wars depend more on political and psychological action than the application of military power. However, so far, the US has focused almost exclusively on the military dimension of the campaign. Thus, whereas the war costs the US $1 billion per month, the US promised to provide only $300 million per year to help in the reconstruction of the country.[66] It has resisted efforts to expand the size of the post-war peacekeeping force (International Security Assistance Force) from its current strength of 5,000 troops. This limitation has made it impossible to create a secure environment for the reconstruction of the country beyond Kabul. Until this issue is addressed Afghanistan's economic and political rehabilitation cannot begin.[67]

In the view of the US, this operation should be the function of the new Afghan army, but it is estimated that it could take as long as five years before this force will be able to challenge the power of the warlords, which raises the question of how to promote security and stability until this force is available.[68] At the present time there have been frequent instances of fighting between different tribes, as well as violence between warlords competing for control of various territories.

The goal of destroying Al Qeada is also damaging the prospects for peace within Afghanistan. To achieve this goal the Americans are supporting several warlords who represent a challenge to the authority of the new government, to which the US has also committed itself! At the same time the presence of US forces in Pashtun areas of the country is alienating the people rather than winning hearts and minds. Pashtuns have complained of the treatment they have suffered at the hands of US forces searching for Al Qaeda. For example, the US 82nd Airborne Division, which is operating in the south west of Afghanistan, appears to have angered many ordinary Afghans and it is believed that such treatment explains the increased frequency of rocket attacks against US forces within the country.[69]

This problem has been exacerbated further by the reliance on long range firepower, which has continued to cause innocent civilian casualties. For example, in July 2002, an AC-130 Spectre gunship opened fire on a wedding party, which killed 48 and wounded over 100 people.[70] The increasing opposition of the Pashtuns can be seen from the resurrection of militant Islamic groups like Laskar Fedayan-e-Islami, which is led by elements of the former Taliban and Gulbuddin Hekmatyar's radical Islamic party. This organisation has declared its support for the use of suicide attacks against American personnel.

In global strategic terms the success of this war is more difficult to assess. The most notable aspect of this relates to the failure to capture Osama bin Laden or the leadership of Al Qaeda. US Defense Secretary Rumsfeld did not see the campaign as a failure simply because it failed to capture Osama bin Laden. He pointed out that the Allies did not capture some Nazi war criminals after the end of World War II, but nobody has suggested that the Allies did not win the war.[71] However, in the case of the Nazi war criminals, once they fled from Germany, they no longer represented a threat. Their base of power was firmly under the control of the

Allied powers within Germany. In contrast, those members of Al Qaeda that escaped represent a very real threat. According to a taped broadcast from Al Qaeda it is claimed that 98 per cent of the leadership of the movement are alive and are planning fresh attacks.[72] It is estimated that at least 20 senior aides and hundreds of Al Qaeda fighters escaped to Pakistan and even Iran. Even though the organisation's infrastructure within Afghanistan has been destroyed[73] it still retains a significant presence in Pakistan, from where it can undermine the new Afghan government.[74]

Whatever the actual scale of the threat, analysts such as Michael O'Hanlon recognise that the escape of Osama bin Laden and his associates was a major strategic failure.[75] Less extensive facilities and a more modest base of support have been identified in the UK, France, Belgium, Germany, Spain, Italy, Albania, Morocco, Algeria, India, Singapore and elsewhere. Clearly the US and its allies are aware of the diffuse nature of this threat and the need to adopt a multifaceted strategy, which they have done. For example, by mid-November 2001, the US, in coordination with over 60 nations, had seized terrorist financial assets worth $24 million.[76] However, the UN has also reported that attempts to starve Al Qaeda of funds are failing because European governments have been unwilling to seize funds without more evidence. As a result, Al Qaeda operatives are managing a global fund of over $340 million.[77]

Both 'Enduring Freedom' and the global war against terrorism are flawed because they rely too heavily on the use of military power to achieve their aims. The function of military power appears to be to deter other states from providing safe havens for terrorist organisations like Al Qaeda, and if this fails, to initiate military operations against the guilty states and the terrorist cells operating within their borders. It is clear that the Americans are prepared to initiate such action and the British have also declared their willingness to conduct such operations.[78]

However, there is a danger that such action could help precipitate more rather than less political instability within the international system and consequently more terrorist action. Terrorism as a strategy seeks to achieve its political goals by creating what Carlos Marighela called a 'militarised situation'. By this he meant that a successful terrorist action could cause the government to overreact and to use excessive and indiscriminate force against the population. At that time the terrorists could present themselves as the defenders of the people and further terrorist attacks would have an important political and symbolic value. As a result, support for the government should steadily evaporate to the extent that it lost control and was defeated.[79]

Although this theory was developed within the context of Brazil's political situation in the 1960s, it has been applied by numerous terrorist groups and possibly forms the underlying logic of Osama bin Laden and Al Qaeda's strategy. Seen in this light, the attacks on September 11 served a clear rational purpose: to cause the Americans to strike indiscriminately and with great force, particularly in the Middle East and cause mass protest amongst ordinary Arab people and their governments. In the immediate aftermath of September 11 Professor Samuel Huntington was asked whether this act of violence proved his thesis that future conflicts would be based on clashes between civilisations. He denied that this act confirmed his theory but added that Osama bin Laden would like to use this act to precipitate such a clash between Islam and the West.[80]

Whether this was an intended outcome or not, the possibility of further American military action in the Middle East has caused ordinary Arabs to become increasingly hostile towards America and the West in general. Many Arabs question whether Osama bin Laden was responsible for the attacks on September 11 and view the evidence that has been presented to prove it with some scepticism. According to one journalist the Arab world believes that America's intervention in the region is merely the latest manifestation of colonialism and, like its predecessor, it is designed to exploit and impoverish the Middle East, through the creation of corrupt and authoritarian governments that support western interests. It is for such selfish reasons that the US brought about a change in regime in Iraq.[81]

Conclusion

Since at least end the of World War II political, ideological and strategic conditions created an environment in which conventional military forces found it difficult to operate in what have been termed unconventional wars. This condition worsened in the post-Cold War era, as new sources of instability and new and more unorthodox opportunities for waging war emerged in the international system. The experience of Bosnia, Somalia, and Chechnya reinforced this perception of failure and even successes like Kosovo highlighted the potential vulnerabilities of conventional ground forces and the political problems created by the use of force. The conduct of OEF suggests that a technological solution to these problems has been found and that US conventional forces can at least look to the future with more confidence.

However, although no one doubts that this feat of arms was an amazing accomplishment, it remains open to question whether this will be the 'silver bullet' that many hope. In truth the distribution of political power and the nature of political discourse within Afghanistan, rather than the unpopularity of the Taliban or the invincibility of the American armed forces, meant that it was relatively easy to overthrow the regime.

The biggest challenge confronting America depends on how successful it is in conquering the country, which will depend on winning the support of both local elites and ordinary Afghans. Unfortunately, the political, strategic and military imperatives that have driven the operation have made it more difficult to undertake this process and there is a danger that the US will snatch defeat from the jaws of victory because the US military have not come to grips with the political, social and psychological aspects of this war. They remain focused on the goal of destroying the enemy, but they failed to realise that they were fighting the symptom rather than the cause of the new terror. In fact, their actions could exacerbate the problem both within the context of Afghanistan and within the Islamic world as a whole.

In sum, OEF was a successful military campaign but it is just the beginning both for Afghanistan and the world as a whole. The greatest danger is that we will learn the wrong lessons from this experience and fail to make effective use of the opportunities created by this successful campaign.

NOTES

The analysis, opinions and conclusions expressed or implied in this study are those of the author and do not necessarily represent the views of the Joint Services Command and Staff College, the UK Ministry of Defence or any other government agency.

1. F. Kitson, *Low Intensity Operations: Subversion, Insurgency and Peacekeeping* (London: Faber 1971); M. van Creveld, *The Transformation of War* (NY, NY: Free Press 1991).
2. Terrorism is defined as: 'the deliberate creation and exploitation of fear through violence or the threat of violence in the pursuit of political change. … Terrorism is specifically designed to have far reaching psychological effects beyond the immediate victim(s) or the object of the terrorist attack. It is meant to instil fear within, and thereby intimidate a wider audience that might include a rival ethnic or religious group, an entire country, a national government or political party, or public opinion in general.' See Bruce Hoffman, *Inside Terrorism* (NY, NY: Columbia UP 1998) pp.43–4.
3. See D. Rumsfeld, 'Transforming the Military', *Foreign Affairs* 81/3 (May/June 2002) pp.20–32.
4. C4ISTAR = Command, Control, Computers, Communications, Intelligence, Surveillance, Targeting Acquisition and Reconnaissance. See General R.B. Myers, 'Six Months After: The Imperatives of Operation Enduring Freedom', *RUSI Journal* 147/2 (April 2002) pp.10–16.
5. For an historical overview of the problems of waging decisive wars, see R. Weigley, *The Age of Decisive Battles* (Indianapolis: Indiana UP 1991) and B. Bond, *The Pursuit of Victory: From Napoleon to Saddam Hussein* (Oxford: Oxford UP 1996).
6. M. Howard, 'When Are Wars Decisive?', *Survival* 41 (Spring 1999) pp.133–4.
7. See A. Horne, *A Savage War of Peace* (London: Papermac 1987).
8. A.J.R. Mack, 'Why Big Nations Lose Small Wars: The Politics of Asymmetrical Conflict', *World Politics* 27/2 (Jan. 1975) pp.175–200.
9. L. Freedman, *The Revolution in Strategic Affairs,* Adelphi Paper 318, (Oxford: Oxford UP for IISS 1998) p.32.
10. Ivan Arreguin-Toft, 'How the Weak Win Wars', *International Security* 26/1 (Summer 2001) p.98.
11. A good illustration of this perspective is provided by Michael Lind, *Vietnam The Necessary*

War (NY: Free Press 1999). Also of interest is Jeffrey Record, 'Weinberger-Powell Doctrine Doesn't Cut It', *US Naval Institute Proceedings* (Oct. 2000).

12. An examination of asymmetric wars over the last 200 years shows the weaker opponent was the victor in at least one third of these conflicts. However, in the period 1950–98 the weaker actor won more often than the stronger opponent: 55 per cent compared to 45 per cent, Arreguin-Toft (note 10) p.96.
13. Ibid.
14. P. Wallenstein and M. Sollenberg, 'Armed Conflict in 1989–99', *Journal of Peace Research* 37/5 (Sept. 2000) p.635.
15. L.B. Tompson (ed.), *Low Intensity Conflict* (Lexington, MA: Lexington Books 1989) p.ix.
16. The Weinberger Doctrine consisted of six tests: Is a vital US interest at stake? Will sufficient resources be committed to ensure victory? Are the objectives clear? Will the commitment be sustained? Is there a reasonable expectation that Congress and the public will support the operation? Have all other options been exhausted?
17. R. Duncan Downie, *Learning From Conflict: The US Military in Vietnam, El Salvador, and the Drug War* (Westport, CT: Praeger 1998), and S.L. Marquis, *Unconventional Warfare: Rebuilding US Special Forces* (Washington DC: Brookings 1997).
18. S. Metz, *Armed Conflict in the 21st Century: The Information Revolution and Post Modern Warfare* (Carlisle, PA: Strategic Studies Institute) pp.14–18.
19. Ibid. p.39.
20. B. Hoffman, 'Responding to Terrorism Across the Technological Spectrum', in J. Arquilla and D. Ronfeldt (eds.), *In Athena's Camp: Preparing for Conflict in the Information Age* (Santa Monica, CA: RAND Corporation 1997) p.340.
21. E.A. Cohen, 'A Tale of Two Secretaries', *Foreign Affairs* 81/3 (May/June 2002) pp.33–46.
22. C. Connetta, 'The Pentagon's New Budget, New Strategy, and New War, *Project Defense Analysis* <www.comw.org/pda/0206newwar.html>.
23. J. Bowyer Bell, *Dragon Wars: Armed Struggle and the Conventions of Modern War* (New Brunswick, NJ: Transaction Publishers 1999) pp.234–6. See also R.H. Scales, *Firepower in Limited War* (Washington DC: National Defense Univ. 1990) pp.3–23.
24. Bowyer Bell (note 23) p.246.
25. Martin Libicki, *Illuminating Tomorrow's War*, Mcnair Paper 61 (Washington DC: National Defense Univ. 1999) pp.47–50.
26. See Larry P. Goodson, *Afghanistan's Endless War: State Failure, Regional Politics and the Rise of the Taliban* (Seattle, WA: Washington UP 2001).
27. Ibid. p.97. Also see A. Rashid, *Taliban* (London: Pan Books 2001) pp.117–29.
28. 'This may turn out to be a pyrrhic victory', *The Independent* (14 Nov. 2001).
29. A.H. Cordesman and A.R. Wagner, *The Lessons of Modern War Volume III: Afghanistan and the_Falklands War* (London: Mansell 1990) pp.7–10.
30. See A. Rashid, 'Pakistan and the Taliban', in W. Maley (ed.) *Fundamentalism Reborn? Afghanistan and the Taliban* (London: Hurst 2001) pp.72–83.
31. 'Some Top Military Brass Favor Status Quo in Iraq', *The Washington Post* (28 July 2002).
32. Global Security, `Operation Enduring Freedom,' <www.globalsecurity.org/military/opsenduring-freedom.htm>.
33. 'Public Support is Overwhelming: Poll Finds 94% Favor Bush's Ordering Strikes on Afghanistan', *The Washington Post* (8 Oct. 2001).
34. 'In Poll, Most Americans Back Bush', *The Washington Post* (8 Nov. 2001).
35. C. Connatta, 'Strange Victory: A critical appraisal of Operation Enduring Freedom and the Afghanistan War', *Project Defense Alternatives* (30 Jan. 2002) p.17. <wwwcomw.org/pda/0201strangevic.html>, See also Center for Defense Information [hereafter] *CDI* 'The Future of US Military Operations in Afghanistan', <www.cdi.org/terrorism/ Afghanistan-future-pr.cfm>.
36. 'The Rout of the Taliban', *The Observer* (18 Nov. 2001).
37. *DoD News Briefing* CENTCOM CINC Gen. Franks (24 May 2002, <www.centcom.mil/news/transcripts/DOD%20Briefing%2024May%2002.html>

38. *DoD News Briefing* CENCTOM CINC Gen. Franks (21 May 2002), <www.centcom.mil/news/transcripts/DOD%20Briefing%2021May%2002.html>
39. 'Afghanistan is Only the tip of the network-centric iceberg', *Signal* 56/8 (April 2002) pp.45–7.
40. A. and H. Toffler, *War and Anti War: Survival at the Dawn of the 21st Century* (London: Little Brown 1994) pp.69–73.
41. *Global Security* .org <www.globalsecurity.org/military/ops/enduring-freedom-ops.htm>.
42. <www.globalsecurity.org/military/ops/enduring-freedom-ops.htm>.
43. 'The US Military Campaign in Afghanistan: The Year in Review', *CDI Terrorism Project* <www.cdi.org\terrorism\afghanistan-one-year-later-pr.cfm>.
44. *Global Security* 'Operation Enduring Freedom –Order of Battle <www.globalsecurity.org/military/ops/enduring-freedom_orbat-01.htm>.
45. E. Luttwak, `A Post Heroic Military Policy,' *Foreign Affairs* 75/4 (July/Aug. 1996) pp.33–4.
46. 'Long and Difficult War Ahead', *The Washington Post* (28 Oct. 2002) and 'Big Gound Force Seen as Necessary to Defeat Taliban', *The Washington Post* (2 Nov. 2002).
47. *DoD News Briefing*, Secretary of State of Defence Donald Rumsfeld and Gen. Tommy Franks, 8 Nov. 2002, <www.defenselink.mil/news/Nov2001/t11082001_t1108sd.html>.
48. See Col. J. Warden, *The Air Campaign: Planning for Combat* (NY: Pergamon-Brassey's 1990), and Col. D. Deptula, *Firing for Effect: Change in the Nature of Warfare* (Arlington, VA: Aerospace Education Foundation 1989).
49. US government estimates that 400 Afghan civilians were killed as a result of the bombing. The human rights group, Global Watch estimates the number of fatalities to be 812. See 'This woman lost everything in a US air raid', *The Guardian* (7 Oct. 2002). Connetta estimates 3,000 killed (note 35) and John Pilger believes that as many as 5,000 Afghan civilians died because of the bombing, 'The Great Charade', *The Observer* (14 July 2002).
50. 'Dawn raids stoke fires of resentment', *The Guardian* (8 Oct. 2002).
51. 'Breakdowns in a Ridgetop Battle', *The Washington Post* (24 May 2002) and 'A Wintry Ordeal at 10,000 Feet', *The Washington Post* (25 May 2002).
52. 'Battle for Gardez', *The Observer* (10 March 2002).
53. M. O'Hanlon, 'A Flawed Masterpiece: Assessing the Afghan Campaign', *Foreign Affairs* 81/3 (May/June 2002) p.48.
54. See Connetta (note 35) p.31.
55. 'A Tougher Target: The Afghanistan Model of Warfare may not apply very well to Iraq', *The Washington Post* (26 Dec. 2001).
56. Goodson (note 26) p.121.
57. Ibid.
58. Rashid (note 27) p.103.
59. M. Mann, *The Sources of Social Power Vol. 1: A History of Power from the Beginning to A.D. 1760* (Cambridge: Cambridge UP 1986) pp.22–5.
60. Rashid (note 27) pp.22–6.
61. Nicolo Machiavelli, *The Prince* [1513] (Harmondsworth, UK: Penguin Books 1971) pp.44–7.
62. Ibid. p.46.
63. 'US deploys elite units to hit al-Qaida', *The Guardian* (5 Aug. 2002).
64. 'Elusive Omar "Back in Afghanistan"', *The Guardian* (30 Aug. 2002).
65. See A. Saikal, 'Afghanistan after the Loya Jirga', *Survival* 44/3 (Autumn 2002) pp.47–56.
66. *CDI Terrorism Project*, 'George Bush's Conundrum – Afghanistan' (April 2002) <www.cdi.org/terrorism/conondrum-pr.cfm>.
67. United Nations, General Assembly and the Security Council, *The Situation in Afghanistan and its Implications for International Peace and Stability* A/56/100-S/2002/737, July 2002, p.2.
68. *CDI Terrorism Project* (note 66) p.2.
69. 'A war that can't be won', *The Guardian* (21 Nov. 2001).
70. See note 50.

71. 'Six Months in to the War: Rumsfeld and Myers' Assesses Progress', *Defense Link*, <www.defenselink.mil/news/Apr2002/n04082002_200204084>.
72. 'Bin Laden is Alive and Planning New Attacks', *The Guardian* (24 June 2002).
73. Russian intelligence estimated that Al Qaeda had 55 installations in Afghanistan, ranging from training camps, accommodation, chemical weapons laboratories, homes for wives and children and even and an operational airfield near the town of Khost.
74. 'In the Lair of the Hunted Taliban', *The Observer* (16 June 2002).
75. O'Hanlon (note 53).
76. 'War on Terrorism Enters New Phase', *Sea Power* 44/11 (Nov. 2001) pp.20–22.
77. 'Al Qaida rich and ready to strike, says UN', *The Guardian* (30 Aug. 2002).
78. Ministry of Defence, *The Strategic Defence Review : A New Chapter* (London: MoD 2002) para.27.
79. C. Marighela, *For the Liberation of Brazil* (London: Penguin 1971).
80. 'So are Civilisations at War?', *The Observer* (24 Oct. 2001).
81. 'America wants to wage on all of us', *The Guardian* (6 Sept. 2002).

United States Special Operations Forces and the War on Terrorism

ANNA SIMONS and DAVID TUCKER

The War on Terrorism

Nine days after the attacks on the World Trade Center and the Pentagon, Secretary of Defense Donald Rumsfeld, echoing and amplifying thoughts expressed by President George W. Bush, told the press that the war on terrorism:

> is something that is very, very different from World War II, Korea, Vietnam, the Gulf War, Kosovo, Bosnia, the kinds of things that people think of when they use the word 'war' or 'campaign' or 'conflict'. We really, almost, are going to have to fashion a new vocabulary and different constructs for thinking about what it is we're doing.

A few days later he told reporters that the war would not begin with something comparable to a D-Day or end with something like the signing of surrender documents on the deck of the USS *Missouri*. 'The truth is,' the Secretary told reporters, 'this is a broad, sustained, multifaceted effort that is notably, distinctively different from prior efforts. It is by its very nature something that cannot be dealt with by some sort of a massive attack or invasion. It is a much more subtle, nuanced, difficult, shadowy set of problems.'[1]

Comments like these about how different the war on terrorism would be from other wars have become less frequent as the war has progressed. The cause of this, perhaps, is that the most visible initial part of the war – the fighting in Afghanistan – turned out to have aims similar to those in many past wars. In Afghanistan the US-led coalition set out to defeat the armed forces of another government as the necessary condition for achieving its political objectives. Even the methods of fighting would have been familiar to students of recent conflicts. As in the war in Bosnia, for example, the coalition succeeded in Afghanistan by joining its air power to an indigenous ground force trained and supported by small numbers of American personnel. In Bosnia this was Croats trained by advisors from Military Professional Resources Incorporated, while in Afghanistan it has been members of the Northern Alliance supported by advisor-combatants from US Special Operations Forces (SOF).

The war on terrorism may see (and now has seen) other campaigns like the one waged in Afghanistan, at least in the sense that the military forces of two or more governments will clash, with the political outcome to be determined by the results of military action. Indeed, the President's new national security strategy leads us to believe that any government that supports terrorism or which employs it in pursuit of its political objectives would be a potential target for sustained military action. We should not be misled, however, by these more traditional aims into thinking that the Secretary and others were wrong in claiming that the war on terrorism will be different still. It both will and will not be given its dual objectives. The first of these is to deter. By demonstrating the ill-effects that come from supporting terrorists, we want to dissuade other governments from harboring or assisting them. This is, in part, what the campaign against the Taliban was meant to do. But the US also had to get through the Taliban to get at Al Qaeda, whose suppression is its second objective. To suppress Al Qaeda requires an altogether different set of tactics, techniques, and procedures. It also demands a different approach and strategy, one that differs from conventional war in the same way – and precisely because – Al Qaeda differs from the Taliban.

Unlike the Taliban, Al Qaeda is not a government and does not use military forces, or even irregular military forces, as a violent means of achieving its objectives. Instead, it employs terrorism. Terrorism is a more directly political and psychological struggle than war, since terrorists maneuver around a country's military shield and strike directly at the political process by targeting the noncombatants who carry on that process. As terrorism is a political and psychological struggle, so must countering it be. Destroying the Taliban or even the leaders of Al Qaeda will not necessarily mean the defeat of the terrorism they support, inspire, and organize. To defeat or suppress such terrorism requires us to deal with more than just the terrorists. In the same way they maneuver around our military shield to strike at the political process, we must maneuver around them to counter their political-psychological support. This is why suppressing Al Qaeda, and organizations like it is the 'subtle, nuanced, difficult, shadowy' problem Secretary Rumsfeld claimed it was.

From this perspective, the war in Afghanistan is only a small supporting operation in a much larger, more complex conflict. The fighting in Afghanistan destroyed Al Qaeda training bases – a conventional military objective – and increased intelligence about the organization sufficiently so that policemen in Europe and Southeast Asia could arrest terrorists and roll up their support networks, and financial analysts could identify bank accounts for closure. Equally important for success, though, was to do this in such a way as to not build additional support for the terrorists and win them more recruits, but to undermine them both in Afghanistan and around the world.

The idea that to succeed against terrorism you must do more than just catch terrorists should not be interpreted to mean that we must appeal to or even appease terrorists' potential supporters. On the contrary, intimidation and fear can be highly effective tools. Indeed, experience suggests that what is needed is some blend of cooption and coercion – or sticks and carrots – the proportion impossible to specify in the abstract but to be adjusted as the campaign goes forward, and according to the character of the target audience. One constraint on the use of intimidation and fear will be the tolerance of the home political community for harsh measures, a tolerance that may change as the terrorist campaign continues. In any event, whatever the mix of rewards and punishments, the point should be to direct them not only to the terrorists, but beyond them to their sources of support, just as the terrorists direct their violence around military forces to attack the political process directly.

One way to conceptualize this strategic struggle is to think in terms of an onion: At the innermost layer is the terrorist organization itself, comprised of strategists and operatives firmly committed to the cause. In the layer immediately surrounding the terrorists are their supporters who provide them logistical assistance and intelligence. They, in turn, are protected by a layer of sympathizers, who help fund and resource them. Then there are the neutrals. Finally, in the outer rings of the onion are individuals who oppose the terrorists, their methods, and their aims. If they are to operate, the terrorists must stay hidden and protected, for which they need their layers of supporters and sympathizers, but they must also convert the neutrals into sympathizers and supporters if they are to grow in strength. They generally do this through suasion, using argument or force. To counter them thus requires stripping away their sympathizers and supporters, and keeping neutrals from being intimidated or seduced. Given the political-psychological nature of this struggle, force may well play a role, but air campaigns, cruise missile strikes, and garrisons full of ground forces will hardly do the trick, and can ultimately prove counter-productive.

This is why the claim that the war on terrorism differs from other wars makes sense if it refers *not* to military engagements like those fought in Afghanistan, but to the less conventionally military efforts undertaken to suppress terrorism by the US over the past 30 years. In this struggle, sources of power other than military have long been used.[2] Indeed, economic and diplomatic sanctions, painstaking police work, and even the fitful effort to build an international consensus against terrorism have all proven more effective than the application of conventional military force. One could even say that the only things that distinguish the current, post-9/11 war from previous campaigns against terrorism are the intensity and seriousness with which the US government is now using these means. Commensurate with what it claims to be at stake – the moral and political, if not physical, survival of the US, and the fate of Western civilization – the government's intensity and seriousness have reached the level at which one can reasonably, though not conventionally perhaps, speak of a war. We should be clear: in this war the relative unimportance of conventional military forces derives *not* from the limited interests at stake, but from the decision by the enemy to avoid the West's overwhelming conventional strength and pursue its objectives via other means.

In choosing these other means, Al Qaeda has placed itself in a tradition of political violence that has proven to be a longstanding and effective alternative to the power typically wielded by nation-states. In many respects, Al Qaeda's campaign is similar to national liberation struggles of the last 50 years, though it is more global and much less confined in scope. Al Qaeda wants to liberate the nation of Islam from its enthrallment to the West. To do this, it uses secrecy and violence to show its self-appointed enemies – the Western powers and, most importantly, the most powerful of those, the US – that they are not in fact so powerful; they can be taken by surprise and they can be hurt. Its methods are both purposive and instrumental, since in causing destruction Al Qaeda rallies support among those it wishes to liberate and also intimidates any among them who oppose its means or objectives.

Because in struggles such as the one engaged in with Al Qaeda, the enemy operates clandestinely in small groups, without the infrastructure of established military organizations, and can easily blend in with ordinary populations, intelligence is decisive. Yet, while our technical means of collection are unparalleled, impressive, and useful, they are also limited. Our best sources of intelligence are likely to be the layers of people among whom the terrorists hide. Gaining their cooperation and eliciting the intelligence they hold is another reason to work on the terrorists' supporters and sympathizers. Peeling them away will not only get us closer to the terrorists themselves, but will limit terrorists' operational effectiveness. It is here that SOF, especially, can help.

Special Operations Forces

Although the term 'Special Operations Forces' has been used interchangeably with 'Special Forces' (SF) since 9/11, and retired Marines have been identified in the media as having special operations expertise, SOF comprise specific units with a range of different, but sometimes overlapping capabilities. SOF units fall under the purview of the US Special Operations Command (USSOCOM), and include US Army Special Forces units (popularly referred to as Green Berets), US Army Rangers, special mission units, the 160th Special Operations Aviation Regiment, Civil Affairs (CA) and Psychological Operations forces (PSYOP); US Navy SEALs; US Air Force special tactics teams, and fixed wing and rotary wing air assets.

Overlap occurs both in the kinds of missions these units train for as well as the means by which they can infiltrate behind enemy lines. For instance, though the term SEAL itself stands for sea-air-land, SEALs are best known for their ability to engage in waterborne operations; all are scuba-qualified. Yet, certain SF soldiers are also scuba-qualified. Likewise, though some SF teams specialize in high altitude low opening (HALO) freefall military parachute techniques, SEALs, too, go through HALO training – which means they also can conduct airborne operations from high altitudes.

A rough division of labor exists within SOF despite such redundancies. Air Force combat controllers, for instance, can be attached to any SOF team in order to call in air strikes. Rangers specialize in seizing airfields. Special mission units train specifically for hostage rescue and anti-terrorism missions, while SF teams train to train others, and work primarily with foreign forces. Depending on the mission, the proximity of the closest available forces, and the desires of the local theater combatant commanders of several different units or teams might be called upon, but also, given their particular expertise clearly only certain SOF units will be assigned given tasks.

At some risk of distortion, we may say that SOF engage in two distinctly different, but complementary kinds of combat mission: those involving direct action, and those in support of unconventional warfare. Direct action missions are short-duration operations directed at specific targets, usually of high strategic or operational value. Direct action missions most commonly involve raids or ambushes, such as that undertaken in October 1993 in Mogadishu, Somalia. There the objective was to capture top lieutenants in General Mohamed Farah Aideed's militia. But the objective for a direct action mission may involve anything from rescuing hostages to eradicating an enemy force, position, or even drug lab.

Closely related to direct action, which can be undertaken in any kind of environment, is special reconnaissance. Soldiers engaging in special reconnaissance must stay well hidden in order to gather intelligence. During the 1991 Gulf War, for example, SF teams dug hide sites behind enemy lines in Iraq in order to monitor road traffic and troop movement. Typically, both direct action and special reconnaissance missions place an absolute premium on stealth. Whenever practicable, too, operators will practice direct action missions over and over again, sometimes even building full-scale mock-ups of the target. Speed and accuracy on the ground are critical to success. Also, direct action and special reconnaissance missions can (and sometimes must) be undertaken with no local support. This is clearly not the case, however, whenever either mission represents a smaller piece of a larger unconventional warfare effort.

There are various ways to think about unconventional warfare, and numerous different definitions have been offered over the years. According to the current US Department of Defense definition, unconventional warfare is:

> A broad spectrum of military and paramilitary operations, normally of long duration, predominantly conducted by indigenous or surrogate forces who are organized, trained, equipped, supported, and directed in varying degrees by an external source. It includes guerrilla warfare and other direct offensive, low visibility, covert, or clandestine operations, as well as the indirect activities of subversion, sabotage, intelligence activities, and evasion and escape. Also called UW.[3]

Members of SF often boil UW down to any effort in which they work by, through, and with indigenous forces. From an SF perspective, the goal of UW is to help win a war by working with – as opposed to neutralizing or fighting around – local populations. UW represents a classically indirect, and ultimately local, approach to waging warfare. It demands that efforts at all levels – strategic, tactical, and operational– be coordinated. To work with indigenous forces, SOF must win their trust. To do this, they live with them, eat with them, and share the same living conditions. They also take the opportunity to study local practices and learn social preferences. Building trust invariably takes time, but the payoff comes in a better understanding of the operational environment, and the ability to solicit the kind of solid intelligence that enables operations.

Civic action is closely related to, indeed, an unavoidable part of such efforts. According to the late Major General Edward G. Lansdale, who claimed to have coined the term in the Philippines in 1950, civic action describes soldiers' 'brotherly behavior':

> ... the soldiers behave as the brothers and protectors of the people in their everyday military operations, replacing the arrogance of the military at highway checkpoints or in village searches with courteous manners and striving to stop the age-old soldier's habit of stealing chickens and pigs from the farmers… The Philippine Army's legal assistance to farmers in land courts, the new start in life given to residents of San Luis, and the care of civilian casualties in military hospitals were all part of civic action.[4]

Certainly, US soldiers sent abroad appear to intuitively understand the value in helping improve living conditions in their immediate vicinity. It earns them gratitude, if not friends. This becomes key to any UW effort because friends will not let friends get hurt. Civic action thus doubles as force protection. It also helps dry up the sea of supporters in which opposing forces swim by providing a more stabilized, improved, and secure local environment. The safer and more secure citizens feel, the more committed they become to staying secure. The exchange relationship is such that the fewer the population's causes for legitimate grievance, the fewer inroads insurgents, guerrillas, or terrorists can make. Or, to rephrase this, by implicitly trading on security for local assistance, civic action can yield militarily useful results, particularly in the realm of intelligence. But here, too, there is a catch. What comprises civic action in a particular locale can usually only be determined once units are on site. To identify the most pressing local needs, and determine what will earn a team the most bang for its buck invariably takes time. Sometimes SF teams have this luxury. Sometimes, Civil Affairs (CA) teams step in instead.

In a certain sense, what CA forces attempt is civic action writ large. CA forces emerged in World War II to administer areas captured or liberated by US forces before civilian administrators were present to take over. Following the war, CA continued to administer Germany, while today CA units typically engage in activities designed to allay civilian fears, address civilian concerns, ameliorate local conditions, and mitigate the effect of military operations. Essentially, CA personnel help stabilize, regularize, or improve civil-military relations in the wake of a US military presence. They accomplish this by engaging in dialogue and what amounts to humanitarian assistance.

Closely linked with CA, Psychological Operations (PSYOP) shape, manage, manipulate, and transmit information. PSYOP's mission is to induce or reinforce attitudes favorable to US objectives, and destroy enemy morale. To do this, PSYOP forces must understand the underlying structure of human communication and the particularities of a given culture. PSYOP's writ is not to deceive, but to selectively present the truth. It does so most famously with leaflet drops and radio or loudspeaker broadcasts. During the 1991 Gulf War, for example, bomb loads dropped from B-52s followed by leaflets warning Iraqi soldiers that they would be next produced over 80,000 surrendered Iraqi troops.

Together, SF, CA, and PSYOP comprise what we might call the UW complex and seem ideally suited to affect those layers of support and potential support that terrorists need. Their skills are particularly useful when we are engaged operationally in a country, as in Afghanistan, but can be equally useful for training and advising indigenous forces to take on these same tasks themselves, as SOF has done since October 2001 with Filipino forces who are fighting Abu Sayyaf (a terrorist group in the Philippines with links to Al Qaeda). In both cases, SOF involvement has helped generate local knowledge and intelligence, which is not to suggest that other military forces have no role in the war on terrorism. It is only to argue that SOF seem specially well suited for UW, both in its classic sense and as is now required by this broader, global war.

However, there are at least two sets of problems with the use of SOF as they are currently configured. One set involves SOF's relations with other military forces. The second has to do with relations among elements of SOF themselves.

The Conventional–Unconventional Rub

Most definitions of UW, to include the current Department of Defense (DOD) definition, treat it as a method, and as a means to an end, with no end explicated. Worse, they do not even describe UW as a *preferred* method under certain conditions. Here, then, is a chronic source of confusion for anyone outside the SOF community. First, if UW is just one among a series of possible approaches, any of which can be applied regardless of conditions, then why would a conventional commander ever choose UW? Most would not. Second, because it is methods, not goals, that distinguishes UW, it becomes all too easy to conflate unconventional *methods* with unconventional *warfare*.

We see this most vividly, perhaps, in reactions to what has been hailed as the most unconventional aspect of the war in Afghanistan – the triple marriage among SF and combat controllers on the ground, Northern Alliance forces, and air assets. This represents only a fraction of what SOF are capable of, and a full-fledged unconventional warfare should involve. Yet, fascination with such efforts and musings that they could herald a paradigmatic shift in warfare merely reinforce the Pentagon's long-standing preoccupation with rapidly achieved, measurable effects. That this happens to be the antithesis of the attitude necessary for supporting the slow indirect methods of unconventional warfare *should* also give us pause, but is not surprising. Unfortunately, the failure of UW to mesh with the Pentagon's preferences is a recurring phenomenon.

For instance, the idea to join SOF to the Northern Alliance in Afghanistan came from the CIA – not from military.[5] Then, following the Taliban's defeat, the military failed to capitalize on the UW skills that helped topple the government, and that then could have been directed at building support among other segments of the Afghan population in order to acquire intelligence and limit the resources going to Taliban and Al

Qaeda remnants. As soon as conventional army forces arrived in the country, and the army gained control over SOF, hunting down Taliban and Al Qaeda became the priority, despite the fact that intelligence was so scarce that these operations turned up little. Conventionalization also intensified. One of the most visible, and widely reported, instances of this was that SF soldiers were ordered to shave off their beards, even though they had grown them both to establish rapport with the locals and to avoid being recognized at a distance as outsiders.

It turns out that much of what occurred in Afghanistan as headquarters elements and conventional commanders arrived on scene was a replay of what happened ove three decades ago in Vietnam.[6] There, SOF were able to operate in an innovative or, at least, unconventional fashion when they worked for the CIA. When the army gained control of their operations, it directed them away from working with and protecting the Vietnamese population toward hunting for and engaging the enemy.[7]

There are two ways to explain this penchant to conventionalize, and why it recurs.[8] First, perspective is everything. From a conventional point of view the order of preference for how to wage any war is via armed force – more is better. From a conventional perspective, armed finesse (UW) and unarmed finesse (CA and PSYOP) may be useful, but only in supporting roles. From an SF perspective, on the other hand, armed finesse is preferable because less can be more. If applied long or skillfully enough armed finesse can even win certain kinds of wars, particularly if armed force and unarmed finesse are used only when needed. Of course, from a CA or PSYOP point of view, when people's minds can be changed or their lives sufficiently improved, finesse trumps force, which may not need to be applied at all.

A second explanation for the tendency to conventionalize is that the less well understood, appreciated, historically proven, or *immediate* a unit's impact, the more skeptical of it most outsiders will be, and the easier it is to rely instead on the tried and true application of force. Nor are such biases completely ungrounded. Waging war by finesse is inherently tricky, in all senses. Or, to return to CA and PSYOP: what they can do represents far more of a gamble than putting steel on target. The catch is, of course, that not all targets are shootable, and where they are not armed finesse can play a role. Nor do all problems have quick, direct action fixes. Indeed, the essence of unconventional warfare is that there is no rapid-fire solution, which is something that SF teams experientially understand. But even so, their knowing this in principle can still be overcome by the seductiveness of direct action, particularly when this is what allies on the ground and commanders at the top clamor for.

SOF's Own Pecking Order

If conventional commanders do not know what to do with SOF, would SOF do better if it were in charge? Interestingly, SOCOM reportedly declined to take the lead in the war on terrorism when it was offered. Perhaps because SOCOM has yet to orchestrate a war, its own leadership felt it could not run one as effectively as a conventional command could. However, something else may also be at work. In theory, as we have argued, it would appear that SOF has unique capabilities not duplicable by other units, and that SOF as a whole should be even stronger than the sum of its stand-alone parts. However, until now, SOF has never had to *act* as a whole, utilizing the full range of its capabilities from quick reaction direct action through years-long UW. Because it has not, the command may be haunted by the fact that not all of its parts work well together, for members of SOF themselves harbor certain prejudices that run counter to a fully unified set of forces.

The tensions are clearest between CA and PSYOP forces, on the one hand, and SF in addition to all direct action-oriented units on the other. Although both CA and PSYOP are critical to winning hearts and minds in a UW environment, neither is considered a first choice assignment by many special operators given the overwhelmingly non-combatant nature of such work. Also helping to further marginalize CA is the fact that most members are reservists. Although CA units are among the most frequently deployed, only one of five is an active duty unit. Typically, members of active duty forces do not regard reservists as their equals. Also, civic action is rarely a unit's first priority. Nor can it be in a conflict zone. Consequently, no matter how pressing civic action can feel once a unit is on the ground, it is often treated as incidental or an afterthought in the planning process. Even in the one simulated UW exercise all SF soldiers attend ('Robin Sage'), civic action occurs last, only after all other phases of the exercise have been completed. Unfortunately, this, along with other factors, would appear to affect attitudes in SF toward CA.

PSYOP also carries a stigma of being second-class. If CA is too touchy-feely, PSYOPers, who pride themselves on their ability to influence and manipulate, are not to be trusted. It does not help that there is a strong preference in SOF for common sense over book smarts, or that PSYOPers are often regarded as nerds who do little more than cook up hair-brained schemes. Skepticism about PSYOP actually has deep roots. Tensions existed during World War II between those responsible for collecting information and generating propaganda on the one hand, and field operatives, on the other. These splits later resurfaced in both the CIA and in SF as SF was being formed. Some argued that UW *was* a psychological operation, therefore PSYOP should be SF's primary focus, and not just a supporting element.[9]

One result of these prejudices is that although their headquarters are co-located, their areas of expertise mutually supporting, and their division of labor completely complementary, SF, CA and PSYOP are informally divided by a pecking order: SF predominates. This is not just a consequence of SF's heft in terms of sheer numbers. It is, as we have just noted, also attitudinal. Indeed, SF's relationship with CA and PSYOP is much more akin to that between the conventional army and SF than SF itself might like to admit, and for many of the same reasons.

Perhaps the best way to sum these up is that the less conventionally military a unit's area of expertise appears to be – if it wages war by pamphlet rather than by applying force – the less the regard in which it tends to be held. Because an independently operating SF team would not and cannot apply overwhelming force, but acts as a 'force multiplier', conventional commanders rarely regard its impact as comparable to that of one of their own units. From an SF perspective, this is just the big Army preferring big over small.

Yet, SF soldiers themselves cannot seem to escape preferring *armed* to *unarmed* finesse. For instance, SF soldiers always make fun of Rangers, who are hyper-conventional and train for direct action missions. They operate at the opposite end of the spectrum from CA or PSYOP. From an SF perspective, Rangers clearly lack finesse – the joke is they also do not think. But when called on, Rangers will bring overwhelming firepower to bear. SF can thus afford to be in a kidding relationship with Rangers in the classic anthropological sense: Rangers are more junior, but no less worthy, and extremely useful in a firefight. This is not the kind of relationship that exists between SF and CA or PSYOP units.

Equally revealing is the relationship between SF and the Navy SEALs, who are more direct action-oriented but also operate in small teams. Here there is clear rivalry when it comes to what both units pride themselves on – armed finesse – and there is considerable chest-pounding, but again, there is mutual respect. Significantly, SEALs too share SF's skepticism toward PSYOP and they tolerate, but probably do not sufficiently appreciate, the value of CA.

SOF and the War on Terrorism

The attitudes that mark SOF's relations with the rest of the military, as well as SOF's internal relations, reveal a status hierarchy that exists in practice, but not on paper or in doctrine. In the same way conventional forces tend to misunderstand and insufficiently appreciate what SOF can do, within SOF, those who practice direct action tend to misunderstand and appreciate insufficiently what UW can do, just as those who practice UW fail to fully understand and appreciate CA and PSYOP.

Identifying the tenaciousness and pervasiveness of this hierarchy is important for understanding the problem the military, including SOF, will have in conducting the war on terrorism because what the war on terrorism, as opposed to wars on nation-states, requires is the opposite of what the hierarchy prefers. The hierarchy prefers conventionalization, direct action, and armed force over armed and then unarmed finesse. The war on terrorism requires the use of CA, PSYOP, their civilian equivalents, and SF teams tasked to do UW. Success in this war will require an emphasis on winning local cooperation. Conventional and direct action forces are least likely to elicit this, while CA, PSYOP and UW forces are most likely to. Meanwhile, the intelligence they gather will make direct action more effective and ideally, over time – and as we succeed – less necessary.

The prejudices that favor force over finesse are so entrenched, however, that it will be difficult if not impossible to overcome them in the near term. Whether we should try at all, of course, depends on our assessment of the historical significance of the current war on terrorism. If it is an aberration and if, in 20 years, confronting China will be Washington's biggest national security challenge, then we should probably encourage efforts to transform the military to make it a faster, more powerful, more flexible version of its current self. If, on the other hand, the war on terrorism signals an epochal change in the way humans use violence against each other, then that transformation of the military should include an effort to ensure that both armed and unarmed finesse are accorded equal status with armed force, and that it is well understood how and why each should be used. An interdependent division of labor such as this would truly represent a revolution in military affairs.

Over the long term, we will likely develop something that approximates a range of reactive and preemptive capabilities, since conventional and unconventional threats are guaranteed to persist. For the present, in the immediate context of the war on terrorism, it will likely take the civilian leadership to intervene in order to shake up the military's attitudinal hierarchy. To the extent that it is being reported in the media, intervention already appears to be underway, although most of the friction between the civilian leadership in the Pentagon and the military seems to center on how to streamline, speed up, and resize the conventional forces, and not on better integrating unconventional capabilities into the military.[10]

Perhaps this is because such a change would require a greater understanding of the nature of terrorism and the capabilities of SOF than currently reside in the civilian leadership, whose background is in conventional military issues. Yet, given the destructive power that is increasingly available to small groups of people willing to use it, nothing may be more important to the future of the country, never mind just the military, than attention to unconventional capabilities.

Whether or not the civilians choose to continue to meddle at the margins rather than in the main, there are a few things they should note. First, thanks to superior radio communications, SOF in Afghanistan were able to coordinate among themselves, and then orchestrate among the various Northern Alliance factions, between Northern Alliance and Pashtun groups, and between military elements and civilians to a greater extent than in any previous marriage of SOF and irregular forces. This is significant because, by achieving more coordination than locals could manage among themselves, SOF was able to subtly direct the war in ways that might not otherwise have been possible. Whether this was done intentionally from the outset, or by pure expedience and happenstance almost does not matter. The fact that it was done at all is consistent with a hallmark trait of indirect or unconventional warfare, which is to turn a constraint – in this case, local infighting – into an opportunity, by uniting factions in such a way that they did not actually have to be united, which (given the situation in Afghanistan) would have been time-consuming and potentially impossible.

What SOF achieved in this case is truly noteworthy, though it does not come without a postscript. SOF's unparalleled success in this feat of coordination may have inadvertently helped convince commanders that SOF operators on the ground could trust those they were advising – and their own abilities to direct their advisees – more than was prudent. This is because, once soldiers develop empathy for those they are advising, they begin to see the world as their advisees see it. In combat, too, their perspective cannot help but narrow, since the longer they spend with fellow-fighters in dangerous (or miserable) conditions, the more they will come to advocate the position of those to whom they are already entrusting their lives.

Whether this explains why various militia leaders were trusted with tasks they then did not perform during Operation 'Anaconda', or whether commanders at higher levels misread or overrode reports from the field remains unclear. Nonetheless, mistakes were made that appear to have cost the US the capture of numerous Al Qaeda members, if not its leaders. Here, the hidden lesson is: Everyone may have been far too precipitate. Although speed was what was most needed, so was accurate intelligence, as well as reliable surrogates on the ground – and the knowledge needed to gauge their reliability.

The civilian leadership should keep two other points in mind. Precisely because SOF seem so well-suited for the war on terrorism, the urge may exist to increase their numbers. If this is done precipitously, it can ruin SOF, much as a sudden ramp-up in numbers almost destroyed SF during the war in Vietnam. SOF succeed because they carefully select their forces. The selection process alone takes months. Then, soldiers must be trained. Experienced, mature, adaptable soldiers who can make it through this training exist in limited numbers. These numbers may not correspond to needs, but this should not alter the rigor with which SOF units are allowed to fill their ranks.

The issue of time also affects another apparently minor, but actually significant issue: that of rotations. Building successful local relationships and establishing rapport as is required in UW takes time. If we employ a rotation system that shuffles SOF units – never mind individuals – in and out of places like Afghanistan and other operational areas too quickly or too often, we will lose everything we are sending them there to do: cultivate connections, gather intelligence, and peel back the layers of the onion. The aim should be to inspire locals to want us to help *them* eliminate the terrorist hardcore. Again, rapport is key; so is making locals feel secure. Meanwhile, units themselves cannot build institutional knowledge, let alone awareness, without putting down local roots. Plus, there is always a psychic cost to SOF operators when they accept a challenge but then feel they have not been allowed to finish their job.

Finally, having dispensed advice freely to the civilian leadership, let us close by offering some to SOCOM. The Command needs to make SOF – and all its capabilities – better understood. SOCOM should spell out the advantages inherent in a holistic, localized approach to rooting out terrorists. It should explain why teams of mature, experienced soldiers who train to remain self-sufficient and self-reliant in hostile environments over long periods of time should be entrusted with shaping the direction of operations from the field, without interference from but always coordinating with conventional commanders. SOCOM should also fight for them to be able to be different – even if this means fighting for beards. Then it should take all of these messages to the big Army, the Joint Chiefs, the civilian leadership in the Pentagon, and to leaders, operators, and planners in other government agencies. At the same time, SOCOM must look within. It must ensure that its own components understand, and respect, the indispensability of each other's roles. Perhaps then – with the civilians pulling and SOCOM pushing – the war might yet go well.

NOTES

1. *DoD News Briefing*, Secretary of Defense Donald Rumsfeld (20 Sept. 2001), <www.defenselink.mil/news/Sep2001/t09202001_t920ruma.html>; George W. Bush, 'Address to a Joint Session of Congress and the American People' (20 Sept. 2001), <www.whitehouse.gov/news/releases/2001/09/20010920-8.html>; "DoD News Briefing,"

Secretary of Defense Donald Rumsfeld (25 Sept. 2001) <www.defenselink.mil/news/Sep2001/n09252001_200109254.html>.

2. For the use of military force to counter-terrorism and a general review of counter-terrorism measures, see David Tucker, *Skirmishes at the Edge of Empire, the United States and International Terrorism* (Westport, CT: Praeger 1997).
3. <www.dtic.mil/doctrine/jel/doddict/data/u/05488.html>.
4. Edward G. Lansdale, *In the Midst of Wars: An American's Mission to Southeast Asia* (NY: Fordham UP 1991) pp.70–71.
5. Bob Woodward and Dan Balz, '10 Days in September: Inside the War Cabinet: At Camp David, Advise and Dissent', *Washington Post* (31 Jan. 2002), <http://ebird.dtic.milJan 2002/e20020131camp.htm>, accessed 1 Feb. 2002.
6. Interestingly enough, this includes SF headquarters, according to SF members who were in Afghanistan from the start of the war. At the outset, it was both circumstances and their ability to operate independently – without oversight or scrutiny by their own layers of command – that enabled teams to practice unconventional warfare (UW).
7. Vietnam was an instance in which SF and the CIA appear to have worked well together. In other instances the relationship has not been so smooth.
8. For more on conventionalization of SOF, and SF in particular, see Anna Simons, *The Company They Keep: Life Inside the U.S. Army Special Forces* (NY: The Free Press 1997) and Thomas K. Adams, *US Special Operations Forces in Action: The Challenge of Unconventional Warfare* (London and Portland, OR: Frank Cass 1998) pp.10–11, 138, 294.
9. Alfred H. Paddock, *U.S. Army Special Warfare, Its Origins*, rev. edn (Lawrence: Kansas UP 2002) pp.119–128.
10. Vernon Loeb and Thomas Ricks, 'Rumsfeld's Style, Goals Strain Ties in Pentagon', *Washington Post*, <http://ebird.dtic.mil/Oct2002/e20021016rumsfelds.htm>, accessed 18 Oct. 2002; Anne Marie Squeo and Gref Jaffe, 'Pentagon Weighs Big Cuts in Major Arms Programs', *Wall Street Journal*, <http://ebird.dtic.mil/Oct2002/e20021015weighs.htm)>, accessed 18 Oct. 2002.

Warfare by Other Means: Special Forces, Terrorism and Grand Strategy

ALASTAIR FINLAN

The terrorist attacks on 11 September 2001 have generated a new strategic environment for the US and its coalition partners in which the bulk of their conventional forces appear asymmetric. The nature of the new war (transnational and focused against an elusive network of terrorists) has forced these nations to wage warfare by other means or in other words turn to Special Forces (SF). These units are the logical military response to the threat posed by Al Qaeda in view of their expertise in unconventional warfare and traditional anti-terrorist role. The employment of SF in Afghanistan in concert with air power and indigenous forces has proved to be highly successful and ultimately created the conditions for the formation of the Afghan Interim Government on 22 December 2001.

The events of 11 September 2001 have etched an indelible mark on global society. Who will forget the Dantean imagery of the 'Twin Towers' of the World Trade Center wreathed in smoke or for that matter, the burning Pentagon? Incredible scenes to those of the modern age but not so surprising perhaps to a survivor of the Blitz, Dresden, Stalingrad or Tokyo.[1] War touched America in 2001 but not in the form that is universally recognised. No hostile warplanes appeared over the targets, and the enemy did not manifest itself nor openly claim the strike. Instead hijacked civil airliners with military precision and timing flew calmly into each tower under the horrified gaze of millions, if not billions of people watching televisions, surfing the Internet or actually standing in the streets of Manhattan. Just under 3,000 people died in the collapsing buildings, not soldiers but instead office workers, businessmen, stockbrokers and the extraordinary firemen and police who rushed to their assistance.

This unique form of attack has been labelled 'terrorism'[2] as it was initiated not by another state but by a non-state entity that the US has identified as the Al Qaeda network led by the infamous Osama bin Laden.[3] To a significant extent, the suicidal assault on the US falls into Christopher Harmon's fifth category of terrorist strategies that encompasses violent acts carried out 'for international effect'.[4]

As it stands, September 11 or 9/11 as it is now commonly referred to raises some awkward strategic questions of the most powerful military state in the world. Surprisingly, the damage inflicted by this group surpasses the combined effort of the German, Japanese and North Vietnamese forces (not to mention the Vietcong) in managing to target the mainland of the US but more significantly destroy or seriously damage two icons of the American nation (one of which was the supreme military headquarters). Furthermore, despite the billions of dollars spent on defence and intelligence each year, the US was completely caught by surprise. Adding to these factors, dominant trends in defense procurement against future threats to the US such as National Missile Defense (NMD)[5] were of limited value against a group of terrorists who crash commercial jets into buildings. The new war was the wrong war in every respect for America's fighting forces.

The enemy, Osama bin Laden, was not that unfamiliar to American military planners and indeed had benefited (during the war in Afghanistan against the Soviet Union) indirectly from US sponsorship in terms of training and weapons. After the end of that war, he set up a network of terrorists to resist US influence in the Gulf region. The most surprising feature of 9/11 is that it was a quantum jump in his efforts against US interests. Previously, attacks had been restricted largely to either the Gulf region, (USS *Cole* in 2000) or East Africa (US embassies in Kenya and Tanzania in 1998). In addition, the character of these attacks (relatively simple) tended to reveal a use of explosives and occasionally (but not always) the sacrifice of an Al Qaeda operative. So 9/11 was startlingly different and stands out as lateral military thinking.[6] Using commercial airliners specifically loaded with maximum fuel for a long distance flight overcame the enormous problems of smuggling explosives into the US. The employment of two sets of terrorists – pilots and hijackers – brought together on the morning of the attack demonstrated sophisticated planning and funding (training pilots alone is very expensive). The coordination of the attack with planes crashing into targets within minutes of each other would do justice to the best military organisations in the world. It is remarkable that such an operation planned over an extended period of time and at an extreme range (in a foreign country) proved to be so successful for a terrorist organisation that has never carried out such an attack before.

Thus 9/11 seems to have ushered in a new strategic environment for the US. The enemy is not a state but a small network of terrorists based primarily in developing countries. They do not wear uniforms, yet are skilled in combat – whether unarmed, with knives or guns. These men – no evidence of women involved yet – also have the capacity to utilise extremely complex Western technology (like airliners), blend in well, and are exceptionally determined (to the extent of killing themselves to achieve a military goal). Within the spectrum of conflict, they are clearly beyond the capabilities of a police force to handle but too elusive and inappropriate for mainstream military forces to engage. Sending a standard infantry unit to deal with terrorists in a hostage scenario is simply too horrific to imagine given the risks of collateral damage.[7]

Conventional forces are designed for battlefields (characterised by massive amounts of firepower) not peacetime urban situations in which force must be applied with almost surgical care. Moreover, the battle may take place in an unfriendly foreign country, and transporting a regular unit with the huge amount of support services it requires may simply not be politically possible.

Special Forces: The Logical Military Response

Western force structures are visibly asymmetric to the threat posed by a small network of terrorists if considered from their orientation towards fighting at the highest end of conventional warfare. Hot war demands a profusion of high technology (in the form of aircraft carriers, tanks, multi-role aircraft and smart weaponry) in order to triumph on the modern battlefield. Nevertheless, within these force structures reside units created 'to influence military strategy in theatre (wherever that might be) that is beyond the capabilities of conventional forces',[8] or in other words, SF. It has long been recognised by military organisations in history that the 'ideal' conventional force structure – infantry, artillery, tanks and battlefield aircraft – possesses certain limitations. In many cases, logistical shortages mean that armed forces must pursue alternative methods of achieving military aims. The Special Air Service (SAS) – arguably the most successful of Western SF – was set up in July 1941 to attack German/Italian aircraft on the ground because the Royal Air Force (RAF) was too weak to do it in the air.[9]

Other strategic environments, like revolutionary guerrilla warfare, demand a different type of military unit – one that can fight like the unorthodox enemy often in very difficult conditions like jungles. British, American and Australian SF played prominent roles in such conflicts in Malaya (1948–60) and Vietnam (1955–75). All of these units share similar qualities: relatively small in relation to conventional units, a perceived elite among soldiers and an ability to operate beyond the conventions of orthodox military thinking.

SF are the logical military response (in close cooperation with intelligence agencies) to dealing with the new threat posed by Osama bin

Laden and the Al Qaeda network. Unlike the bulk of regular military units, these multi-skilled soldiers train in both conventional and unconventional warfare. Since their inception in World War II, SF have been noted for their unusual approach to modern warfare. According to Tim Jones, 'special forces like the Commandos, SAS, SBS, SOE and the Chindits, pioneered heterodox military practices, including guerrilla hit-and-run raids, small unit short- and long-duration patrols, ambushes, and the use of air-supply for small and large unit forces in physically testing conditions'.[10] These qualities alone make SF stand out within the orthodoxy of Western military forces as being the most appropriate response to an enemy who fights purely within the medium of unconventional warfare.

It must also not be forgotten that terrorism is not new to SF and several units have dedicated anti-terrorist capabilities[11] that can effectively neutralise (under favourable conditions) the additional firepower of the terrorist with reduced amounts of collateral damage.[12] This focus on anti-terrorist operations emerged as a response to the upsurge of Palestinian terrorism in the 1970s and the botched operation by German authorities to free Israeli athletes from the Black September splinter group on a Munich airfield in 1972. In this disastrous incident, all of the hostages were killed.[13] With regard to Britain, SF have been deployed in areas of significant terrorist activity within urban environments with great success for over 25 years.[14]

The small size yet significant firepower of these units offers a rapidly deployable force in the field whether by overtly working closely with friendly governments[15] or covertly by parachute, submarine or helicopter. SF can work for extended periods (measuring weeks) without re-supply in the field that dramatically reduces the need for cumbersome (and detectable) supply lines. They do need a logistical umbrella but not one exclusively offered by conventional forces: American SF in South East Asia in the 1960s often worked closely with the CIA that provided the supplies for operations.[16]

Looking at the history of SF since World War II, chasing and capturing key political members of a terrorist organisation in a foreign land has been achieved on several occasions. In the jungles of Malaya, it was the SAS patrols operating in the difficult swamp area of Telok Anson that captured the notable political leader of the Chinese Terrorists, Ah Hoi in 1958.[17] Without such figures, terrorist organisations rapidly lose their cohesion and in the case of Malaya by the early 1960s, the Emergency (as it was euphemistically called) was largely over.

The War in Afghanistan

The Afghan War of 2001/2002 is unique. From the start of hostilities on 7 October to the creation of the Afghan Interim Government under Hamid Karzai on 22 December, Operation 'Enduring Freedom' destroyed a repressive political regime, the Taliban, and forced the remains of the Al Qaeda terrorist network[18] to scatter across Asia. What makes this campaign remarkable is that it was carried out by a very small number of soldiers, fewer than 3,000 US ground troops supported by a few hundred coalition forces in concert with air power.[19]

It is too early to produce a definitive account of the activities of SF in Afghanistan but enough material exists to draw certain conclusions about their deployment. At least seven different types of SF have been openly acknowledged as being in theatre up until 22 December: from the US, the Green Berets, US Navy Seals and Delta Force; from Britain, the SAS and Special Boat Service (SBS); and from Australia/New Zealand, their own SAS units.[20]

The use of these forces can be encapsulated in two phases of operations that reflected a clear shift of thinking within Central Command (the US Army's formation with responsibility for this region of the world headed by General Tommy Franks) in how to use SF once the campaign had started. The initial response (Phase I) was predictably dominated by air power[21] with a degree of confusion surrounding the role of SF being apparent in the raid on Mullah Omar's compound on 20 October. After this date, with increasing hostility in the media to collateral damage, air power and SF were closely coordinated (Phase II), which produced spectacular effects on the ground with the advance of the Northern Alliance. In addition, SF were utilised in the latter parts of the campaign as a strategic strike force to either put down a prison riot or winkle out terrorists in caves.

Phase I

The first indications of SF on the ground in Afghanistan were made just over a week after the September 11 attack. On 20 September, it was reported that a four-man SF team was spotted and attacked outside of Kabul but the unit withdrew successfully.[22] By all accounts (if true), this bears the hallmark of a British SF mission. During World War II and the Cold War, Britain devised two specific roles for SF, first as a specialised strike force (often deep behind enemy lines) and second to provide battlefield intelligence on enemy forces by first-hand observation. These reconnaissance techniques were perfected in the jungles of Malaya and particularly in the Indonesian Confrontation (1962–66). Ken Connor provides a personal perspective about one of these patrols in 1964:

> We were hiding on the edge of a brown, swift-flowing river, just watching, listening and waiting. The only sounds were natural: the slap of water against the riverbank, the calls of birds in the forest canopy high above us and the distant cry of a hornbill. The four of us had been there for ten days, communicating only in signs and clicks of our fingers and tongues. It was our third trip to the same area trying to verify intelligence reports of an Indonesian army camp upstream, so far without success.[23]

By good fortune, British SF were in the region prior to the attack on the US for an exercise in Oman.[24] It would be logical to deduce that these forces, due to their proximity alone, were the first into Afghanistan. The involvement of British SF would have brought to Central Command a tried and tested formula for the successful use of these forces either in a reconnaissance role or as a strategic strike force. On 29 September, the Pentagon (but not the British Ministry of Defence) admitted that SF were on the ground in Afghanistan and revealed interestingly that the British forces 'are better at this than we are'.[25] Interestingly, the subsequent appointment of Lieutenant-General Cedric Delves[26] as the senior British liaison officer to Central Command on 17 January 2002 added a significant amount of experience about SF and their roles to the planning process at the top of the chain of command.[27]

The attack on Mullah Omar's compound outside Kandahar on 20 October 2001 by a reinforced squadron of Delta Force (about 100 soldiers) supported by blocking units of Rangers (about 200 in total) is an indictment of how the US Army has traditionally struggled to deploy this unit effectively. The most notable feature of this night of operations was the videotape of another unit of Rangers parachuting on to an airstrip 60 miles south west of Kandahar that was liberally distributed to Western media the following day.[28] Delta Force is a highly effective unit. Colonel Charlie Beckwith set it up in 1977 and mirrored it on the British SAS.[29] The history of the unit has been fraught with misfortune not due to the soldiers themselves but rather to those in the US Army who have tried to deploy it.

The failure at Desert One in Iran (Operation 'Eagle Claw') on 24 April 1980 was not the fault of Delta Force though it had been put in an almost impossible position by too many units in the US armed forces trying to have a finger in the pie.[30] Again, Delta Force was forced to work with the Rangers whose contribution to the covert mission was to blow up an Iranian fuel truck with an anti-tank weapon that burned like a beacon around the highly secret landing site.[31] Helicopters (or the lack of working helicopters) ultimately doomed the mission, though the collision of a helicopter with a Hercules aircraft gave the mission disaster status.[32]

The other most well known mission of Delta Force, once more in concert with Rangers as a blocking force, was the attempt to intervene in the deteriorating conditions in Somalia on 3 October 1993. Popular perceptions, recently invigorated by the latest Hollywood movie of the incident, *Black Hawk Down*, focus on the fact that 18 or 19 US servicemen were killed in this operation. In reality, the Delta Force mission was a complete success with the capture of two of General Aideed's henchmen.[33]

It all started to go wrong when the two Black Hawk helicopters were shot down and the combined Delta Force and Rangers were isolated on the ground. Bowden's authoritative account of the subsequent battle makes it clear that the highly experienced Delta Force made the difference between just 18 men being killed (six from Delta) instead of all of them.[34] The Rangers were, despite their reputation, just very young soldiers who at one stage fired on the Delta assault team by accident.[35] The failure of the mission must be attributed to the military planners who decided to launch such an operation in broad daylight, which immediately compromised the element of surprise that is so essential for SF and made them (as well as their helicopters) very vulnerable to hostile fire.

The SF attack on Mullah Omar's compound on 20 October 2001 seems almost formulaic in comparison with these two failed missions. Like the previous two missions, covert forces were used in an explicit manner, whether by design (Mogadishu) or by accident (Desert One), that effectively neutralised the element of surprise. In this case, AC-130 gunships armed with mini-guns pounded the area around Mullah Omar's compound prior to the assault. Delta Force stormed the compound – found nothing of significance – and while exiting ran into serious opposition from the Taliban, who managed to wound 12 members of the SF unit.

In addition, the ferocity of resistance from the Taliban forced Delta Force to abandon a secondary aim of leaving behind a covert observation team.[36] This operation outside of Kandahar was another misuse of the highly valuable Delta Force. The purpose of the mission appears somewhat nebulous from official sources, apart from gathering intelligence.[37] The account from General Richard B. Myers (the senior military adviser to the President) of this incident is revealing:

> Question: Why the targets?
>
> Myers: Primarily for their intelligence value. One of them was a Taliban command-and-control facility, so we're hoping to find intelligence there. The other, the airfield was similarly, we thought of intelligence value.

> Question: Were you hoping to find commanders as well as intelligence at this command and control facility?
>
> Myers: We did not expect to find significant Taliban leadership at these locations. We of course were hoping we would, but we did not expect it, and we did not find senior Taliban or al Qaeda leadership.
>
> Question: The al Qaeda leadership. Were they expected to be in this area? Can you characterize that in any way?
>
> Myers: Yes, I'll characterize the one target as one of the locations where Omar lives, and it's a fairly large complex. It's a command-and-control compound for the Taliban leadership.[38]

The involvement of Delta Force suggests that perhaps the US military had hoped more than acknowledged by General Myers to find Mullah Omar in the compound. The idea of finding valuable intelligence from this complex is also questionable (Mullah Omar could not read or write). This botched operation had the potential to be another Mogadishu if members of Delta Force or the Rangers had been killed and/or left behind.[39] The propaganda coup for the Taliban was considerable in any event with the wreckage of the undercarriage of one of the helicopters being left behind.

In stark contrast to Britain, the US armed forces, particularly the Army, have struggled to deploy this enormous capability offered by Delta Force for years due to a lack of understanding as to their roles. Perhaps the veil of secrecy surrounding this unit has generated too much ignorance in the higher command concerning this unique element of SF. In Britain, in the last 20 years, several former officers of the SAS have managed to make it to the top levels of the military hierarchy with the most recent being General Sir Charles Guthrie, the former Chief of the Defence Staff. Consequently, senior planners better understand the roles and functions.

Furthermore, Delta Force appears tied by a virtual umbilical cord to the Rangers on major operations. The units could not be more different, and Rangers, despite their motto of 'Rangers Lead the Way', are not SF. [40] They are highly trained infantry with specialised raiding skills. To what degree, this close association is due to high-level Army politics and the Rangers desire a slice of the action is debatable. However, on the three occasions that Delta Force has operated with the Rangers since 1981, the missions have experienced serious mishaps or failed completely.

Phase II

The shift in US military thinking towards the deployment of SF was most apparent in the greater coordination of air power with ground troops and the open support for the Northern Alliance. Prior to 30 October 2001, the coalition forces (predominantly from the US) had executed precision strikes from aircraft in the same fashion as the air campaign in Kosovo in 1999. Like the air campaign in Kosovo, these strikes appeared to have little effect on the opposition's ground forces.[41] After 30 October, the use of B-52 bombers[42] directed by SF on the ground symbolised the new strategy, and the rapid advances of the Northern Alliance from the capture of Mazar-i-Sharif on 8 November to the capture of Kabul on 13 November was testimony to its effectiveness.

Air power has traditionally promised more than it can actually deliver. The earliest theorists like General Giulio Douhet in his book, *The Command of the Air* (1921) conceived that a bombing offensive could tear the guts out of a nation without having to defeat armies in the field.[43] However, World War II proved this theory wrong. The subsequent age of the precision guided munitions (PGM) from the 1970s onwards appeared to offer the converse of Douhet's idea. Air power armed with laser-guided bombs seemed to promise the capability to defeat armies (with precision strikes) without recourse to strategic bombing, which was now politically and publicly unacceptable in the post-war era. Again, experience in the Gulf War of 1991, Bosnia in 1995 and Kosovo in 1999 suggested that air power only works in concert with massive numbers of ground forces. Afghanistan supports this trend, though with a refinement that small numbers of SF working with indigenous forces removes the need for large deployments of coalition ground forces and the heightened risk of politically unwelcome casualties.

US Special Forces in the form of the Green Berets (set up in 1952)[44] played an important role in coordinating attacks from the air with the advancing Northern Alliance forces. One such team of Green Berets, Texas-One-Two under the command of Captain Jason Amerine has recently made public its role in Afghanistan: 'We thought that we'd send in teams and link up with a conventional unit', Amerine said. 'Special Forces is all about getting on the ground and making the best of what could be a bad situation.' He talked about going in behind enemy lines and linking up with a 'G Force' – *guerrillas* – and a Pashtun tribal chief named Hamid Karzai. 'We had weapons, ammo and provided humanitarian assistance (food)', he continued.

> We re-established a headquarters in Tarin Kot, a place where the Taliban began, and where a psychological victory for Karzai took place. People began switching sides. The Taliban sent 500 soldiers and 100 trucks to a region 50 miles south of Kandahar to put down the uprising ...The Taliban didn't know that F-14s and F-18s would bomb the convoy. Daily offensives were directed through air strikes. We re-established security, trained and organized G forces. The bombing continued, humanitarian assistance continued. We swept south

> towards Kandahar, the last major city where we had to develop trust. Firefights ensued and we launched counterattacks.[45]

Texas-One-Two was withdrawn from Afghanistan after a stray bomb from a B-52 on 5 December landed near the unit killing three members and ten Afghan *guerrillas* and wounding many more SF as well as Afghans. One of those who was slightly wounded in this incident was Hamid Karzai.[46] What is surprising about this revelation is the contrast between Britain and America in terms of publicity about SF and their relationship with wider society. Members of Texas-One-Two (in uniform) discussed their experiences in front of political science students at the University of Maryland. Such openness has two benefits: first, society is better informed about the activities of these units and second, the potential pool of recruits (particularly officers) is widened. In Britain, however, under the strict rules of the Ministry of Defence not to discuss these units, such a display of SF would be inconceivable.[47]

The participation of the Green Berets and other SF in this role undoubtedly provided substantial momentum to the high-speed advance of the Northern Alliance between November and December 2001. Acting as a nexus between tribal warrior and sophisticated twenty-first century air power, SF were a substantial force multiplier that ultimately helped to crack the Taliban regime from within Afghanistan itself.

The other major role for SF in this second phase of operations was to act as mobile strike units to neutralise Taliban and Al Qaeda forces that held out in fortified positions. One of the most controversial uses of SF in this role involved the suppression of the revolt by Taliban/Al Qaeda prisoners of war in a fort called Qala-i-Janghi between 25 and 27 November 2001. The causes of the uprising are still being debated. What is clear is that the failure of the Northern Alliance to completely disarm the prisoners (many of whom had concealed weapons like knives and grenades) and the small number of guards to prisoners (just 50 to look after over 400) were key factors. On the first day of the revolt, a CIA Agent, Johnny 'Mike' Spann was killed as the prisoners attacked the guards and acquired a large number of weapons from the fort's well-stocked arsenal. Putting dangerous prisoners of war close to such weapons must be regarded as one of the more questionable decisions of the Northern Alliance. Both British and American SF arrived on the scene; the Americans 'were in uniform the SAS in plain clothes'.[48] These units coordinated the attempts by the Northern Alliance to take control of the fort and called in air strikes from both F-18s and AC-130 gunships on hostile positions. One of the bombs (dropped on 25 November) accidentally wounded five of the American SF when it landed off target.[49]

A notable feature of the revolt was filming of British SF in action by an Afghan cameraman that was subsequently shown on Channel 4 News on 13 December. Apart from the Iranian embassy siege in 1980, there are very few examples of British SF being caught carrying out an operation on camera. Perhaps with the growth of global media and digital information highways, the activities of these 'shadow warriors' will become increasingly more visible to international society.[50]

By 27 November, after a huge amount of firepower had been applied to the fort, the bulk of the prisoners had been killed and those that remained surrendered. One of the more unorthodox/lateral methods used to persuade the prisoners to surrender was the pumping of cold water into the bunkers – an inexpensive yet highly effective means of wearing down the will of the prisoners to continue fighting.[51]

This action involving SF has already raised uncomfortable questions with regards to the legitimacy of quelling the revolt by force given that the Taliban/Al Qaeda had prisoner of war status. Amnesty International's request for an inquiry has been rejected by both the British and American governments;[52] however, this debatable use of SF is likely to remain a topic of discussion for a significant time in the future.

The most complex operations to neutralise Taliban/Al Qaeda concentrations of forces involved attacks on fortified caves. Assaulting a cave is arguably one of the most dangerous types of operation given that tunnels may extend for many hundreds of yards, and in all likelihood, SF would have limited knowledge of their internal layout prior to the attack. Furthermore, clearing tunnels would require very close quarter combat skills, as the enemy would literally be around or in each bend and cranny. It would be very difficult to carry out such an attack without incurring significant friendly casualties on the basis that the environment overwhelmingly favours the defender.

One of the most well documented attacks took place (at the same time as the prison revolt – approximately 25 November) on a cave in mountains near Kandahar. An entire squadron of the British SAS was tasked with clearing the cave; an operation that has been described as 'one of the most daring engagements that 22 SAS Regiment has undertaken in 30 years'.[53] Four hours of intense fighting left four SAS soldiers wounded, 18 Afghans killed, 17 taken prisoner[54] and the cave captured.

The subsequent assaults on the more infamous Tora Bora caves, the headquarters of Osama bin Laden, between 17 and 18 December 2001 also faced stiff resistance that was eventually overcome by a combination of SF and air strikes, but the Al Qaeda leadership was not found. The employment of SF in this particular manner (clearing difficult complexes) is a variation of their direct action role and the anti-terrorist skills of these units, particularly in relation to close quarter combat,[55] and makes them the most appropriate military units to assault such difficult targets.

Conclusion

'The War on Terrorism' as it is popularly called in the US has created a new strategic environment. Like geopolitical theory that encourages the study of the world not in terms of national boundaries but rather as geographically contiguous land masses so too does this new strategy require a global approach.[56] The threat stems not from the nation-state but instead from a section of the world's population stretching across several continents.[57] Unfortunately, the bulk of military forces in the West are geared towards defending the nation-state from another hostile nation-state not a well-financed band of globetrotting international terrorists.

However, the existence of SF ensures that the US and its coalition partners can wage warfare by other means. These units have the capability to take the fight to the terrorist in any land and in whatever guise – uniformed or plain clothes. The remarkably swift war in Afghanistan has demonstrated how effective these forces can be in terms of rapid deployment and counter-terrorist activity. Their ability to link up with opposition groups, train and organise military resistance as well as harness the immensely powerful but often unwieldy option of conventional bombing into a well-focused application of firepower brought down a political regime very quickly.

The costs of deploying SF in Afghanistan have been very favourable in relation to the gains achieved. To date just four SF soldiers (all Green Berets) have been killed, three of them by a stray bomb the fourth in an ambush (a CIA agent was wounded in the same incident) on 3 January 2002.[58] A host of SF have received wounds in Afghanistan that bears witness to the intense levels of fighting that these units have experienced in what is ostensibly a quick but not casualty-free war.

Interestingly, while Western nations are enormously sensitive to the deaths of young soldiers in foreign lands, particularly Vietnam and Mogadishu, the issue of deaths among the much older members of the SF reveals significant societal levels of toleration. In Britain, SF have been killed on a regular basis (but not in large numbers) since the 1950s in various conflicts with the most recent soldier mortally wounded in action in Sierra Leone on 10 September 2000,[59] yet at no stage has widespread opposition to their use been voiced. The employment of SF perhaps overturns the widespread belief that Western nations cannot sustain casualties and if so, offers a great deal of political latitude.

The initial strategy in Afghanistan placed primary emphasis on air power in the same manner that had been used in peace enforcement operations in the Balkans in recent years. Likewise, the use of Delta Force against Mullah Omar's complex was an expensive (in terms of wounds) as well as potentially disastrous operation that revealed that the US was still struggling to deploy this unit effectively.

After the failure of both traditional approaches, a new strategy emerged after 30 October 2001 that placed greater weight on the activities of Special Forces on the ground (coordinating efforts of the Northern Alliance) with air power in a supporting role. This new approach has proved to be highly effective. Furthermore, the employment of SF as strategic strike forces to neutralise fortified Taliban/Al Qaeda positions (prisons or caves) has been a logical use of the specialised skills of these units.

Questions, though, will remain about the role of SF (British and American) in suppressing the prison revolt in Qala-i-Janghi and why negotiations and containment (given the prisoner of war status of the Taliban/Al Qaeda fighters) were not the preferred options. The assaults on the cave complexes and fortified positions have been in the main successful but accidents have occurred. It has recently been admitted that US Special Forces (US Navy Seals) may have killed up to 16 civilians (by mistake) in a night operation in Uruzgan province on 24 January 2002.[60] Overall, operations in Afghanistan have shown the immense value of SF in general and that these units have an ability to generate a strategic effect far out of proportion to the numbers of the soldiers on the ground.

The war against terrorism will continue for some time ahead. It is likely in view of the elusive and now scattered remnants of the Al Qaeda network that the war will be prosecuted in far-flung countries. Nevertheless, the nature of the new war does, however, raise some awkward questions for SF, notably concerning the issue of overstretch. The numbers of SF (not raiding forces like Rangers) are very limited, particularly in the case of coalition partners like Britain.[61] Rapid expansion of such forces will also be difficult bearing in mind that only one in ten applicants who apply for the best SF meet the required grade[62] unless standards are dropped with the concurrent impact on operational effectiveness.

This is the dilemma facing military planners on both sides of the Atlantic: SF are the most appropriate military response but they are limited in numbers and not easily replaced. Furthermore, the anti-terrorist campaign is transnational in scope and limited manpower is easily diluted. In addition, Afghanistan may well prove to be an isolated case with warfare being fought in mountains and desolate countryside for control of a few strategic cities.

The next campaign(s) in the hunt for the elusive Osama bin Laden and the destruction of his allies, apart from the jungles of the Philippines, will perhaps take place in more urban environments and offer a distinctly different challenge. It is clear in the light of recent events that when the leadership of the Al Qaeda network is located, the means (or the weapons of choice) for the US and its coalition partners to apprehend them will undoubtedly include a significant package of SF.

NOTES

1. All four cities suffered extensive damage from conventional bombing during World War II and in each case thousands of civilians were killed by the air attacks. With regard to London, one of the most famous images of the Blitz was St Paul's Cathedral covered in smoke.
2. Paul Wilkinson in his seminal book *Terrorism and the Liberal State* (London: Macmillan 1977) suggested that terrorism could be described as 'a kind of unconventional war', see p.49.
3. Osama bin Laden, the bearded Saudi dissident, is a rare kind of terrorist. A rich man (whose wealth is measured in millions), he has rejected a life of comfort for one of earnest struggle against first, the Soviet Union and subsequently the US. A man of great will-power who has managed to stay one step ahead of the enormous resources – political and military – that the US has deployed against him.
4. Christopher Harmon, 'Five Strategies of Terrorism', *Small Wars and Insurgencies* 12/3 (Autumn 2001) p.44.
5. NMD is designed to intercept rogue intercontinental ballistic missiles launched from hostile nations. As such, it is a derivative of the enormously expensive anti-ballistic missile research in the 1960s and the even more expensive Strategic Defense Initiative of the 1980s. The cost of a limited NMD is estimated to be $60 billion. See Charles L. Glaser and Steve Fetter, 'National Missile Defense and the Future of U.S. Nuclear Weapons Policy', *International Security* 26/1 (Summer 2001) p.42.
6. The ability to think laterally and apply such thinking to a military environment has been a hallmark of SF since the inception of the Special Air Service (SAS) in 1941. In this respect, the planner or planners of 9/11 share an important characteristic with SF.
7. Collateral damage is a military euphemism for accidental damage to non-military targets whether people or buildings.
8. Alastair Finlan, 'British Special Forces in the Falklands Conflict of 1982', *Journal of Small Wars and Insurgencies* 13/3 (Autumn 2002) pp.75–96.
9. German and Italian numerical superiority in terms of fighter aircraft in Egypt was a major concern in 1941 for senior British officers in the region. See Correlli Barnett, *Engage the Enemy More Closely* (London: Penguin 2000) pp.332–3 for an illustration of the fears of Admiral Sir Andrew Cunningham (the most senior naval officer) about this critical issue in a March 1941 letter to the First Sea Lord.
10. Tim Jones, *Postwar CounterInsurgency and the SAS 1945–1952 – A Special Type of Warfare* (London and Portland OR: Frank Cass 2001) p.145.
11. Some of the more prominent units include the British Army's SAS Counter Terrorism Warfare team, the Royal Navy's Special Boat Service (SBS), the US Army's Delta Force and the US Navy's Seal Team Six. All of these units are either dedicated anti-terrorist

units like Delta Force and Seal Team Six or contain specialist anti-terrorist teams like the SAS and SBS. See the following texts for the best accounts of the creation of these specialised forces: Tony Geraghty, *Who Dares Wins – The Special Air Service 1950 to the Gulf War* (London: Little, Brown 1992) pp.413–56; John Parker, *SBS – The Inside Story of the Special Boat Service* (London: Headline 1997) pp.233–59; Colonel Charlie Beckwith and Donald Knox, *DELTA FORCE – The U.S. Counter-Terrorist Unit and the Iranian Hostage Rescue Mission* (London: Guild Publishing 1984) pp.94–180; and Richard Marcinko and John Weisman, *Rogue Warrior* (London: Arrow 1993) pp.235–319, for an account of the history behind Seal Team Six.

12. The most famous anti-terrorist operation is clearly the Iranian Embassy Siege of May 1980 in which the SAS stormed and cleared the building (killing five out of the six terrorists – the survivor was arrested) in just 11 minutes.
13. Anthony Kemp, *The SAS - Savage Wars of Peace – 1947 to the Present* (London: Penguin 2001) pp.143–4.
14. See James Adams, Robin Morgan and Anthony Bambridge, *Ambush – The War Between the SAS and the IRA* (London: Pan 1988) for one of the best accounts of Special Forces in this environment.
15. The recent deployment of US Special Forces to the Philippines in order to fight the Al Qaeda linked Abu Sayyaf rebels is one such case. See David Usborne, 'US forces move on Filipino militants', *The Independent* (17 Feb. 2002).
16. Laos in 1959 was one such case. See James Adams, *Secret Armies* (London: Pan 1989) p.46.
17. Ken Connor, *Ghost Force – The Secret History of the SAS* (London: Orion 2000) p.50.
18. Despite its remarkable success, Operation 'Enduring Freedom' failed to capture Osama bin Laden or the highly camera shy Mullah Omar.
19. See White House document, 'The Global War on Terrorism' (21 Dec. 2001), <www.whitehouse.gov/news/releases/2001/12/print/100dayreport.html>.
20. I have deliberately excluded units such as the 160th Aviation Group or the so-called Night Stalkers or US Air Force Special Operations Detachments because their functions are distinctly different from ground-based Special Forces.
21. The Gulf War of 1991 (a good example of the influence of Air/Land Battle doctrine in the US armed forces) has set a pattern for US military involvement in large scale conflicts (of whatever nature) in which the initial response is the use of strategic air power demonstrated in Bosnia in 1995, Kosovo in 1999 and Afghanistan in 2001/2002.
22. 'SAS in Taliban gun battle', *The Guardian* (23 Sept. 2001).
23. Connor (note 17) p.118.
24. Severin Carrell and Robert Mendick, 'Delta Force, the SAS and the Shadowy War of Misinformation', *The Independent* (30 Sept. 2001).
25. Julian Borger and Richard Norton-Taylor, 'Special Forces in Afghanistan', *The Guardian* (29 Sept. 2001).
26. 'SAS Chief takes top Afghan war job', *BBC NEWS* (4 Jan. 2002).
27. Lieutenant-General Cedric Delves has a distinguished background in SF and played a significant part in the recapture of the Falkland Islands in 1982.
28. See Seymour Hersh, 'Escape and Evasion – What Happened when the Special Forces landed in Afghanistan?', *The New Yorker* (5 Nov. 2001).
29. Colonel Charlie Beckwith served as an exchange officer with the SAS in 1962 and went on operations in Malaya with the unit. He also served with distinction in Vietnam as a Green Beret at Plei Mei in 1965 and in command of an airborne battalion in 1968. See Beckwith and Knox (note 11) pp.11–89.
30. See Adams (note 16) p.130.
31. Beckwith and Knox (note 11) p.269.
32. Ibid. pp.276–9.
33. Mark Bowden, *Black Hawk Down* (London: Corgi 2000) pp.81–2.

34. Ibid. p.502.
35. Ibid. pp.57–62.
36. Hersh (note 28).
37. See Pentagon Briefing on US Ground Operations in Afghanistan, 'U.S. Special Forces Attack Terrorist and Taliban Targets', 20 Oct. 2001, <http://usinfo.state.gov/topical/pol/terror/01102005.html>.
38. Ibid.
39. The death of the 18 US soldiers in Somalia led directly to the US withdrawal from the region after images of the bodies being dragged through the streets by angry Somalis were screened around the world.
40. Bowden (note 33) p.22.
41. See Martin Aguera, 'Air Power Paradox: NATO's "Misuse" of Military Force in Kosovo and its Consequences', *Small Wars and Insurgencies* 12/3 (Autumn 2001) pp.115–28 for an account of how the use of limited precision strikes failed to effectively influence the Yugoslav Third Army in Kosovo.
42. The B-52 bomber is a dinosaur in relation to modern aircraft. First built in the middle of the twentieth century, the B-52 was designed primarily to carry large quantities of nuclear weapons but could also carry enormous payloads of conventional weapons. Interestingly, the B-52 was considered 'obsolete' in the late 1970s – see William Keylor, *The Twentieth Century World* (Oxford: OUP 2001) p.385.
43. See John Pimlott, 'The Theory and Practice of Strategic Bombing', in Colin McInnes and Gary Sheffield (eds.) *Warfare in the Twentieth Century* (London: Unwin Hyman 1988) p.119.
44. Adams (note 16) p.39.
45. Glenna L. Linville, 'I Would Do It Again': Soldiers Recount Life on Afghan Front, Special to the *American Forces Press Service* (11 Feb. 2002), <www.defenselink.mil/news/Feb2002/ n02112002_200202113.html>.
46. Ibid.
47. A recent report in a British newspaper suggests that the Ministry of Defence may change its policy concerning the blanket security imposed on official accounts about missions involving SF. See Michael Evans, 'SAS exploits could be made public', *The Times* (19 Feb. 2002).
48. Matthew Campbell, 'The Fort of Hell', *The Sunday Times* (2 Dec. 2001).
49. Justin Huggler, 'The Castle of Death', *The Independent* (30 Nov. 2001).
50. The much publicised (except it seems to the Northern Alliance who almost fired on the British forces) and filmed deployment of the SBS at Bagram airfield on 15 Nov. 2001 is another example of how visible these forces are in the media age. See Nigel Morris, 'Alliance Nearly Opened Fire on UK Troops', *The Independent* (23 Jan. 2002).
51. Campbell (note 48).
52. Colin Blackstock, 'British Role in Firefight', *The Guardian* (14 Dec. 2001).
53. James Clark, 'Cave Warfare', *The Sunday Times* (2 Dec. 2001).
54. Kim Sengupta, 'British Forces to Take Part in Assault on Cave Complex', *The Independent* (3 Dec 2001).
55. With regard to the British SAS, a soldier undergoing specialist anti-terrorist training will fire 5,000 rounds in a week. Such high levels of practice produce a highly competent marksman. See Adams, Morgan and Bambridge (note 14) p.63.
56. Keylor (note 42) p.30.
57. The exception to this rule was Afghanistan and now the 'Axis of Evil' nations, Iraq, Iran and North Korea.
58. Steve Vogel, 'Special Forces Soldier Killed In Afghanistan', *Washington Post* (4 Jan. 2002).
59. See Richard Connaughton, 'Operation Barass', *Small Wars and Insurgencies* 12/2 (Summer 2001) pp.110–119, for an account of how the SAS soldier was killed in action.

60. Patrick Cockburn and Andrew Buncombe, 'US admits troops may have killed civilians in raid', *The Independent* (6 Feb. 2002).
61. The SAS has four regular squadrons (about 60 men each) and the SBS has three regular squadrons (of roughly the same size). See Kemp (note 13) p.218 for an organisational table of the larger SAS.
62. The British SBS, as an example, has a 90 per cent failure rate – see Ewen Southby-Tailyour, *Jane's Amphibious Warfare Capabilities* (Coulsdon, UK: Jane's Information Group 2000) p.530.

Muslims, Islamists, and the Cold War

GHADA HASHEM TALHAMI

It is not all that uncommon to endow a nation's foreign war with moral qualifications, viewing the enemy through the eternal dichotomy of good and evil. During the First World War, the Germans were dubbed the Huns, evoking images of pre-Christian barbarism and primitive force. When the Germans faced off against the Western powers during the Second World War, they earned the title of Nazis and the eternal enemies of democracy and international law. Indeed, following the discovery of Germany's genocidal policy towards the Jews and other minorities, Hitler's Germany became synonymous with evil. Germany and its allies became known as the Axis powers, implying a senseless alignment of states with nothing in common but their hostility to the Allies.

This same Germany, however, was allowed to shed its evil characteristics following its acceptance as a NATO ally and was allowed to transform itself into a beacon of democracy and a valued partner in the war on communism. When the Soviets replaced the Axis powers as the fulcrum of a new evil empire dedicated to the elimination of economic freedom and the enslavement of freedom-loving nations of the world, they replaced the Nazis as the new satanic power in the world.

Recently, a new axis of evil has been identified, and was also assigned characteristics and alien values and beliefs just like the former Communists. A new US foreign policy emerged which was christened the 'war on terror', and was described as a holy crusade. The enemy, once again, was painted in moralistic hues and dressed in religious garb. A religion, Islam, of one-sixth of the world's population is now the new enemy, the incomprehensible evil, evoking terror and bewilderment in the minds of most humankind.

Why, one may ask, are the real concerns of successive American administrations never shared with the public at large in a forthright and realistic manner? No simple answer exists although it has been made abundantly clear by now that this indulgence in excessive moralization not only deters the public from a badly-needed appreciation of foreign policy issues, but also makes it extremely difficult to reverse positions when the need arises. It is not enough to point to America's Puritan past as an explanation for the tendency to paint cosmic events in shades of black and white. It does not suffice to draw attention to the masterpieces of American literature such as *Moby Dick* (1851) which captured the irrational obsession with evil as a powerful Puritan trait and a visible thread running from Wilsonian foreign policy to the Cold War pronouncements of Secretary of State John Foster Dulles. Or could it be that this phenomenon is a necessary adjunct to the conduct of foreign policy in a populist democracy such as the US where the public's clamor for information is often satisfied with declarations and assertions that meet the need for a simplistic understanding of foreign policy? There are no definitive answers to these questions, but the indisputable fact is that US foreign policy is mired in symbolism, polarization, and a thick layer of morality.

US and European Scholarship on Islam

If a foreign policy which obscures reality is bad enough in terms of keeping the public in the dark, the reluctance of the academic community to define that reality is truly astonishing. Yet, it is not surprising that this academic failure affects mostly Middle Eastern and Islamic studies. A relatively new field in the US, this area has only recently been informed by the contributions of area experts and native-born scholars. For much of its history, US scholarship on Islam and the Middle East suffered from the confusion of culture with social science, a tendency to mute authentic voices, and a jaundiced view ascribing permanency to changeable phenomena and passing trends. Although we can never be sure as to when this skewed view of the politics, religion and culture of one of the world's most troubled areas began to inform the perspectives of American foreign policy makers, a thread connecting the two has always existed. Through prestigious vehicles for the dissemination of establishment views such as the journal *Foreign Affairs*, some academics have gained notoriety through their generalizations on the Middle East. The case of Samuel Huntington's 1993 article 'The Clash of Civilizations' which appeared first in *Foreign Affairs* is a point in hand. After causing a furious debate among scholars and writers inside and outside of the US, Huntington's thesis was almost buried and forgotten as one of academia's occasional and bizarre forays into the realm of public policy. His thesis, however, experienced a surprising reincarnation as a result of the September 11 terrorist attacks on the World Trade Center. The Huntington view of history came to be regarded as the most prophetic and definitive thesis on Islam versus the West.

Huntington seemed to have captured the struggle between globalization and tribalism by painting it in large visionary strokes focusing on Islam. Arguing that the newly emerging world conflicts can no longer be viewed through the old prism of ideological struggle, he pointed to civilizations as the reason for recent and future global confrontations. He then proceeded to describe a 'civilization identity' and to describe seven or eight major and potentially antagonistic civilizations. His main focus, however, was on the imminent and inevitable clash between Islam and Western civilization. According to the eminent cultural critic, Edward Said, Huntington's thesis was informed by a 1990 essay 'The Roots of Muslim Rage', which was penned by Bernard Lewis, historian of Islam. Neither a scholar of Islam nor of the Middle East, Huntington took the liberty of creating and personifying huge entities which he called 'Islam' and the 'West'.

Huntington and Lewis for that matter had no patience for analyzing the internal dynamics of the current world of Islam, nor of its visible and multiple communities which defy generalizations and static characterization. The entire world of Islam, thus, suffered a cartoon-like simplification and lost its historical complexity which extended not only to its geography but to its world of ethnic, sectarian and sub-cultural complexities. Said views this polarization between Islam, which is all evil, and the West, which is destined to triumph since good always triumphs over evil, as an example of 'demagogy' if not absolute ignorance. That one man presumes to describe and speak for an entire civilization, whichever way defined, suffers indeed from reductionism and unscholarly generalizations. Said wonders how many Indonesians, Moroccans, or Egyptians did Huntington survey before he reached his dubious conclusion about Muslims who are obsessed with the superiority of their civilization while convinced deep below of how inferior they were to Western power.

Not that Huntington lacks defenders, particularly after the attacks of September 11, when people as divergent in their background as Italian rightist Prime Minister Silvio Berlusconi, and former Pakistani Prime Minister Benazir Bhutto, seemed to echo Huntington's sweeping generalizations. Berlusconi, on his part, bragged about how it was the West and not the world of Islam which produced Mozart and Michelangelo, and Bhutto who now recognized in the attacks another facet of Islam's inability to adjust to modernity, a reminder of her own trouble when she sought the leadership of Islamic conservative Pakistan. The British weekly *The Economist* in its 22–28 September 2001 issue, directly praised Huntington for his perceptive assessment of Islam.

Why is if difficult for all these scholars, pundits, leaders and opinion-makers to see the September 11 attackers for what they really are, a small group of religious fanatics who used grand Islamic references to attack innocent people and destroy what is left of the thin line connecting the world of Islam to the West?[1] Said concludes his article by summarizing what Huntington's thesis was all about:

> These are tense times, but it is better to think in terms of powerful and powerless communities, the secular politics of reason and ignorance, and universal principles of justice and injustice, than to wander off in search of vast abstractions that may give momentary satisfaction but little self-knowledge or informed analysis. 'The Clash of Civilizations' thesis is a gimmick like 'The War of the Worlds', better for reinforcing defensive self-pride than for critical understanding of the bewildering interdependence of our time.[2]

Another academician, Francis Fukuyama, sought to reassure the world that his earlier prediction pertaining to the inevitable march towards capitalism and democracy, which he defined as the twin institutions of modernity, upon the collapse of communism was still valid, especially following the events of September 11. In his well-known 1989 essay 'The End of History and the Last Man', he had predicted that the world is not destined to witness 'a clash of civilizations', as Huntington would later predict, but an orderly march towards modernity. Even though some parts of the world resisted this global tendency upon the collapse of communism, there was no alternative to capitalist democracy since all the forces previously aligned against it were now openly discredited. Since the worlds of fascism, socialism, monarchic rule and other authoritarian varieties have publicly failed, the world's march will be in one direction only, hence his prediction of the impending 'end of history'.

Huntington's gloomy prediction is not warranted, wrote Fukuyama, even after the September 11 attack. Fukuyama had also bet on culture, rather than internal and changeable dynamics, to explain his vision. He argued that democracy and capitalistic theory do not succeed everywhere and that: 'It is not an accident that modern liberal democracy emerged first in the Christian West, since the universalism of democratic rights can be seen in many ways as a secular form of Christian universalism.'[3] He then states that Islam, or at least its fundamentalist branch, makes it clear that it does not accept modernity. This affirmation of his faith in the superiority of Western culture and its clear receptivity to rational democracy and liberalism in no way diminish his prediction of triumphalism of the West. He concludes:

> But the struggle we face is not the clash of several distinct and equal cultures struggling amongst one another like the great powers of 19th century Europe. The clash consists of a series of rearguard actions from societies whose traditional existence is indeed threatened by modernization. The strength of the backlash reflects the severity of this threat.[4]

Middle East scholars who, unlike Huntington or Fukuyama, specialize in this region, generally decry the sweeping generalizations of the grand theorists of the West versus Islam school. In reality, the record shows no monolithic Islamic block but a divergent mix of states with divergent interests. Fred Halliday reached this conclusion after analyzing the membership of the most professedly Islamic institution in the world, namely the Islamic Conference Organization. Numbering 54 states (today 55 with the addition of Ivory Coast), these nations have a record of occasional cooperation on certain issues but a great deal of disagreement on others. Often, their collaboration does not extend beyond public declarations of Islamic solidarity.

Several cases illustrate this trend, such as failure or refusal of Arab states to take the side of Turkey over that of Greece in the Cyprus issue. Islamic Iran, likewise, does not take a position of open support on the questions of Chechnya, Kashmir, and China's Muslim provinces. Iran also does not support the Muslim side in the Nagorno-Karabagh dispute. Debates between Muslim states and Western countries, upon close examination, are seen to revolve around ordinary political and economic issues which divide normal nations. Rarely are these differences colored by the religious affiliations of these states, particularly in the economic field such as disputes over oil prices. Neither are military and strategic bilateral and multilateral relations based on religious view points.

This is not to say that Middle Eastern and Islamic states eschew the use of religious or cultural language when expressing frustration with the more developed countries, such as references to Western support for Israel, and Western animosity towards Muslims. Even criticism directed at globalization by Muslims and Middle Eastern groups is clearly not opposed to the phenomenon of world integration on a technological and commercial level, but at the resultant domination by Western powers over entire regions. Thus, inequality and not religion incite people to reject systems imposed by the great powers. The confusion of religion with sovereignty issues is such that even countries like Iraq, with its decidedly official secular ideology, have often been described as an anti-Western Islamic state.[5]

Halliday perceptively points to the rhetoric and phraseology of Islamic groups as further evidence of the nationalist, rather than religious, nature of their cause. Despite frequent references to the classic Islamic sources of legal theory such as the *Quran* or *Hadith* (the Prophet's sayings), the main complaints of Islamic groups remain typically Third World issues such as Western imperialism, inequality between nations, and Western domination and exploitation. Indeed, it is not an exaggeration to say that Khomeini's rhetoric resembles that of other radical Third World leaders such as Mao, Peron, Castro, Nasser and yes, even Gandhi as he challenged Britain's right to rule India.[6] Halliday concludes with a plea against terrible simplifications:

> What the Muslim world wants from the West is not conversion to Islam but equality, respect and opportunity.... First, we must be aware of the diversity of the places we are talking about. The first form of simplification or stereotyping is to treat as one, in political or cultural terms, that which is not. The Middle East is not a generic Arab or Islamic entity. There are many differences between Arab peoples, on the basis of shared core items of faith; there is also a wide range of cultures and opinions.[7]

Another cautionary note against sweeping generalizations and simplification of Muslims and their issues by the Western countries of the world comes from the ranks of anthropologists. These show the greatest concern with defining and understanding the worst behavioral attribute attached to Muslims by the West, namely, terrorism. A phenomenon that is neither avoidable nor easily understood, terrorism is definitely predictable. Terrorism always aims at the attainment of political goals that appear unattainable through other means. To those who claim that terrorism is always state-sponsored, anthropologists see it as an outgrowth of the perceptions and actions of disadvantaged communities. When under extreme pressure, these communities resort to violence against groups that oppose and oppress them. Often this retaliation extends to outward groups not directly related to the aggrieved community's suppression. What is indisputable, however, is that this lashing out is the result of a group's marginalization by the international system of states. As the community comes under siege, experiencing multiple pressures, it begins to accept violent behavior in defense of its goals. Justifying the terrorism, these beleaguered communities claim that no other avenue was open to them.

Therefore, despite the Western view (and specifically the American view) that without state-sponsorship there will be no terrorism, reality proves otherwise. Once the community-inspired causation of terrorism is acknowledged, state-sponsored terrorism becomes irrelevant even though it may appear as the main cause of this violence. Eliminating the sponsor still does not cancel the causes of a community's aggrieved condition. And as one author reminds us, communities that produce terrorists are neither of recent vintage nor limited to the Middle East. The American Revolution spawned its own terrorist groups, such as, the Sons of Liberty, and others could be included under this general category of Western groups, such as Canadian separatist groups. One of the most outstanding examples of such terrorism was the Jewish underground before Israel's statehood. Terrorism, clearly, is not confined to specific communities and geographic locations, but will rear its head as a result of specific perceptions and the presence of generalized conditions of oppression and powerlessness.[8]

Islam and the Christian West

What adds to the validity of this thesis is the Muslim and Arab deeply ingrained perception of their victimization by the Christian West. This perception is, moreover, supported by history and historians of this subject who are convinced essentially of the perpetual violence governing this relationship. For instance, right from the earliest date of the Christian–Muslim encounter, Muslims were treated as nefarious to the civilizational impact of religion on the world. The Byzantine Empire regarded Islam not as a coequal and comprehensive religion, but as a Christian heresy, just as the legions of Christian heresies similar to the 'Arians' and Nestorians, whom the Byzantines battled over a span of five centuries. Another violent Christian–Muslim confrontation was the Crusades, which pitted the European Catholic Church against the natives of the Middle East. This conflict resulted in the Christian invasion of the Holy Land with all that implied of the finality of a relationship that should have been expressed in dialogue rather than deadly combat.

Still viewed today as a colonial episode of European control over the Muslim Middle East, the Crusades presaged the violence of succeeding colonial centuries when one side victimized the other through the loss of sovereignty over their own lands. Even native Arab Christians were casualties of this confrontation. Indeed, today the Crusades are used by Muslims as a metaphor for colonialism and Western, religiously-based domination and intolerance.

The Catholic Church inaugurated another period of extreme violence against Muslims when the latter lost control over Spain. The *reconquista* treated the Muslims of Spain with absolute vindictiveness, offering them only the option of conversion if they chose to stay. There were no Saladins in this encounter, who offered the departing Crusaders upon his re-conquest of Jerusalem the option of redeeming their freedom as a condition of safe departure.

The Protestant missionary episode in the Middle East, which sought to spread the true faith through conversion during the nineteenth and twentieth centuries also tolerated no other religious variants, not even native Christians and followers of ancient faiths. The relationship between missionary and native, whether Christian or Muslim, was built on an ingrained sense of religious and cultural superiority. The act of conversion, moreover, was never a guarantee of equality since the missionaries, as advanced agents of empire, sought to create a system of domination based on ethnic and racial factors.[9]

Turning Huntington's claim about Islam having bloody boundaries on its head, then, forces a new examination of history and a new frame of reference for the violence. In the twentieth century, nevertheless, the violence that is inherent in the Christian–Muslim relationship is more likely to be of a political and philosophical nature. It is a negative relationship, which in many cases generated a loathing of Arabs and Muslims and a religiously based validation of Israel. At the center of this development is Christian guilt over the Holocaust, which is the cause of a new theology that can best be described as 'Holocaustianity'. Some elements of the Christian church, particularly in the US, apparently hold political views that are extremely different from mainstream organizations like the National Council of Churches with its familiar support for the concept of a Palestinian state with Jerusalem as its capital. These elements have moved accordingly to a different theology which believes that the Holocaust, and not the resurrection of Jesus Christ, is the central event in history. This thesis generalizes guilt for the Holocaust to cover all humanity, including even people remotely related to the scene of the actual Holocaust such as the Japanese, Africans and the like.

Generalizing the guilt as a new perspective on a very significant event in recent European history would not be so egregious were it not for the fact that it results in idolization of the State of Israel and the belief in the survival of Israel as a necessary condition guaranteeing Christian salvation. Since some seminaries are actually engaged in the teaching of this theology, its impact on general Christian–Muslim understanding cannot be exaggerated. Muslims are once again victimized by a religious interpretation of world events that marginalizes them and throws Christian support behind the state of Israel irrespective of political facts and the terms of international debate. Could this be a perception of a new Muslim threat, particularly as Muslims are a substantial demographic presence in major European cities and in North America? Could a new confrontation be looming on the horizon as the points of Muslim–Christian contacts become multiplied across the globe?[10]

Afghanistan before the Invasion of the Soviets

No one understands the radical changes overtaking the Islamic collective psyche in recent years particularly before the invasion of Afghanistan by the Soviets than area experts who are also knowledgeable about Islam. Tracing reaction to global marginalization of certain Arab Muslims, these experts see the Afghan imbroglio as a significant flashpoint of the Western–Muslim confrontation which began deceptively as a Cold War clash of ideological and strategic proportions. The early and constant involvement of Saudi Arabia in this conflict, a state with strong Islamic credentials of the Sunni variety, appeared to reflect regional policies but in reality betrayed strong ideologically Islamic proclivities.

A simple understanding of the growth of formal Islamic institutions in Afghanistan illustrates clearly the intersection of ideology, religion, and political strategy in a part of the world where political regimes always sought to legitimize themselves through religion. The same has always been true for Saudi Arabia, which quickly became drawn into the Cold War struggle of Afghanistan as a result of its self-image not only as the guardian of Islam's holiest places but also as the embodiment of one of Islam's most conservative sects, namely Wahhabism. An eighteenth century phenomenon, Wahhabism integrated the rigorously conservative Hanbali school of the shariah with a new Puritanism which opposed any and every political and social innovation as a threat to the faith. It was no accident that this sect developed in the most isolated and insulated corners of the Muslim world, namely eastern Arabia, at a time when European winds of change were beginning to influence some parts of the world of Islam. Emphasizing the Hanbali variant of civil and criminal shariah law, Wahhabism and its sponsoring Saudi regime, legitimized only regimes of like disposition and ideological outlook.[11]

This Saudi variant on sectarian Islam received a new boost with the discovery of vast sources of oil in the Arabian peninsula and the regime's urgent need to create its own favorable strategic environment in a world riveted by secular winds emanating from Egypt and communist incursions in nearby Islamic countries.

Saudi Arabia's involvement in Afghan politics began slowly as an effort to support a fellow Sunni state. At the beginning of its history as a modern Islamic nation-state, Afghanistan emerged in 1721 from its struggle against takeover attempts by its neighbor, Safavid Shii Iran. In the 1880s, Afghanistan defeated another attempt to become part of the Shii world by the Imami Shii Hazara group, an ethnically distinct people who survive today as 15 per cent of the total population. At first, the new dynasty sought closer relations with the Naqshabandi Sufi and revivalist order which reached Afghanistan from India under the direction of Sayyid Ahmad Barelvi (today's Ahl-al-Hadith movement), and later with the Jamaat-i Islami (founded 1941) of Abu al-Ala al-Mawdudi. Through intermarriage, the royal family also established ties to the Qadiri Sufi order.

But the Afghani government was always apprehensive about semi-educated Muslim clergy (the ulema class) who were prone to preaching jihad against local leaders, as well as about pro-British and Indian educated clergy. Thus, the quest for loyal and educated ulema began with the inauguration of a faculty of theology attached to Kabul University. This move could not have been feasible without cooperation from Al-Azhar University in Egypt, which provided scholarship for Afghani students to study at the Muslim world's oldest Islamic institution of higher learning.

What the regime expected from Al-Azhar and what resulted from this association turned out to be two different things. At the beginning of the twentieth century, Al-Azhar lived by the reputation of such modernists as Muhammad Abduh, who preached reconciliation between Islam and the modern world. More importantly, Abduh's slant on the faith accepted the rule of modernizing and secular dynasties as that in Afghanistan. But by the 1950s and 1960s, the Azhari environment and Egypt's ideological wars brought the Afghani student clerics in contact with the commanding figures of the Egyptian Islamic revival, such as the Muslim Brotherhood's new theorists such as Sayyid Qutb (c1906–66). These same students upon assuming teaching duties in Afghanistan were also absorbing Mawdudi's diatribes against the secular state. Greatly influenced by Qutb's deadly confrontation with Nasser's socialist regime, they found his ideas ready ammunition for their ideological wars against campus Marxists of the same period.

The University of Kabul, and particularly its faculty of theology, spearheaded the rise of new Islamic organizations such as Sazman-i Javanan-i Musulman (Muslim Youth Organization), which was led originally by Burhanuddin Rabbani, who served at that time as a founding professor of the shariah faculty. The first meeting of this organization designated Gulbuddin Hekmatyar, another leading figure of the civil wars of the 1990s, the coordinator of political activities. Another leader of the Islamic student movement was Ghulam Rasul Sayyaf, who, like the others, received his education either in Saudi Arabia or in Egypt.[12]

When pro-Soviet figures began to seize certain areas of the government's authority following the *coup d'état* of 1973, the main Islamic activists left for Peshawar, the capital of Pakistan's Northwest provinces. The search for funding in order to sustain their activities in exile took the Islamists to Saudi Arabia. After spending six months in that country, Rabbani received support which was channeled, it was assumed, through Rabitat al-Alam al-Islami (Muslim World League). When the Soviets invaded Afghanistan in 1979, the Afghani Islamist activists were already well connected to Saudi and American secret services. These linkages were achieved through the support of the Saudi royal family and the Pakistani military regime of General Zia ul-Haq, both of which functioned as US surrogates in the Persian Gulf region. Thus, the Islamic direction of the national, anti-Soviet struggle in Afghanistan was acquired and enhanced through state sponsorship of the US and interested Islamic regimes.

Saudi Arabia's contribution to the strategic and political quagmire of Afghanistan had a great deal to do with the Saudi loathing for foreign innovations and their rejection of non-Muslims. Wahhabism became known as a Salafi school when Abd al-Wahhab's ideas foreshadowed those of Qutb about a century and a half later. This thesis, however, cannot be extended to cover all of the Saudi system of international relations since other considerations intruded on their overall strategy.

Specifically, the Saudis feared contamination by the anti-imperialist logic and leftist propaganda of Nasserite Arab nationalism, as well as the revolutionary rhetoric of Islamist Iran. Rabitat al-Alam al-Islami was specifically created in 1962 for the purpose of disseminating Sunni Muslim ideas in a world that was raked by these destabilizing winds of change. Al-Rabitat turned out to be the first in a series of institutions which engaged in a massive printing and distribution of Qurans and other Islamic texts and funneled funding to Islami centers throughout the world. The recipient institutions adhered to preaching a very traditional form of Islam which approximated closely the Saudi preference for Salafi Islam. The ideological battlelines with Egypt were clearly marked just as forces of Yemeni military reformism battled Saudi-backed Yemeni traditional forces. An ideological war of the first order, the Yemeni civil war (1962–67) split the Arab World along religio-ideological lines while the two sides professed to be within the Islamic mainstream.

One side-aspect of the Yemeni confrontation was Saudi Arabia's alliance with the Muslim Brotherhood (founded 1929) which was also fighting Nasserism in Egypt. The Brotherhood at the time had managed to exorcise the spirit and influence of Qutb and had passed under a moderate leadership advocating 'the Islamization of society', and led by Hasan Hudaybi and Omar Talmasani. This group willingly went along with President Anwar Sadat's policy in the 1970s, which used the Islamists in its battle against the remnants of Nasserism in Egypt. This policy was also reflected in a worldwide effort by al-Rabitat to support the Brotherhood and its branches throughout the Arab World. While the Brotherhood refrained from organizing a branch in Saudi Arabia itself, the latter continued to support conservative groups such as Pakistan's Jamaat-i Islami.[13]

The challenge paused by the Iranian Islamic Revolution of 1979 was even more serious than Nasserism. Here, another Muslim state presented itself as an alternative to Saudi Arabia's leadership position in the Muslim World. The Afghanistan war was, thus, a great opportunity for the Saudis to create a warrior brand of Sunni Islam in Afghanistan which up to that point has been largely infused with Sufi organizations. Such Sunnism was expected to become seriously anti-Shia, reprising the historic Sunni–Shii conflict between Iran and Afghanistan. This involvement had already experienced a close alignment between the foreign policy of Afghanistan and the Saudis following the detachment of East Pakistan in the 1970s.

Despite a brief period in which the Jamaat was excluded from any access to the state under Prime Minister Zulfiqar Ali Bhutto, this fiery brand of

Sunnism succeeded in infiltrating the ranks of the military institution. According to some experts, this task has been made easier by the changing nature of the Pakistani military whose officer class was becoming less aristocratic and British-trained (exemplified by Field Marshal Ayub Khan until 1969) and more middle class and Punjabi-based (such as Zia ul-Haq). The latter group, based on their class affiliation and education, were more receptive to Islamist ideas. It was not surprising, therefore, to see Zia base his legitimacy on the grassroots support of an increasingly Islamized Pakistan after his seizure of power in 1977. The Jamaat-i Islami were among his greatest supporters and a few years later, so was President Ronald Reagan and the Saudi regime, who were anxious to create a strong Islamic front against the Soviet invasion of Afghanistan. To the US, Pakistan and Saudi Arabia were best situated to replace the fallen power of America's surrogate in the region, namely the Shah of Iran. But the Islamic front in Afghanistan and Pakistan was eventually shattered into various splinters.

The Ahl al-Hadith faction in Pakistan and Afghanistan proved to be the most militant of the Salafi groups which preached a puritanical and rigid form of the faith. Ahl al-Hadith also received a great deal of funding from Saudi Arabia and established religious schools along the northwest border of Pakistan. The same movement was instrumental in bringing Islamic fighters of the Salafi persuasion from the Gulf countries to fight in Afghanistan's war.

Afghanistan and the anti-Soviet War

With the start of the Communist invasion of Afghanistan, most of the population accepted the challenge to its sovereignty as a religious struggle under the Salafis' definition of a jihad. The reason for failure to organize nationalist and traditional resistance was due to Pakistan's mistrust of their irredentist claims on its territory, and to the exclusive privilege of Islamic groups as recipients of external funding. The US, Pakistani and Saudi intelligence services joined hands in support of the Islamic fighters known as Mujahidin. Both in the US and in the Arab world, support for the Afghani fighters came largely from rightist groups which relished taking on the Soviet colossus. People like the Egyptian Sheik Omar Abdurrahman declared a jihad, expressing an unusual pride in the revival of a long-deceased practice.

Hoewever, the most significant role was performed by the Pakistani Inter-Services Intelligence (ISI) agency which directed military operations and was in charge of the distribution of funds. Weapons were given out, apparently, not only for specific operations but also as a reward for completing military tasks in the traditional style of government-tribal relations. Soviet distribution of weapons also contributed to the easy availability of arms. The US increased its aid to Afghanistan during the late 1980s from $30 million to more than $600 million annually. This same amount or even slightly more was contributed by Saudi Arabia and other Gulf states.

Overseeing this huge financial operation in addition to the Pakistani ISI were the American CIA and the Saudi al-Istikhbarat al-Ammah (General Intelligence Agency) headed by Prince Turki al-Faisal al-Saud. The Rabitat continued to finance religious schools for Afghani refugees along the northwest Pakistani border. Another Saudi Committee headed by Prince Salman ibn Abd al-Aziz, the Governor of Riyadh, was in charge of financing Arab volunteers who were recruited by the Muslim Brotherhood from various Arab countries.

At the same period, the Islamic Salvation Foundation, created by Osama bin Laden from his family's wealth amassed in the construction industry of Saudi Arabia, supported specific Arab and Afghani fighting groups. According to some Arabic accounts, bin Laden was working closely with Prince Turki's agency as late as 1988.

Several NGOs, which supported the Afghani refugees and various civilian projects, were organizations under the auspices of the Islamic Coordination Council in Peshawar. This was headed by a Palestinian named Abdullah Azzam, who wrote once explaining his reasons for joining the Afghani jihad as being severe disillusionment with the secular ideology of the Palestinian Liberation Organization.

What enhanced the religious nature of the Afghani struggle was not only the availability of volunteers and generous funding but also Pakistan's insistence on dampening the fires of Pashtun nationalism in order to arrest its infectious influence over some groups within Pakistan. Thus, only religious groups, as opposed to Afghani nationalist groups, were tolerated in Pakistan.[14]

While some fought for political reasons, others were decidedly fighting as a fulfillment of the Islamic obligation of jihad. Osama bin Laden had confessed in an interview in 1988, that originally the Afghanis approached him for funding, not for volunteers. He decided to join their ranks for purely personal religious reasons, or in accordance with the way in which he interpreted the jihad. Other Arab fighters shared this view, which said the *uma*, the one single Muslim nation of the scriptures, threatened in Afghanistan, therefore calling for the application of the jihad principle.[15] Because of the revivalist interpretation of Islam which swept the Arab World following the decline of secular Arab nationalism in the 1970s, the finer nuances implied in the concept of jihad were totally lost. None of the classic authorities on the law of war were remembered. But indeed, Muslims had arrived at a just war theory which places great limitations on the act of fighting as early as the end of the eighth century. In Al-Shaybani's famous work *Siyar,* the meaning of jihad is given as 'effort' or 'striving' and the use of force is prohibited except in the case of a definitive war of self-defense.[16]

The 1991 Gulf War had a great impact on the Mujahidin, although Soviet troops pulled out of Afghanistan by February 1989. First of all, the approaching storm engulfing the Arab World in 1990, split the ranks among supporters of Saudi Arabia, such as the Salafis, and the Muslim Brotherhood and the Islamic Jihad groups in Egypt, who opposed this close Saudi-Western alliance. Saudi invitation for Western forces to be stationed on their territory was particularly opposed by the most radical wing of the Afghan fighters and the Jamaat-i Islami and certain elements within the Pakistani ISI. The government of Pakistan, as well as some Mujahidin factions, remained supportive of the Saudi position. The Saudi plan to bring 2,000 Afghan fighters to Saudi Arabia as a gesture of support to the American military was sabotaged by radical elements and the Pakistani military.

The 1991 Gulf War also meant a final cessation of the flow of Saudi funding to Pakistan, which added to the dismay of different fighting groups. The US had ended its support upon the departure of the Soviets. By 1994, Saudi Arabia was treating Osama bin Laden as a hunted man and revoked his citizenship. Bin Laden then moved to the Sudan but remained highly involved in Afghanistan.[17]

The Rise of the Taliban

The involvement of the same intelligence services which were active in the anti-Soviet war and later in the murky background of the Taliban government betrays the same trends. By 1994, Pakistani military intelligence headed by the Interior Minister, Naseerullah Babarm, and according to some, with the help of the CIA, helped create the Taliban faction whose militant Islamist predisposition was conveniently overlooked by Washington. The Pakistani government sold the idea of a Taliban regime to Washington on the theory that such a militant Sunni government would stop the advance of any Iranian Shii force in Afghanistan and would guarantee US and allied access to the oil-rich territories of the Muslim states of the former Soviet Union.

The Saudi government and that of the United Arab Emirates (UAE) also approved the idea of a Sunni and anti-Iranian regime in Afghanistan and were the only two governments beside Pakistan to recognize the Taliban. Riyadh was motivated by its sectarian and ideological competition with Islamic Iran while the UAE government was hoping to use its influence over the Taliban to settle its claims over the Iranian-disputed Gulf islands of

Abu Musa and the Greater and Lesser Tunbs. Thus, Saudi and UAE funding, Pakistani military and logistical support, as well as Washington's tacit approval, enabled the Taliban to win against the Burhanuddin Rabbani-Massoud brief control over Kabul and allowed the Taliban to take almost complete control of the country by September 1996.[18]

Washington's silent approval of the Taliban regime proved to be short-lived, especially after the well-publicized ideological excesses of the Sunni zealots in power. The US State Department was particularly aggravated by the Taliban's consenting behavior towards the narcotics trade, the revenue of which increasingly went to the support of more militant Islamist groups. Finally, the August 1998 attack on the US embassies in Nairobi and Dar al-Salaam, which was attributed to bin Laden, aroused Washington's anger at the entire worldwide Islamist network supported by the Taliban.

The Taliban's rejection of Washington's demand for the handing over of bin Laden, led to further friction and pressure on Pakistan to help seize the Saudi poster-child of Islamist terrorism. According to some reports, the US was almost successful in persuading the Nawaz Sharif government to cooperate when the latter denounced the Taliban publicly because of their support for Islamist activists within Pakistan.

The success of the Pakistani military and ISI in toppling Sharif and replacing him with General Pervez Musharraf, finally restored power to the very groups which engineered the Islamist Taliban victory over Afghanistan, as well as Pakistan's incursions into Kashmir. On 2 August 2000, Musharaf said in a BBC interview that Pakistan had an abiding national interest in keeping the Afghani Pashtuns on the side of Pakistan. This Pakistani policy of seeking to control Afghanistan dates back to the period of Zia ul-Haq (1977–88) which sought to pit the Pashtuns against the other minorities in an effort to create a dependent government in Afghanistan. Zia's idea was that controlling Afghanistan provides Pakistan with strategic depth in its perpetual struggle against India. This policy would prevent the eventuality of waging a two-pronged war simultaneously, one in Afghanistan and one in India.[19]

Conclusion

What had happened in Afghanistan following the end of the Cold War was no different from what had transpired in other corners of the world, namely the phenomenon of the unraveled state. As Afghanistan descended into increasingly anarchic conditions, it became the most suitable theater for Arab and Islamist extremists. It was even suspected that many an Arab regime, including Saudi Arabia, hoped that Afghanistan would become a magnet for this disgruntled class and a battlefield from which they might never return. Unfortunately, the US and other Western countries for a brief moment mistakenly saw the Taliban as a possible instrument in the new Great Game that promised to unlock the energy and oil riches of the Muslim Asian republics. In the words of a former CIA station chief in Pakistan, US and other foreign oil companies hoped to build a pipeline to transport the natural and energy resources of Turkmenistan to the markets of Pakistan. The Taliban were in control of most of the pipeline routes by 1996, but a year later the Taliban lost their bid for a total control of the country. At the time of chaos and renewed civil war, many of the Afghan Arabs began to drift back to Afghanistan in search of a new jihad to occupy their misdirected energies.[20]

An understanding of this multifaceted and complex recent history of the Afghani quagmire is a necessary precursor to understanding America's war on terrorism and the various implications of that war. According to Third World experts, Arabs and Muslims targeted by the US war on terrorism, as well as the apprehensive Arab masses abroad, the September 11 episode was the most serious, although not necessarily the only, clash between the West and Islam. It was no accident that the first to be identified as the perpetrators of the crime were Osama bin Laden and Palestinian organizations.

What riled Middle Eastern observers was the conviction that the search was conducted within the boundaries of Arab geography and Islamic airspace and never encompassed any other communities. According to that viewpoint, identifying the exact identity of the criminals was not as important to the US as identifying a certain ideological and cultural framework as the guilty party. This framework turned out to be the Arab and Islamic one, which stood in opposition to the 'free world' and the ideology of liberalism.

The advocates of a war between world civilizations are only too eager to target Islam as an ideology of resistance, just as they targeted before that liberation theology in Latin America. These advocates are not concerned with the finer differences between religious sects or the involvement of outside forces in religious wars, but merely in directing the war not only against radical Muslims but also against all Muslims and Islamic civilization. Perhaps it would not be inappropriate then to ask: is this war on Muslims another Crusade?[21]

The terrorist challenge to America, additionally, cannot be understood outside of the context of the Cold War. The involvement of the CIA in Afghanistan's wars must be accepted and accounted for, as well as that of Pakistani and Saudi regional policy makers. Clearly, Saudi Arabia, Pakistan and the US saw the Afghani imbroglio as an opportunity to further their state and regional interests. Afghanistan, after all, was always on the cusp of clashing empires and civilizations. The Cold War was one more phase of the Great Game which saw Tsarist Russia and Britain struggle for strategic advantage across much of Asia in the past.

What is also hard to grasp and understand is the juxtaposition of the imperial interests of the US, the regional interests of Saudi Arabia and Pakistan, and the anti-national predilection of the Arab Afghani and Pakistan Mujahidin. Only a dissolving political state and anarchic polity can invite the participation of these disparate elements at once. Clearly, the interest of Saudi Arabia in maintaining its status as the world's foremost Islamic state and the interest of the Mujahidin in fighting in defense of the Islamic *uma* are bound to clash. Clearly, the interest of Pakistan in safeguarding its strategic northern flank was bound to conflict with US economic and strategic interest in maintaining control over Afghanistan.

In retrospect, none of these parties which fought side by side against the Soviets were ready for the chaos which descended on Afghanistan in the late 1980s and early 1990s. Moreover, none anticipated the changing strategic priorities of the US when terrorism finally reached its shores. The war on Muslims is, therefore, a multi-headed Hydra which seems to target Islamists and Muslims irrespective of sect and national origin. It is a war built on academic myths perpetrated by the likes of Huntington and cultural and political generalizations of medieval proportions.

More importantly, the current war on Muslims has no relevancy to democracy or the Arab Muslim peoples' receptivity to the concepts of human rights, religious freedom and tolerance, as well as peaceful existence among all people. The war on terrorism should more aptly be termed the war on an ally who turned bad. The fact that this former ally happened to represent a minority of a minority in the Muslim and Arab World needs to be emphasized.

A final point to bear in mind is the alien nature of violence to Islam. No one familiar with Huntington's thesis can afford to minimize his emphasis on the violent nature of Muslims and Islam. Of all the claims made in his general and unsupported thesis, reference to the historic bloody clash between Muslims and non-Muslims captured the imagination. The Afghanistan dimension of Bin Laden and his Taliban allies, however, clearly point to the political and socio-economic causation of that violence. The military experience of almost a decade of warfare was bound to inculcate militaristic values in the Taliban and their Arab and Pakistani allies. The fact that the Mujahidin emphasized a militaristic and tribal version of Islam should in no way reflect badly on the rest of Muslims around the world.

Indeed, one can readily argue that the theory of violence of bin Laden which justified a war on civilians and members of the other monotheistic faiths is more related to the anti-colonial rhetoric of the 1960s and 1970s than to the teachings of Islam. Even the idea of the liberating impact of violence on the victims of colonial and imperial violence never received unanimous approval. Frantz Fanon (1925–61), the ideologue of Third Worldism, actually aroused a ferocious debate whenever he espoused such an idea.

However, in the real world of wars of liberation, violence was not only accepted, it was also romanticized. It is interesting that the perpetrators of the theory of an inherently violent Islam never bothered to follow the debates on violence which permeate the literature of anti-colonial liberation.[22]

Perhaps we should accustom ourselves to the notion that all modern wars are based on deception, but we do not have to accept generalizations which go to the core of what is sacred among and between civilized people. The current war on terrorism approximates a clash of civilizations only in so far as it theorizes about colossal and historically misunderstood relationships. Nevertheless, the theory remains a theory which is strictly divorced form the historical context and floats by itself in a sphere of generalizations, misconceptions and dramatic but erroneous visions of the history of a very significant portion of humankind.

NOTES

1. Edward W. Said, 'The Clash of Ignorance', *The Nation* (22 Oct. 2001) pp.11–13.
2. Ibid. p.13.
3. Francis Fukuyama, 'History Is Still Going Our Way', *Wall Street Journal* (5 Oct. 2001) A14.
4. Ibid.
5. Fred Halliday, 'The British Isles and the Middle East: Inventing an Islamic Threat', the Peter Mansfield Memorial Lecture, *Middle East International* 624 (5 May 2000) p.24.
6. Ibid. pp.24–5.
7. Ibid. p.25.
8. William O. Beeman, 'Terrorism: Community Based or State Supported?', *American–Arab Affairs* 16 (Spring 1986) pp.29–35.
9. Yvonne Haddad Speaks at al-Hewar Center about Christian-Muslim Relations (17 Dec. 1997), <www.alhewar.com/Haddad.htm>.
10. Ibid.
11. Hamid Enayat, *Modern Islamic Political Thought* (Austin: Univ. of Texas Press 1982) pp.41, 67, 69.
12. Barnett R. Rubin, 'Arab Islamists in Afghanistan', in John L. Esposito (ed.) *Political Islam: Revolution, Radicalism, or Reform?* (Boulder, CO: Lynne Rienner 1997) pp.181–3.
13. Ibid. pp.183–5.
14. Ibid. pp.187–90.
15. Ibid. pp.195–6.
16. John Strawson, 'A Western Question to the Middle East: 'Is There a Human Rights Discourse in Islam?', *Arab Studies Quarterly* 19/1 (Winter 1997) (Special Issue titled: *Human Rights in the Arab World*) pp.37–8.
17. Rubin (note 12) pp.198–9.
18. Amin Saikal, 'The Role of Outside Actors in Afghanistan', *Middle East Policy* 7/4 (Oct. 2000) p.51.
19. Ibid. pp.51–3.
20. Milton Bearden, 'Afghanistan, Graveyard of Empires', *Foreign Affairs* 80/6 (Nov.–Dec. 2001) pp.24–8.
21. Anwar Badr, 'Man takhdum luabat sinaat al-mutahamin?' (Whom Does the Game of Manufacturing Guilty Parties Serve?), *al-Huriya* 865 (29 Sept. 2001) p.14.
22. See Emmanuel Hansen, *Frantz Fanon: Social and Political Thought* (Columbus: Ohio State Univ. 1977) pp.115–76; and David Macey, *Frantz Fanon, a Biography* (NY: Picador Press 2000) *passim*.

An Ambivalent War: Russia's War on Terrorism

STEPHEN J. BLANK

Ostensibly Russia is an ally in the war on terrorism. Since 1998 it has consistently denounced terrorism as a threat to its interests and security, claimed to be fighting it in Chechnya, and tried to forge an anti-terrorist bloc in Central Asia, the second front of what Moscow regards as a two-front war where its vital interests are directly engaged. Russian analysts also like to claim that Russia's contribution to the US victory in Afghanistan was also the greatest of any ally although proof is lacking.[1] Many Western analysts, as well believe that Russian support was very instrumental in the fall of the Taliban. Certainly Russia, since September 11 has supported the anti-Taliban crusade and intensified weapons shipments to the Northern Alliance, allegedly paid for by Washington.[2] Indeed, Alexei Arbatov states that it coordinated this aid with Washington's redirection of its bombing campaign in October–November 2001 to produce a decisive victory for the Northern Alliance against the Taliban.[3] There are also many reports of extensive intelligence collaboration as well as many earlier reports, which have been denied, alleging earlier US-Russian plots to assassinate Osama bin Laden or to attack Al Qaida and the Taliban before September 2001.[4]

Today Russian leaders advocate a global campaign against terrorism under the auspices of the UN, whose authority in Chechnya and elsewhere in the Commonwealth of Independent States (CIS) Russia has steadfastly refused to accept. Although they acknowledge that Chechnya ultimately must be settled on the basis of a political solution, official spokesmen tend to emphasize the prosecution of military victory over terrorists rather than discuss the notion, commonly found in Western discussions of terrorism, of attacking the socio-economic and political roots of that phenomenon or states who sponsor it[5] Indeed, recent reports state that Russia is trying to kill Aslan Maskhadov, the leader of the Chechens, thus calling into question its commitment to a negotiated political settlement.[6]

They also insist that the anti-terrorist coalition should be based on equal status and no double standards, namely no foreign criticism of its campaign in Chechnya or contact with or support for the Chechens.[7] Indeed, they argue that the extent of Russia's partnership with the West will be determined by the extent of support they give to it against what it claims to be terrorism in

Chechnya. Moreover, criticism of Russia's Chechnya campaign or support for the Chechens will, they threaten, cause the breakdown of the anti-terror coalition, making the talk of partnership meaningless.[8]

And yet a deeper examination of the war in Chechnya and of Russia's military efforts in Central Asia and the broader CIS suggest a strikingly more ambivalent, even contradictory picture. In fact, rhetoric to the contrary notwithstanding, in many respects Russia's war on or against terrorism resembles a Matrioshka doll. The deeper you look into it, the less there is. Certainly Russian perspectives on how to fight terrorism strongly diverge from Western ones. For example, owing to the aforementioned disparity in Russian and Western perspectives, Russian policy in Chechnya increasingly tends to resemble a policy akin to that of Joseph Conrad's character Kurtz in the short story *The Heart of Darkness* (1902), that is 'exterminate all the brutes'. Thus Russia now demands of Georgia that it compel Chechens who fled to the neighboring Pankisi Gorge in Georgia, including both Chechen fighters (terrorists or not) and civilians, return to the Chechen war zone lest Russia further threaten Georgia as it has bombed it thrice since 11 September 2001.[9] This demand flies in the face of virtually every international convention pertaining to refugees and civilians and suggests goals beyond simply restoring Russian sovereignty over Chechnya.[10]

Yet even as Russian authorities strongly denounced terrorism and bin Laden since 1999, apparently to the extent of plotting to kill him, the CIA and FBI believe that Russia or Russian agents were involved in the attack on the destroyer USS *Cole* in October 2000 and that the Russian spy Robert Hanssen gave Russia high-tech encryption technology that Moscow then sold to bin Laden![11] Similarly during 2000–2001 Russian military and political authorities frequently threatened to launch military strikes and perhaps an invasion of Afghanistan against the Taliban and Al Qaida to help defend Central Asia and Russia against terrorism.[12] Yet not only did no attacks take place, there are equally frequent statements from high-ranking military or political figures indicating their belief that there was no threat of a Taliban invasion of Central Asia and expressing confidence in being able to deal with the threat of indigenous terrorists.[13]

Certainly many Central Asian states, as did China, displayed a marked unwillingness to fight with the Taliban as well as some confidence that they could reach an accommodation with it through purely political means.[14] Moreover, close analysis of all the activities of CIS defense structures generated by Moscow indicate a lot of paper shuffling and rhetoric but little or no action. Central Asian leaders and elites were less than impressed by Russian deliveries of 'assistance' that had been lavishly promised in 2000–2001.[15] Likewise, Russian forces in Central Asia, clearly possessing some undefined intelligence ties to the Islamic Movement for Unity (IMU) escorted Juma Namangani, its leader, out of Central Asia in early 2001, hardly a sign of a resolute anti-terrorist policy.[16] And while Russia supported the Northern Alliance in Afghanistan against the Taliban, in Tajikistan it was simultaneously opposing the drug runners and indigenous terrorists linked to that largely Tajik group, a feat that is as hard to accomplish as it sounds.[17]

Thus despite regular invocations of the threat of a 'terrorist international' from Manila to Sarajevo that does in fact exist, the threat to Russia is and was less than it publicly stated.[18] And often Moscow apparently colluded with the bearers of this threat. This does not mean that there was or is no threat. Since 1999 there have been numerous signs of Al Qaeda and other terrorist groups' interest in Russia beyond Chechnya.[19] Certainly Russian counterintelligence was warning throughout the 1990s of real threats to blow up or seize nuclear powerplants.[20] Likewise, there was much terrorism in Chechnya and Dagestan as part of the broader thrust for Chechen independence during 1997–99. This terrorism certainly aimed to detach Chechnya and Dagestan from Russia and set up a Muslim state, thereby justifying a severe military and police response.[21] Nevertheless, as President Jacques Chirac of France reminded President Vladimir Putin in January 2002, there is much more to Chechnya than terrorism.[22]

However, the lessened intensity of the threat and Russia's ambiguous and often self-serving response to it suggests that invoking international terrorism may have been as much a political ploy with clear domestic and foreign policy objectives as it was an accurate intelligence estimate. Understanding that rhetoric aside the threat was less than publicly depicted helps us explain Moscow's curious and ongoing failure to devise and/or deploy any kind of appropriate military riposte to it.

This failure persists, for example at the meeting of the Shanghai Cooperation Organization (SCO or Shanghai-6) in January 2002 where the members voted to cooperate more closely against terrorism, in particular three groups, the Chechens, the IMU, and the Uighur insurgents in Xinjiang.[23] Despite intelligence cooperation among these states; they can hardly offer Moscow and Beijing major assistance in Chechnya or Xinjiang. And the IMU is apparently moribund having suffered military defeats between 2000 and 2001 and Namangani's death in US bombing raids in Afghanistan. Thus between two and three years of high-level rhetoric and meetings has generated little effective development of combat-ready or capable military-political organizations to confront Central Asian terrorism.

Another example of this ambiguity is nuclear and other WMD proliferation. Undoubtedly Russia knows that Iran and Syria (and previously Iraq) are terrorist states, yet it continues to sell all these states conventional weaponry and know-how that is then used for terrorist purposes, mainly but not exclusively, against Israel, by their clients to whom these weapons have been transferred.[24] In fact Russian media and spokesmen like to deny that Iran sponsors terrorism or that the country is contributing to it since Iran supposedly scrupulously observes International Atomic Energy Agency agreements. And in any case everyone's special services are supposedly helping to organize or outfit forces that their adversaries call terrorists.[25] Nor have they done anything to oppose Iran's recent escalation of threats to Israel that are made on behalf of Iran's client the terrorist group Hizballah in Lebanon or Tehran's attempt to collaborate with the Palestine Liberation Organization inside Israel.[26] Despite calls for partnership with America against terror and advocacy of equality in this pursuit, Moscow has previously ruled out any action to stop the proliferation of conventional weapons and WMD capabilities to these states even as it continues to sell them weapons, technology, and know-how.[27] And not only does Moscow aid and abet them, it 'categorically' opposed military action against Iraq and emerged as a major economic partner of Iraq although that position may have softened under American pressure just before the invasion.[28] Moscow's support of the influential military and economic lobbies in Russia, who weigh heavily in state policy to support Iran and Iraq, hardly suggests a wholehearted resolve to fight terrorism and its sponsors.

Similarly Moscow likes to lump together, as at the SCO's conferences, the threats of terrorism and separatism. While Moscow forthrightly denies that it supports terrorism or separatism, it is quite clear that its forces are the main military-political backers of the separatist and breakaway statelets of Transdniestria, Abkhazia, and Nagorno-Karabakh. Nor can we deny that these statelets are and function as instruments of Russian neo-imperial power against former Soviet republics who were insufficiently solicitous of Moscow's interests.[29] Thus here separatism is clearly a critical instrument of Russian policy. Indeed, Moscow occasionally threatened to support the Kurds inside Turkey, a movement that Turkey labels as terrorist and separatist, if Turkey aided the Chechens or otherwise displeased Moscow, and there are occasional charges that they still are supported by Armenia and behind that Russia.[30] In all these areas the war on terrorism, proliferation to sponsors of terrorism, and support for separatists, Moscow's record, to be frank, comes up short.

Chechnya

Russian spokesmen have consistently outlined two fronts in the campaign against terrorism: Chechnya and Central Asia. Yet, officials like Defense Minister Sergei Ivanov have made clear Moscow's exclusive interest in

Chechnya and disinterest in bin Laden.[31] On both fronts Russia has displayed the ambivalence and ambiguity of its responses to terrorism albeit in different ways. While Al Qaida and the Taliban undoubtedly had links to both theaters and the insurgents there, Moscow's portrayal of the threat and its response to it has differed in each theater.

Moscow portrays the Chechen threat as being directed at Russia's integrity and as aiming to establish a Muslim terrorist theocracy in the North Caucasus if not elsewhere. Putin actually invoked a Russian version of the domino theory to justify the war.[32] Russian leaders did not invent this Chechen goal but it surely was the aim of the outsiders who usurped effective control in Chechnya from Aslan Maskhadov's government. They succeeded because Russia refused to construct a political solution after 1996 and because Maskhadov failed to establish control over an admittedly difficult situation.

Furthermore there is good reason to believe that during the wave of kidnappings, drug running, and general acts of terrorism that originated in Chechnya during 1996–99 Russian military, political and police officials were deeply involved in various forms of highly profitable collaboration with the 'terrorists'. For example, officers in the North Caucasus Military District, the army's main fighting force in Chechnya, *routinely*, sold soldiers to the Chechens as slaves or to become drug couriers and addicts through August 1999. There is also considerable evidence of corruption of the Federal Security Service (FSB) through its toleration of and occasional protection of Chechen criminals and rackets in Russia.[33]

Likewise Boris Berezovsky, Yeltsin's right-hand man, kingmaker, and family financier, and for a while Secretary of the CIS was publicly known to be involved in negotiations with the kidnappers that the FSB now charges (for acutely self-interested reasons) were the way in which he was funding the terrorists. It seems inconceivable that if Berezovsky was transferring money to the terrorists, he did so without the knowledge and support of key elements in the government, including the FSB. Indeed he admits his participation in a general sense in such negotiations and claims to have acted with these organs' full knowledge.[34]

Similarly the charges that the Chechens launched the bombings in Moscow and Vologodonsk in September 1999 that decisively shaped public opinion have never been satisfactorily proved while the FSB was caught supposedly running a simulation of such an explosion in Ryazan, and Berezovsky has publicly charged the FSB with those bombings.[35] Those bombings and the war against the Chechens that began with their invasion of Dagestan in August 1999 along with Putin's accession to office appear to have been an almost providential series of events for a government besieged on all sides, lacking domestic support, and obsessed with the fear that Russia might fall apart.

Therefore we must grasp the reasons why the Russian army responded to Chechnya by resorting to total war. Certainly in September 1999 the then Minister of Defense, Marshal Igor Sergeyev, proposed a limited invasion of Chechnya culminating at the Terek River in Northern Chechnya, a natural frontier.[36] Instead the government, led by Yeltsin and Putin, opted for a total invasion of Chechnya as proposed by Chief of Staff, General Anatoly Kvashnin. Essentially this option of total war went beyond defense against a real, serious, and justifiable threat to Dagestan and Russia's integrity to confront four other threats to the Yeltsin regime.[37] One clear threat was the domestic opposition that was expected to win the Duma elections in December 1999 and then launch investigations, arrests, and trials of members of the government and even Yeltsin's family (and to impeach Yeltsin). Undoubtedly this would have put Yeltsin himself and the succession to him at risk and was thus an unacceptable risk for the party in power. The still unexplained bombings in Moscow in September 1999 plus the initial military successes against the Chechens helped ensure a patriotic consensus around Putin and his victory in the Duma elections and the presidential elections in June 2000.

A second threat to the regime owed much to intra-military politics. Kvashnin and Sergeyev, by the end of 1999, were bitter antagonists with each one pushing rival threat assessments and thus prescriptions for defense spending. For Sergeyev, the threat was a high-tech conventional war, as in Kosovo or a war that would require the first use of Russian nuclear weapons since the conventional forces were clearly unavailing against a Western thrust. However, the likelihood of this was low as long as Russia preserved and extended its nuclear deterrent. In this relatively low-risk environment defense investment for procurement should go primarily to the nuclear arm, the Strategic Nuclear Forces (S.Ya.S) with the residual going to the conventional forces until such time as the economy revived and could support them.

However Kvashnin saw Kosovo not as a high-tech war but as a secessionist nightmare. The General Staff had long since seen Chechnya as another Kosovo where a breakaway minority, claiming oppression as it sought alleged self-determination, would ultimately win foreign support leading to a Western operation on the scale of Kosovo to support them. This was the nightmare version for Russia and led Russian strategists to include the option of using tactical nuclear weapons (TNW) in a first strike in such a war to gain intra-war escalation dominance and force NATO to negotiate. And despite the simultaneous planning for Chechnya and funding constraints, the armed forces mounted this operation as the climax of Zapad-99, its largest exercise since 1991 in mid-1999. Zapad-99 featured a NATO invasion from Poland and the Baltic states and culminated, due to the general purpose forces' weaknesses in this use of TNW followed by peace talks.

Thus the General Staff's agenda primarily entailed funding to confront the threat of conventional wars like Chechnya in order to win them quickly and deny NATO another Kosovo option. Kvashnin and his allies also strongly desired to avenge their defeat by the Chechens in 1996, which the military generally laid at the politicians' doorstep. Indeed, after 1996 a rather dangerous stab in the back mentality appeared among the officer corps. Numerous military men have publicly said that the government betrayed the military on that occasion, stealing defeat from victory and preventing them from winning. Major military figures like retired General M. A. Gareyev, President of the Russian Academy of Military Sciences and a major military theorist, openly stated that the government is the enemy of the country, writing that, 'For 150 years the political leadership of this country has placed the military into extremely unfavorable and intolerable conditions from which it has had to extricate itself. Moreover, eventually the military winds up "guilty" of everything.'[38]

Gareyev was hardly alone, the young military historian Alexander Kirov, whose military career was terminated because he wrote the truth on Hungary in 1956, writes as if it was the party alone who was responsible for this and other military deformations. Thus, he writes:

> Over the postwar years our civilian government sacrificed military leaders, the defenders of our country, more than once, suggesting that they issue criminal orders to their subordinate troops and that, if they did not carry out these orders, then the full force of the law and the contempt of the Soviet people would bear down on them, on generals and privates alike. Unfortunately very few Soviets thought this through; most of us did not even try to understand or accept it. Soldiers could never question the constitutionality and legitimacy of an order. Thus the party and the state (but not the military-SB) nomenklatura could manipulate the armed forces and social awareness to its own interests.... Today some are prepared to lay the entire blame on the army. But unfortunately they were neither wise enough, nor brave enough, to point this out at the time.[39]

Marshal Sergeyev echoed this sentiment when he asserted that the underlying cause of the *Kursk* submarine disaster in August 2000 was the lack of funding of the military that had led to lack of equipment, resources, etc.[40] Likewise General Shamanov, commander of the forces in Chechnya threatened a mutiny if he was not allowed to pursue a decisive victory.[41]

Subsequent revelations demonstrate how this intra-military split and anger at the government affected the planning for the war and showed what the war in Chechnya is really all about. Plans to invade Chechnya, confirmed by former Prime Minister Sergei Stepashin, developed from March 1999 when the Chechens kidnapped Internal Forces (MVD) Major General Gennady Shpigun, to August 1999.[42] By May 1999 the Ministry of Foreign Affairs was confidentially telling US analysts that there would be war in Chechnya by August.[43] Russia's press also stated that an operation against Chechnya to be led by the Ministry of Interior's Internal Forces (VVMVD) was underway or being planned.[44] Stepashin claimed that this operation was to stop at the Terek River, namely Sergeyev's option.[45] Unfortunately things developed differently.

There is also good reason to suspect that the Chechen invasion of Dagestan in August was both a real threat to Dagestan and a provocation incited by those on both sides who wanted a war to give a pretext for launching (or getting Yeltsin to sign off on launching) the invasion plan.[46] Although the army had made many statements of its readiness the forces on the border were utterly surprised and the VVMVD failed operationally. It was the hastily dispatched regular army, under the General Staff's command, that then expelled the Chechens from Dagestan in September 1999 after two incursions into that republic. At this time Kvashnin and Putin made their deal. The General Staff got carte blanche to occupy all of Chechnya, exterminate the terrorists (which meant massive depopulation of the area due to bombing), and do so with few operational controls from Moscow.[47] This accord would heal the breach between the military and the government and also supposedly suppress the internecine fighting within the armed forces. Meanwhile Putin anxiously sought ways to defeat the opposition in upcoming Duma elections. Thus both he and Kvashnin needed what the other could offer. According to British analyst Mark Galeotti,

> The result was an unholy pact. Russian intelligence sources have confirmed for me that it went something like this: Kvashnin would give Putin a victorious little war. In return Kvashnin expected a higher profile for the general staff; funding that would more than cover the cost of the invasion; and a completely free hand to fight the war as he saw fit, free of political interference. A deal was struck on September 20 with a final proviso: if it could all be done without too many Russian casualties – never a vote winner – Putin would get a suitable victory just before the Duma elections. Thus war returned to the Caucasus.[48]

Russia perceived a third threat from Chechen and Islamist agitation for separatism in 1999. Throughout the period after the collapse of the ruble in August 1998 there were widespread fears of economic or political moves that would bring about the de facto disintegration of the Russian Federation, a fear that clearly gripped the elite in the government. This fear of separatism within the federation is also visible in Putin's vigorous moves to recentralize power in Moscow from the start of his tenure. And it demonstrates that the war in Chechnya stands at the bloody crossroads of the federal and civil-military issues of Russian politics and represents the ongoing failure to achieve a democratic resolution of these two issues.

Finally, Russian military-political leaders discerned a fourth threat in the North Caucasus from NATO's alleged designs to move into the Transcaucasus. The General Staff had argued for a tough policy here since 1998. Its views on the threats facing Russia and the military forces needed to counter them emerged from a pre-Kosovo threat assessment in November 1998 that was written by lower-ranking but knowledgeable members of the General Staff.

This article, written as Kosovo's crisis approached its apex, blasted NATO for acting unilaterally out of area and imposing a new world order by bypassing the UN and OSCE. This article accused NATO and specifically the US of trying to go beyond the Washington Treaty and convert NATO into an offensive military bloc that was expanding its 'zone of responsibility' by punitive, military means.[49] The authors charged that:

> At the same time, it is not unlikely that NATO could use or even organize crises similar to that in Kosovo in other areas of the world to create an excuse for military intervention since the 'policy of double standards' where the bloc's interests dictate the thrust of policy. *The possibility of the use of military force in Kosovo against the Yugoslav Army and simultaneous disregard for the problem of the genocide faced by the Kurds in Turkey, the manifestation of 'concern' at the use of military force in the Dniester Region, Chechnya, and Nagorno-Karabakh* is typical of the alliance's actions [author's emphasis].[50]

The authors went beyond hinting that war in Chechnya was already on the agenda to forewarn NATO openly about Russia's likely reaction to an operation against Serbia. Rather than accept a NATO-dictated isolation from European security agendas and the negating of organizations like the UN and OSCE, Russia would act because this crisis provided NATO with an opportunity to project military force not just against Serbia but against Russia itself. This was because the main objective of NATO enlargement was to weaken Russia's influence in Europe and around the world. Therefore the following scenario was possible. 'Once our country has coped with its difficulties, there will be a firm NATO ring around it, which will enable the West to apply effective economic, political, and possibly even military pressure on Moscow.'[51] Specifically,

> When analyzing the development of events in the Balkans, parallels with the development of events in the Caucasus involuntarily suggest themselves: Bosnia-Herzegovina is Nagorno-Karabakh; Kosovo is Chechnya. As soon as the West and, in particular, NATO, has rehearsed the "divide and rule" principle in the Balkans under cover of peacekeeping, they should be expected to interfere in the internal affairs of the CIS countries and Russia. It is possible to extrapolate the implementation of "peacekeeping operations" in the region involving military force without a UN Security Council mandate, which could result in the Caucasus being wrested from Russia [it bears mentioning that this applies as well to the independent states of the Transcaucasus, an involuntary hint of the continuing neo-imperial mindset of the General Staff-author] and the lasting consolidation of NATO's military presence in this region, which is far removed from the alliance's zone of responsibility. *Is Russia prepared for the development of this scenario? It is obvious that, in order to ensure that the Caucasus does not become an arena for NATO Allied Armed Forces' military intervention, the Russian Government must implement a well defined tough policy in the Balkans, guided by the UN charter and at the same time defending its national interests in the region by identifying and providing the appropriate support for this policy's allies*. [author's emphasis][52]

Thus the army was let loose upon Chechnya at least as much to resolve sectoral and personal interests as it was sent to repel terrorists. Yet it soon became apparent that the concept of operations or of victory was deficient from the outset. Indeed, on 31 January 2000 Deputy Chief of Staff, General Valery Manilov admitted that one could not speak of victory regarding this war.[53]

Indeed, by early 2001, recognizing the failure to prevail militarily, Putin gave control of the war to the FSB, Russia's domestic intelligence agency.[54] He thereby indicated that neither the Army nor the MVD could formulate a victorious strategy but wanted not to be tarred with the brush of defeat. Yet by 2002 with victory no closer Russian reports said that Putin was now transferring control to the MVD, another sign of frustration.[55]

Putin's first transfer of authority also suggested an open resort to a policy of anti-Chechen terror. Certainly the FSB's forces cannot conduct a real military campaign, particularly the partisan warfare that this war has become and which is one of the most stressful kinds of war imaginable. Therefore the new strategy would basically be one of terror, much like the old KGB's troops' activities against various forms of opposition inside the USSR. Not surprisingly, it was about this time that some observers and participants began to invoke the examples of Northern Ireland or the guerrilla wars of 1944–53 in the Baltic states and Ukraine against Soviet occupation, which involved massive use of KGB forces and mass deportations to the Gulag. Yet within months, it also became apparent that the FSB could not run the campaign, and the supposed withdrawals of regular army troops was halted indefinitely.[56] In 2002 Kvashnin admitted that some 86,000 troops from Russia's multiple militaries are still in Chechnya.[57] Finally, this decision may also have reflected just how unable Russia's multiple militaries still are to collaborate.

Since September 11, Putin has supposedly launched an initiative to begin negotiations if the Chechens would lay down their arms. Despite preliminary feelers nothing has been accomplished as of yet; and Russian authorities still insist on unacceptable conditions prior to any talks, for example extermination of Chechen leaders. This suggests they still seek a decisive victory and believe that such an outcome is possible even though nobody can define what it would look like.[58] Yet this pursuit is clearly doomed to frustration. The armed forces and perhaps Putin seek it for their own personal sake and power, as there is no longer majority public support or a discernible and viable national interest in a war that by all accounts is essentially about repeated looting, bloody internecine rivalries among Russian intelligence and police agencies for loot and turf that includes protection of so-called terrorists, and the commission of an unending series of quasi-genocidal brutalities as attested to by Russian and outside observers.[59]

Russian generals fully know that their troops are drunkards, criminals, etc.; military crimes against soldiers may have risen in 2001.[60] Indeed, at least one observer suspects more Russian soldiers were killed by acts of brutality in the Russian Army, *Dedovshchina* (translated as hazing but a much broader phenomenon) in the 1990s then during the war up to June 2001, and there are an estimated 5,000 annual desertions in the Russian Army, surely a sign of soldiers' fear of this brutality.[61] The numerous atrocity stories, the discovery of mass graves, accounts of Russian and Chechen death squads that target civilians, widespread accounts of Russian troops looting, repeated 'cleansing' operations that are merely excuses for another round of looting of the population, Russian journalistic revelations that officers regularly steal their men's salaries and bonuses and that they and officials have stolen almost all the funds earmarked for Chechnya's civil reconstruction, and the many instances of collaboration between Russian forces and various protected Chechen 'terrorists' or more exactly gangsters confirm these findings concerning the quality of the forces and operations in Chechnya and even throughout Russia.[62]

On the basis of these reports one can only conclude that the forces in Chechnya are not much better than an armed gang or rabble. Indeed, abundant reports also suggest that intelligence and regular Russian agencies collaborate with so-called terrorists and fight each other as much as they fight Chechens. While the military seeks to cover up such revelations, even by force, it is clear that this war increasingly has little or nothing to do anymore with terrorism but has declined essentially into a pursuit of loot, glory, and power.[63] These instances of anomic military behavior in a particularly nasty version of the protracted ethnic wars of our times are not uncommon in these wars. But given Russia's importance for Eurasian security and its governments' pretensions to a major security role globally, the implications of this continuing moral disintegration are quite frightening.

Today Russia clearly aims to destroy Chechnya as an autonomous political community. However, that would not extinguish the profound political crises in the North Caucasus and beyond. Instead it would only intensify them further. Nevertheless the numerous reports of atrocities against civilians offer grounds for fearing that the Chechen political community as such is not the only strategic target, but that Chechens who claim a genocide in the making on the basis of what they have seen and experienced are correct. Indeed, NGO studies charge that Russian conduct in Chechnya exceeds Serbian actions in Kosovo.[64]

This war's unending tragedy is not just that Moscow still neither knows how to conclude a political settlement to the war nor has a viable concept of what it would entail. Nor is it just that plus the fact that Moscow still refuses to negotiate with any truly authoritative figure who can end the war and command internal support in Chechnya. Rather, by its action Moscow may have precluded the emergence of any such authoritative figure, for there are many who believe that Maskhadov lacks sufficient control over the Chechen forces to negotiate with Moscow.[65]

Moscow's efforts to put Chechen clients in power and restore a political order either depend on Russian military support or have fallen apart. Therefore, this war could escape political definition or control, the framework within which Clausewitz tells us political violence must be bounded lest it become violence and war for its own sake. Then the entire Russian Federation and perhaps parts of the CIS would become the theater or theaters of war as internal war becames its own justification. The arrest, in August 2001 of alleged plotters to overthrow the government in two other North Caucasus provinces, Kabardino-Balkaria and Karachayevo-Cherkessk and Tatarstan's reported desire for a status like that of Quebec in Canada indicate that this war has not quieted calls for a devolution of power away from Moscow.[66]

However, infinitely more dangerous is the real possibility of the war going beyond Russian borders to embrace neighboring states, particularly

Georgia. Russian commanders have sought pretexts for intervening in Georgia since the Chechen war began. In fact Yeltsin asked Georgian President Edvard Shevarnadze for the right to cross into Georgia's Pankisi Gorge against the Chechens. As Shevarnadze realized, not only would this widen the war, it would destroy Georgia as well. Therefore he wisely refused to authorize Russian intervention.[67] Nevertheless he has been under constant Russian pressure to intervene and this war has now linked up with Georgia's ongoing conflict with the Abkhazians, provides a constant and not always resisted temptation for Georgia to strike at Russian and Abkhaz interests there.[68]

It also provides Russia with endless opportunities for threatening Georgia. Thus Russia has thrice bombed Georgia since September 11, allegedly due to this Chechen presence there. Russian commanders regularly charge that Georgia and the dissenting Russian president of Ingushetia, Ruslan Aushev, are offering sanctuary to Chechens and regularly threaten to invade them. Those threats suggest a Russian failure to fully assimilate the lessons of past wars in which commanders threw good money after bad and widened their fronts with disastrous consequences.[69] Moreover, it is clear that Russian threats pushed the US to intervene as it did in February 2002, announcing that it would send trainers and advisors to Georgia to train Georgian forces to deal with terrorists.

Thus endless war and frustration of Russian goals might yet tempt Moscow to expand the front in a vain effort to achieve a conclusive victory. While this is a common error in modern military history, it has never led to victory. Simultaneously, a clear and strong connection exists between this war and rising domestic repression, centralization, and more expressions of the FSB's search for traitors, spies, etc. across Russia.

Central Asia

In Central Asia the linked threats comprise destabilization of the Central Asian republics on Russia's southern flank and the potential rise to power of fundamentalist and extremist Muslim parties, the generation of a massive refugee crisis (mainly of fleeing Russians), and the further explosion of drug money and trafficking into Russia. Quite properly Moscow listed drugs as a national security threat in 1999, and the connection between drugs and terrorism in Central Asia is incontrovertible. Certainly the drug trade is one of the main sources of terrorist revenue and perhaps an object of struggle between rival forces as much as insurgency for political purposes is their motive.[70] Still Moscow's responses to this threat are no less ambivalent and self-serving as in Chechnya even if they have not included military operations. As Ahmed Rashid observes with respect to 1997–2001, it was in Russia's interest to destabilize the region and prevent American plans for pipelines from succeeding by arming the anti-Taliban forces.[71] More generally for 1996–2002 he writes that,

> Russia acted as a responsible superpower at one level, helping to control militant incursions, whilst feeding the conflicts with arms and encouraging localized state repression to continue. Moscow is also suspected of having maintained a clandestine intelligence relationship with the IMU.[72]

Although Moscow began warning about terrorism in 1996–97 with the rise of the Taliban, it first reacted to that threat by pushing the resolution of the civil war in Tajikistan to a decisive political conclusion.[73] It did not use this occasion to create a or strongly push for a military and intelligence union of Central Asian states with Russia until 1999–2000. The war in Kosovo, the war with Chechnya, NATO's concurrent growing interest in the CIS, the collapse of the CIS as a functioning military organization, the rise of the GUUAM (an organization comprising Georgia, Ukraine, Uzbekistan, Ukraine, Azerbaijan, and Moldova) as a potential rival military organization, and CIS members' rising attraction to the US all galvanized Moscow to attempt to recreate a military-intelligence union with those states under its auspices. Certainly a major strategic factor in driving Moscow to this conclusion was the fact that after 1996 disillusionment with the capacity of the CIS to work as an institution and with Moscow's ability to provide genuine security assistance substantially increased. As Houchang Hasan-Yari wrote,

> Disillusionment with the CIS, especially due to its incapacity to resolve regional problems, was great in Central Asia. At a January 1998 conference in Ashgabad, the region's five states proclaimed that they did not consider the CIS to be a political or even a juridical entity. Accordingly, member countries are free to participate or not participate in CIS programs as they choose. That same year these countries revised their 1994 Central Asian Union, and opted to include regional security under the agreement. They chose to adopt coom [*sic*] programs for diversifying military procurement and training, and endorsed their active participation in PfP (Partnership for Peace). Toward the end of the year, Kazakhstan and Kyrgyzstan signed a separate pact obligating each to respond militarily in the event the other were attacked.[74]

In this context it would appear that Uzbekistan's withdrawal from the CIS and adhesion to GUUAM in early 1999 may have been a decisive turning point in raising Moscow's fears and heightening its efforts to threaten terrorism as well as announce its readiness to defend against it.

Uzbekistan's actions came shortly before assassination attempts against its President Islam Karimov, attacks which we now know to have heralded a terrorist offensive in Central Asia but which were believed by CIS officials at the time to have been instigated in some way by forces connected to Moscow.[75] While that suspicion appears to have been misplaced, its existence is revealing about the true nature of the Russian war on terrorism and how it was perceived in the CIS. Nevertheless Moscow's efforts to create a collective CIS force against terrorism and to threaten the rising power of the Taliban in Afghanistan who, with Al Qaeda and Pakistan, supported these insurgents, clearly centered on Uzbekistan and pivoted around efforts to lure it back into the fold. Thus throughout the period until September 11 a complicated minuet ensued among Russia, the Central Asians, the insurgents, including the Taliban, and the US. As is now known, Washington had become more and more involved with Uzbekistan militarily since 1997–98, and this involvement allowed Karimov to undertake a series of constant oscillations from Russia to China and Washington in search of military assistance with the aim of maximizing his freedom of maneuver and independence.[76]

His objective was to obtain military aid but certainly not to have Uzbekistan become another theater of war. Thus every threat by Moscow to Afghanistan which was met by an equal Taliban threat to expand insurgency in Central Asia and especially Uzbekistan led him and the neutral Turkmenistan, and even occasionally other states like Kazakstan to seek a negotiated settlement with the Taliban. While a long series of meetings duly occurred in 2000–2001 announcing the creation of various institutions of a CIS defense force and Putin and his subordinates publicly urged this process on to the point of demanding the insertion of pro-Russian cadres in defense and intelligence posts throughout the CIS, little beyond paper declarations was accomplished.[77] Russian aid was small and late in coming, the troops already in Tajikistan were clearly corrupted by the drug trade and involved in mysterious ways with the insurgents, Russia's capabilities for fighting were in any case insufficient, and the threat of Russian intervention was no more palatable than was insurgency.[78] Still the reality of annual spring insurgencies threatening Tajikistan, Kyrgyzstan, and especially Uzbekistan intensified through 2001, but there was no common will to act against it in concerted fashion. Apparently the only truly lasting achievement was increased defense spending and repression by Central Asian regimes.

This frustrating sequence dovetailed for Moscow with its steadily improving relations with China, another state gravely concerned about Islamic terrorism, this time in Xinjiang, but also having links to Afghanistan and Pakistan. Chinese fears of Western penetration of Central Asia tallied with those of Russia, and both must have been aware of Tashkent's unreliability and collaboration with Washington before September 11. Given their mutual fears about terrorism and about American policy more generally, and their shared desire to suppress Central Asian insurgency and the Western presence, they quickly found a vehicle for joint operations in the SCO which grew out of the former confidence building mechanism of the Shanghai-5.

The recent documents coming out of the annual meeting of the former Shanghai-5, now known as the SCO, Shanghai-6 with Tashkent's membership, or Shanghai Forum open the door to ad hoc Russo-Chinese military exercises and operations, in the name of peace and stability in Central Asia, a fundamental change in Chinese policy. Indeed China's commitment to act militarily in Central Asia at the request of an invaded treaty partner to counter terrorism, separatism, or secessionism represents China's unprecedented willingness to project its military power abroad.[79]

Apart from its significance for the larger issues of Sino-Russian relations and efforts to block US influence in Central Asia, this treaty also represented a continuation of Russian efforts going back to the mid-1990s to leverage the support of other major neighbors of Central Asia to provide legitimacy and support for its efforts to play the role of a regional gendarme there. Evidently as well this organization was also linked to efforts to create multilateral alliance systems against the terrorists and their sponsors in Pakistan. Since India, like Iran, China, and Russia, is deeply concerned about Pakistani based efforts to incite and organize Muslim insurgents (always called terrorists by their enemies) in Kashmir and Central Asia, in April 2001 India and Iran essentially ratified their own strategic partnership directed against Pakistani based threats in Central Asia, Afghanistan and Kashmir.[80] This common threat obviously constitutes a basis for Russo-Chinese-Indian-Iranian common concern and possible action in Central Asia.

Thus the expansion of the scope and membership of the SCO represented both Russian interests in strengthening its position vis-à-vis the real threat of terrorism in Central Asia, but also the possibility of a true multipolarity there among outside rivals for influence which both Russia and China resented, and China's desire to play an ever larger figure in Asia by fighting insurgency at home in Central Asia as well as in Xinjiang.

These twin ambitions emerge very clearly in President Jiang Zemin's speech to the 2000 summit of this organization in Dushanbe. While he began by stressing that the international community as a whole should adhere to China's five principles of peaceful coexistence and the UN charter, he proceeded to stress the linked nature of the threat confronting the members. Thus, he stated that,

> However, we should not be blind to various kinds of domestic and foreign factors inside and outside our five nations that interfere in and undermine the peace and stability of the region and we should maintain a sober understanding and high vigilance. The development of the situation not only has further increased the necessity and urgency of strengthening cooperation between our five nations, but also has set a higher demand on the level and priority of such cooperation in [the] future.[81]

He then stressed the need to substantiate and improve the SCO's mechanism by expanding both the fields of inter-state cooperation and the regular multilateral cooperation among the governments involved in all these areas.

Second, the SCO should cooperate at a deeper security level and act jointly 'to crack down on the activities of all brands of splittist, terrorist, and extremist forces in the region'.

Third, the members should strengthen bilateral and multilateral trade, technological and economic cooperation. He tied this proposal to China's strategy for developing Xinjiang. Obviously this would greatly broaden the SCO's purview and make it a kind of regional economic organization as well as a security and confidence-building structure. He particularly stressed construction of major transportation, infrastructure, and telecommunications projects in Xinjiang.

Fourth, Jiang Zemin urged strengthened cooperation in international affairs to safeguard and strengthen the UN's and particularly the Security Council's authority, and to safeguard and respect state sovereignty, non-interference in states' internal affairs. These supposedly 'established' principles should lead the members to oppose 'hegemony and power politics', that is the US, and promote multipolarization to inhibit the US' capability to act against China and Russia. Finally he tied the work towards these goals to the achievement of a 'fair, rational, and new international political and economic order'.[82]

This joint move to formalize and expand the parameters of the organization accelerated during 2000–2001. Most importantly it provided the impetus for both Russia's reintensified campaign to launch a CIS wide military force against insurgents and terrorism and to use the organization as a vehicle to attack US policies, particularly missile defense.[83] Russian Foreign Minister Igor Ivanov clearly supports the idea of minimizing as far as possible American and other foreign involvement in Central Asia which was just what the communiqué stated.[84] Subsequently both sides acted to intensify the integration of Central Asia in general and the members of this organization in particular with Russia and China in both economics and defense. At the same time the members agreed, in April 2001, to establish an anti-terrorism center or joint rapid deployment force. That decision could lead to the stationing of Russian and/or Chinese troops in Central Asia.[85]

The 2001 summit added Uzbekistan to a new, revamped Shanghai-6 or Shanghai Forum and again attacked America's supposed proclivities for bypassing the Security Council and for unilateral construction of missile defenses. But it went far beyond this step. Its communiqué advanced beyond the intelligence sharing and coordinated discussions and efforts to counter Muslim militants. It formalized a joint pact committing the signatories to 'Join hands to battle the 'three evil forces of terrorism, separatism and extremism.'[86] In effect this communiqué and summit formalized the organization' evolution into a collective security pact committing all the members to defend each other against attacks that are manifestations of terrorism, separatism, and extremism. This conforms to Russian and especially Chinese objectives.[87] Thus Jiang Zemin said afterward that the Shanghai pact 'forms a legal foundation for jointly cracking down on terrorism, separatism, and extremism and reflects the firm determination of the six states to safeguard regional security'.[88] The communiqué and pact referred to joint military exercises which would introduce Chinese troops to foreign exercises for the first time in its history and beyond that, the collective security element commits Beijing to defend the other signatories from such attacks and them to defend China.[89] There also was a further formalization of the process called for by Jiang Zemin in 2000 to make this a truly regularly functioning and broadly based organization.

Jane's Terrorism and Security Monitor rightly observed that the key development here was the legalized expansion of China's capability to project power abroad for the first time in its history. It speculated that the 'long-term result of the gathering is the tacit surrender of defence elements of sovereignty by Central Asia to their "superpower neighbours".'[90] Pakistani analysts saw it as a strategic alliance against the US and for that matter European efforts to build the Transport Corridor Europe-Caucasus-Asia (TRACEA) transport corridor or Silk Road from Europe to China, bypassing Russia. They also noted Iran's clear intention to affiliate itself with the organization and vice versa, clearly as part of a broader anti-American alliance bloc. Iranian statements and actions over the recent past confirm this Iranian desire.[91]

However, beyond the profound significance of China practically committing its forces for action abroad in a new military alliance embracing Central Asia is the fact that the treaty can be used to defend China if it should feel obliged to go to war against the threat of Taiwanese independence. While there is no religious or terroristic element in the Taiwan issue, Chinese statesmen and analysts have long made clear their belief that this problem is one of separatism and foreign support for an 'insurgent' movement to prevent China from realizing and regaining its integrity. Thus China could potentially use the mutual defense pact signed in Shanghai to justify military help from Russia or the other signatories against American defense of Taiwan. As a senior Chinese official told former Reagan administration official, Constantine Menges, the Moscow treaty did not explicitly include military cooperation because past agreements, including the Shanghai treaty generated a situation where 'we have ample agreements on that issue'.[92]

Yet even before September 11 and certainly afterwards there were signs that this elaborate organization and collective security system was a facade. As we now know, US military cooperation with Uzbekistan was already established.[93] Likewise, China too had a decidedly checkered record in dealing with terrorism. In its case Beijing and Pakistan had always been allies, had analyzed US cruise missiles fired in 1998 for the Taliban, and were supporting Maoist guerrillas in Nepal and Sri Lanka. Similarly both Moscow's and Beijing's hegemonic ambitions in Central Asia were well known to local leaders and each other. And since September 11, Russian policymakers apparently are conveying broad hints that their support for Western military presence in Central Asia should be interpreted as a sign of joint Russo-Western concern about China's policy goals there and joint interest in Central Asia.[94]

All these accumulated local misgivings about both Russian and Chinese policies led Central Asian governments on their own to support Washington after September 11 and have led Moscow to acquiesce in the expanding US presence in Georgia and Central Asia. While on the one hand many in Russia's security establishment bitterly oppose state policy and this presence, it is possible that some more enlightened souls have realized that only Washington can militarily extirpate the terrorist threat on Russia's southern peripheries and that the gamble on projecting military power in perpetuity into the CIS to keep those states in Moscow's orbit has failed conclusively because Moscow can neither sustain those forces nor gain external support for doing so. Indeed, those actions diminish support for Russia abroad.

Conclusions

In many respects Russia's war on terrorism resembles a Matrioshka doll, the more you look, the less there is. Moreover, what there actually is does not portend a satisfying conclusion as victory in Chechnya is both indefinable and elusive, and Central Asia is slipping out of Moscow's grasp. Even though its fundamental aim since 1992 has been to retain the option and capacity to interfere in the domestic politics of all the post-Soviet successor states, and it has resorted to destabilization tactics of armed intervention under the guise of peacemaking, subversion, support for separatists, undercover intelligence operations, and attempts to stack governments with pro-Moscow creatures, none of these tactics has succeeded or given Moscow real control over those states' policies.

In both Central Asia and in Chechnya as well the ostensible war on terrorism represents the triumph of imperial notions of security and a commitment to purely military and police/intelligence means of dealing with security threats, which increasingly appear to have failed. Russia has not been above exploiting separatism and insurgency for its own ends but cannot bring these conflicts to satisfying resolution. Instead, finally it has had to acquiesce in the presence of the US, its greatest rival or in formal treaties with China, a quite likely future enemy. While the American option is certainly more palatable, the growing US presence suggests that the consequences of Russia's recklessness which mortgaged too much of its security policy to an unreformed military and archaic notions of security are now decisively making their presence felt.

If this analysis be correct, the moves initiated by Putin in September 2001 should culminate in a massive rethinking and restructuring of Russian security and the organizations responsible for providing it. It is quite clear that those agencies, as presently constituted, not only cannot provide adequate security to Russia, but that they are consistently tempted to engage in strategic overreaching and tactics that are not always indistinguishable from those that they attack. The previous policy that originated in 1992 in the military's desire to strike at its domestic rivals and anti-reformers longing for a neo-imperial position to counter Yeltsin's reforms, may soon run its course as it leads only to protracted wars of the Chechen type and freezes the CIS into an insecurity that can only be overcome by the invitation of foreign troops, either Western or Chinese.

If Russia really wants to be a partner in the war on terrorism and reclaim its Western vocation, one test of this partnership must be this reorganization of its thinking and institutions for defense of national security. Otherwise Russia will merely blunder along the path of discredited and unsustainable policies that put it at ever greater risk of another perpetual war against insurgents, and their allies abroad, be they terrorists or not. Not only is such a Russia undesirable as an ally, under those conditions and given the failure of military reform and the growing dependence upon outside support, it may not be long viable as a state.

NOTES

1. Alexei G. Arbatov, 'A Russian Note of Caution. The Day After: An Assessment', *Survival* 43/4 (Winter 2001–2002) p.152.
2. Conversations with Canadian analysts at Wilton Park, England, March 2002, *Nezavissimaya Gazeta*, in Russian (Moscow, 29 Sept. 2001), *Foreign Broadcast Information Service, Central Eurasia*, (Henceforth *FBIS SOV*) (1 Oct. 2001).
3. Arbatov (note 1) p.152.
4. James Bone, Zahid Hussain, Michael Binyon, 'Russia and America Become Allies in Battle Against the Muslim Pimpernel', *The Times* (25 Nov. 2000).
5. Vladimir A. Orlov, 'Russian-U.S. Cooperation in Preventing Megaterrorism', *Program on New Approaches to Russian Security* (Ponars) Policy Memo, No.231 (Dec. 2001), Sergey B. Ivanov, Minister of Defense, Russian Federation, 'Countering International Terrorism by Miliary Force', Speech to the Munich Wehrkunde Conference (3 Feb. 2002), <www.securityconference.de>, 'Putin Calls for Global Fight Against Terrorism Under UN Flag', *Deutsche Presse Agentur* (15 Feb. 2002).
6. 'Federal Security Service Leader Says Rebel Leaders Must Be Liquidated in Chechnya', *Interfax* (24 Jan. 2002).
7. 'Russia Supports War on Terror – No Missiles to Iran Says Ivanov', *Deutsche Presse Agentur* (4 Feb. 2002).
8. *Interfax*, 4 Feb. 2002.
9. C.W. Blandy, *Pankiisokye Gorge: Residents, Refugees, & Fighters* (Camberley, Surrey: Conflict Studies Research Centre, Royal Military Academy, Sandhurst 2002) pp.2, 17–18.
10. Ibid.
11. Jerry Seper, 'Software Likely in Hands of Terrorist', *Washington Times* (14 June 2001) p.A1, *Al-Watan al-Arabi*, in Arabic (Paris, 10 Nov. 2000), *FBIS SOV* (9 Nov. 2000).
12. Stephen Blank, 'Karimov's Free Hand as a Dominant Military Power', *Central Asia Caucasus Analyst* (13 Sept. 2000).
13. *Khabar Television*, in Kazakh (Almaty, 9 Nov. 2000) *FBIS SOV* (9 Nov. 2000); *Segodnya,* in Russian (Moscow, 6 Oct. 2000), *FBIS SOV* (6 Oct. 2000).
14. Blank (note 12), Ahmed Rashid, *Jihad: The Rise of Militant Islam in Central Asia* (New Haven, CT.: Yale UP 2002) pp.196–9; *Voice of the Islamic Republic Of Iran*, in Persian (Mashad, 26 Nov. 2000), *FBIS NES* **[???]** (26 Nov. 2000).
15. Presentation to the Council on Foreign Relations by S. Frederick Starr, Director of the Central Asia Caucasus Institute of Johns Hopkins University School for Advanced International Studies, Washington DC, Jan. 2001, Simon Petermann and Stanislav Tkachenko, *The Military Cooperation of the CIS Countries and NATO* (Final Report NATO Institutional Research Fellowship June 2001) pp.72–87.
16. Rashid (note 14) p.178.
17. Adam Garfinkle, 'Afghanistanding', *Orbis* 43/3 (Summer 1999) pp.403–18.
18. 'Vstrecha Prezidenta RF s Rukovodiahschim Sostavom Diplomaticheskoi Sluzhby MID Rossii', *diplomaticiheskii Vestnik* 2 (2001) pp.7–13.
19. For example, Bashkir volunteers have been found among Al Qaeda detainees.
20. Orlov (note 5).
21. This is regularly admitted by dispassionate observers as well as frequently claimed by the Russian side.
22. *Radio Free Europe Radio, Liberty Newsline* (16 Jan. 2002).
23. Jean-Christophe Peuch, 'Central Asia: Conference Participants Pledge to Combat Terrorism', *Radio Free Europe Radio Liberty Newsline* (8 Jan. 2002).
24. On Iraqi and Iranian ties to terrorists see Jeffrey Goldberg, 'The Great Terror', *The New Yorker* (25 March 2002) pp.52–75; Douglas Frantz and James Risen, 'A Secret Iran-Arafat Connection Is Seen Fueling the Mideast Fire', *New York Times* (24 March 2002) pp.A1, 20.
25. Alexander Pikayev, 'Russia, Iran and Non-Proliferation', unpublished paper; Yevgeny Zvedre, 'Export Controls in U.S.-Russian relations', unpublished paper; idem., 'Russian-U.S. Nonproliferation Dialogue: The Iranian Factor and Collaboration in Export Control,' *Yaderny Kontrol' in Russian* (14 April 2000), *FBIS SOV* (15 July 2000); Zvedre is Senior

Counselor in the Security and Disarmament Department of the Ministry of Foreign Affairs of the Russian Federation, Martin Sieff, 'Russia, Tentative Partner in Terror Fight', *United Press International* (3 Feb. 2002).

26. Frantz and Risen (note 24) pp.A1, 20. Interestingly enough, this tie between Iran and the Palestinian authority was evidently forged in Moscow when Arafat was meeting Putin in 2002. This leads to some interesting questions about the extent of Russian knowledge of and involvement in this relationship.
27. Stephen Blank, 'Russia Seeks to Profit from Iranian Rearmament', *Jane's Intelligence Review* (April 2001) pp.23–5; Zvedre, Pikayev (note 25).
28. *The Monitor* (8 March 2002); Scott Peterson, 'Russia Rethinks Its Longtime Support for Iraq', *Christian Science Monitor* (13 March 2002) p.1; Mark Matthews, 'U.S. Believes Russia is Shifting on Iraq', *Baltimore Sun* (5 March 2002).
29. Charles King, 'The Benefits of Ethnic War: Understanding Eurasia's Unrecognized States', *World Politics* 53/4 (July 2001) pp.538–43.
30. *Azadlyg,* in Azeri (Baku, 8 Dec. 2000), *FBIS SOV* (8 Dec. 2000); *Ortadogu* (Ankara edn.), in Turkish (Istanbul, 24 Nov. 2000), *FBIS SOV* (24 Nov. 2000).
31. 'Feeling the Heat', *The Hindu* (23 Dec. 2001), available from Lexis-Nexis.
32. *Nezavisimaya Gazeta* (electronic version) (Moscow, 17 March 2000), *FBIS SOV* (17 March 2000); *Vek* (electronic version) (Moscow, 26 Nov. 1999), *FBIS SOV* (29 Nov. 1999); *ITAR-TASS*, (Moscow, 1 March 2000), *FBIS SOV* (1 March 2000).
33. *Kommersant* (electronic version), in Russian (Moscow, 23 July 1999), *FBIS SOV* (10 Aug. 1999).
34. *Radio Free Europe Radio Liberty Newsline* (4 Feb. 2002); Natlia Yefimova, 'Berezovsky: I Gave Cash to The Chechen Rebels', *Moscow Times* (1 Feb. 2002) p.3.
35. *Jamestown Foundation Monitor* (29 Aug. 2001); Francesca Mereu, 'Russia: New Book Alleges FSB Ordered Political Hits, Apartment bombings', *Radio Free Europe Radio Liberty Newsline* (29 Aug. 2001); Berezovsky made his charges publicly in London, based on this evidence in March 2002.
36. *Nezavisimaya Gazeta* (electronic version), (Moscow, 14 Jan. 2000), *FBIS SOV* (18 Jan. 2000), Michael R. Gordon, 'A Look At How the Kremlin Slid Into the Chechen War', *New York Times* (1 Feb. 2000).
37. Stephen Blank, 'Chechnya and Its Consequences', in Michael H. Crutcher (ed.) *Russian National Security Perceptions, Policies, and Prospects* (Carlisle Barracks, PA: Center for Strategic Leadership, US Army War College 2002) pp.135–55.
38. General M.A. Gareyev (trans. by Robert R. Lowe), 'Applying Zhukov's Command Heritage to Military Training and Reform in Today's World', *Journal of Slavic Military Studies* 12/4 (Dec. 1999) p.83.
39. Alexander M. Kirov, 'Soviet Military Intervention in Hungary', in Jeno Gyorkei and Mikolos Horvath (eds.) *1956: Soviet Military Intervention in Hungary* (Budapest: Central European UP 1999) p.188.
40. Patrick E. Tyler, 'Budget Cutbacks Blamed by Russian in Fiasco With Sub', *New York Times* (22 Aug. 2000) p.1.
41. *Nezavisismaya Gazeta* (27 Nov. 1999) pp.1–2.
42. *Nezavisimaya Gazeta* (note 36), Gordon (note 36).
43. This was told to the author by one of the US analysts who were told this information.
44. This becomes quite clear if one goes through the *Current Digest of the Post-Soviet Press* for March–Aug. 1999.
45. *FBIS SOV* (18 Jan. 2000); Gordon, (note 36).
46. *Novaya Gazeta* (electronic version) (Moscow, 24 Jan. 2000), *FBIS SOV* (24 Jan. 2000); C.W. Blandy, *Dagestan: The Storm: Part I – The 'Invasion' of Afghanistan* (Camberley, UK: Conflict Studies Research Centre, RMAS March 2000) pp.3–40, Amy Knight, 'Political Power and Elections: The Role of Russia's Security Agencies', paper presented to the Project on Systemic change and International Security in Russia and the New States of Eurasia (Washington DC Feb. 2000).
47. Ibid.

48. Mark Galeotti, 'Why There's a War in Chechnya', *Washington Post Weekly* (20 and 27 Dec. 1999) p.25.
49. *Nezavisimoye Voyennoye Obozreniye*, in Russian 42, (Moscow, 6–12 Nov. 1998), *FBIS SOV* (9 Nov. 1998).
50. Ibid.
51. Ibid.
52. Ibid.
53. *Radio Free Europe/Radio Liberty Newsline* (31 Jan. 2000).
54. 'Putin Talks Up Endgame in Chechnya, Calls In Secret Service', *Agence France Presse* (22 Jan. 2001), *Johnson's Russia List* 5043 (22 Jan. 2001).
55. *Gazeta.ru*, in Russian (Moscow, 18 Jan. 2002), *FBIS SOV* (18 Jan. 2002).
56. Susan B. Glasser, 'Putin's War Persists As Sentiment Shifts', *Washington Post* (28 July 2001) p.1; *The Monitor*, 9 May 2001; Artyom Venidrub, 'Chechnya: An Order Too Tall for FSB', *Gazeta.ru* (7 May 2001).
57. *Kavkaz.strana.ru*, 22 Jan. 2002; *Jamestown Chechnya Weekly* 3/4 (29 Jan. 2002).
58. 'Federal Security Service Leader Says Rebel Leaders Must Be Liquidated in Chechnya', (note 6).
59. Human Rights Watch, '*Welcome To Hell': Arbitrary Detention, Torture, and Extortion in Chechnya* (NY: Human Rights Watch 2000) is an early example of these reports. Sadly little seems to have changed since then.
60. *Radio Free Europe/Radio Liberty Newsline* (17 July 2001).
61. Alexander Golts, 'Russian Journalist Accuses Federal Troops of Exploiting Chechen Oil Plants', *BBC Monitoring* (29 June 2001).
62. Anatol Lieven at the Carnegie Endowment for International Peace's Conference on Russia After Ten Years, 7–9 June 2001, <www.ceip.org/files/programs/russia/tenyears/transcript14.htm>; see also the forthcoming PhD dissertation of Miriam Lanskoy from Boston University.
63. Alexander Golts, 'Blaming Generals Masks Military's Deeper Problems', *Russia Journal* (26 Dec. 2000), <www.russiajournal.com/weekly/article.shtml?ad=4116>.
64. Human Rights Watch (note 59).
65. Lieven (note 62).
66. 'Russia Says Coup thwarted in Southern Republics', *Reuters,* 16 Aug. 2001; Paul Goble, 'Is There A Quebec In Russia's Future?', *Radio Free Europe/Radio Liberty Analysis* (24 July 2001).
67. *Chechnya Weekly* 2/14 (3 April 2001); 'Georgian Troops Repelled Chechen, Rebel Bid to Enter Abkhazia', *Agence France Presse* (27 Aug. 2001); 'Tbilisi and Sukhumi Prevent Chechen Guerrilla Raid', <*allnews.ru*/english/200108/27/chechnya>.
68. *Radio Free Europe/Radio Liberty, Lifeline* (11 and 26 May 2000); Vladislav Shurygin, 'Chechen Fighters' Secret Sponsors, General Aushev and Other Russian Commanders', *APN* (30 May 2000); 'German Spy Agency Fears Widening of Chechnya War', *Reuters* (17 April 2000).
69. Sarah E. Mendelssohn, 'The Putin Path: Civil Liberties and Human Rights in Retreat', *Problems of Post-Communism* 47/5 (Sept.–Oct. 2000) p.6.
70. Rashid (note 14) *passim.*
71. Ahmed Rashid, *Taliban:Militant Islam, Oil & Fundamentalism in Central Asia* (New Haven, CT: Yale UP 2000) p.179.
72. Rashid, *Jihad* (note 14) p.231.
73. Yevgeny Primakov as Foreign Minister in 1996–98 made the resolution of this civil war his first priority.
74. Hoochang Hassan-Yari, 'Pushing Too Far, Too Fast? NATO, the Caucasus, and the Central Asian Republics', in David G. Haglund (ed.) *New NATO, New Century: Canada, the United States, and the Future of the Atlantic Alliance* (Kingston, Ontario: Queen's Univ., Centre for Int. Relations and the Canadian Inst. of Strategic Studies 2000) p.164, Petermann and Tkachenko (note 15), pp.72–87.
75. Taras Kuzio, 'Geopolitical Pluralism in the CIS: The Emergence of GUUAM', *European Security* 9/2 (Summer 2000) p.98. This is based on Kuzio's conversations with an official of the Ukrainian Foreign Ministry.

76. Blank, 'Karimov's Free Hand' (note 12), Rashid, *Jihad* (note 14), pp.196–9.
77. Stephen Blank and Theodore Karasik, '"Reforms" That Hark Back to Stalinist Times', *Los Angeles Times* (20 July 2000), Petermann and Tkachenko (note 15) pp.72–87; *Nezavisismaya Gazeta*, in Russian, (Moscow, 1 Aug. 2001), *FBIS SOV* (1 Aug. 2001).
78. Blank, 'Karimov's Free Hand' (note 12).
79. '"Shanghai Five" Change Turns China in a new Strategic Direction', *Kyodo* (18 June 2001), retrieved from Lexis-Nexis; Robert A. Karniol, 'Shanghai Five in Major Revamp', *Jane's Defence Weekly* (27 June 2001) p.5; Bates Gill, 'Shanghai Five: An Attempt to counter US Influence in Asia?', *Newsweek Korea* (May 2001), <www.brookings.edu/views/op-ed/gill20010504.htm>.
80. Smita Gupta, 'Threats of Terrorism Bring India, Iran Closer', *The Times of India* (15 April 2001).
81. *Xinhua Domestic Service*, in Chinese (Beijing, 5 July 2000), *FBIS CHI*, 5 July 2000; *Zhongguo Tongxun She,* in Chinese (Hong Kong, 9 July 2000), *FBIS CHI* (9 July 2000).
82. Ibid.
83. Richard McGregor, '"Shanghai Forum" Unites Against US Missile Plan', *Financial Times* (16 June 2001).
84. Kazakh Television First Channel, Astana, in Kazakh 1510 GMT 13 Jan 2002, 'Russia Seeks To Strengthen Influence in Central Asia', BBC Monitoring.
85. See Note 79.
86. *Xinhua News Agency*, Beijing (15 June 2001).
87. Ibid., see also note 79.
88. See note 86.
89. Ibid., see also Karniol (note 79) p.5.
90. See note 79.
91. 'Foreign Minister Discusses Bilateral Ties With Chinese Official', IRNA News Agency, 20 Feb. 2001, Retrieved from Lexis-Nexis.
92. Constantine Menges, 'Russia, China, and What's Really on the Table', *Washington Post* (29 July 2001) p.BO2.
93. Rashid, *Jihad* (note 14) pp.172–4, 189–93.
94. 'Putin's Unscrambled Eggs', *The Economist* (9 March 2002) p.53.

11 September 2001 and the Media

PHILIP TOWLE

There were prolonged and troubled debates in all of the countries about the reasons for Al Qaeda's attacks of 11 September 2001 and the nature of the support which should be offered to Washington. In Japan the debate was primarily constitutional; in Pakistan it raised, in particularly acute form, the issue of the connection between the state and religion; in India it posed the question of the country's relationships with Pakistan and with the US; in Britain the debate revolved round race relations, military strategy and the country's position in the world. The pivotal nature of the choices was shown by the way in which the debates evoked each country's history to illuminate the way ahead.

The Japanese Debate

The Japanese media identified immediately with the United States' suffering and reacted with horror and disbelief to the events of 9/11. Two days later one newspaper opined, 'the entire world community has been brutally victimised. Japan should share the anger of the American people and take an active role in joining international efforts to ferret out those responsible for the act'. An emergency rescue team was immediately assembled in case it was needed by the US. Within the first week, the Japanese Defense Agency was reported to be considering reinterpreting the law on emergencies to enable it to take more action against terrorists in Japan's neighbourhood.[1] Within two weeks Prime Minister Junichiro Koizumi had visited Washington and promised to take very far-reaching measures, including the dispatch of Japanese warships to a potential war zone for the first time since 1945. An extraordinary session of the Diet began on 27 September 2001 to consider how the pacifist Constitution could be reconciled with such actions.[2]

Newspapers reflected the dilemma. *The Asahi Shimbun*, with its circulation of nine million readers, wanted Japan to respond appropriately. But its columnists worried that 'once Japanese destroyers engage in joint operations with US naval task forces, there will be no going back, and Japan could be forced into silent submission whenever the US makes fresh demands'.[3] At the same time, article after article referred back to the criticisms of Japan during the 1991 Gulf War for failing to aid the coalition militarily. Takeshi Kondo, a Member of the Upper House, was quoted as saying, 'I never want to go through the humiliation I felt at that time.'[4] On the same day, one editorial argued,

> as country after country pledged solid support, material as well as moral, bitter memories of Japan's diplomatic blunders during the Gulf War ten years ago came flooding back to many policy makers... avoiding a replay of the Gulf War fiasco requires that Japan legislate to remove these legal limitations.[5]

The nationalistic mayor of Tokyo, Shintaro Ishihara was dismissive of the whole debate, 'anything written by humans should be reinterpreted and rewritten freely. It's the duty of politicians to go beyond and implement new policies.' Yet, as one former prime minister put it, 'what we have been preserving for decades as a result of our own war experiences' could not just be jettisoned overnight.[6]

The problem was actually greater in 2001 than in 1991 because Japan's economic position had weakened so much. In 1991 Japan could make the largest financial contribution to the liberation of Kuwait of any country outside the Gulf. This sacrifice was not sufficiently recognised either in the Gulf or the US, but it was harder now to achieve even this degree of gratitude. An editorial in the *Asahi Shimbun* on 14 September 2001 warned that Japan is 'now one of the weakest links among major economic powers'.[7] The *Nihon Keizai Shimbun* feared that the attacks could trigger 'a Japan-led global economic crisis' if corrective measures were not taken by the Japanese government such as writing off bad loans and stimulating domestic demand.[8]

Newspapers reported that the Japanese tourist industry was particularly badly hit after the attack on the Twin Towers with three quarters of a million Japanese cancelling overseas trips. The public affairs manager of the Japan Association of Travel Agents complained that 'Japanese tend to overreact whenever a calamity occurs in a foreign country. This is not the case with Western tourists.'[9] He did not dilate on the striking contrast between Japanese courage 60 years before and their caution today.

Despite these difficulties, while Prime Minister Koizumi struggled manfully to push reforms through Parliament and to mobilise the Self Defense Force (SDF), Japan was increasingly asked for financial help as though the stagnation of the last ten years had never occurred. Already, by the end of September, Pakistan had been promised $40 million and President Musharraf subsequently asked Koizumi to write off Pakistan's five billion dollar debt to Japan. The Japanese government did promise to provide Pakistan with 4.7 billion yen to support Afghan refugees and it jointly chaired an international meeting in New York in November to coordinate international efforts to restore the shattered Afghan economy.[10]

The Japanese were hurt by US comparisons of the terrorist attack with the naval raid on Pearl Harbor in December 1941. Yet their newspapers were among the first to make the comparison. One wrote on 13 September, 'the deadly strike was probably more shocking than the attack on Pearl Harbor 60 years ago'.[11] The Japanese seaborne strike had targeted servicemen, the Muslim attack had been on civilians. The distinction had, therefore, been terrorism and a conventional, albeit pre-emptive, assault. These were moral terms in which the debate was not generally conducted elsewhere. The parallels drawn outside Japan were to the failure of US intelligence to predict either of the attacks and to the nature of the response. The Japanese debate was defensive and uncertain. It increased their desire to help and hence the depth of the agonising over the constitutional dilemma. The US administration tried to help Tokyo over its difficulties; President Bush stressed that Japan had become one of 'America's finest allies' during his speech commemorating the 60th anniversary of Pearl Harbor.[12]

Governmental critics argued that the US could feel that it was standing up for universal values, such as freedom and democracy, while Japan did not stand for anything since its Prime Minister continued to visit the war shrine honouring Japanese soldiers from the Second World War. Members of the opposition Democratic Party of Japan grumbled that Koizumi had reacted too late and had not taken sufficient account of Middle Eastern reactions.[13] However, he was caught whichever way he turned. When Japanese naval vessels were sent for logistic and intelligence support to US forces in the Indian Ocean, *The Asahi Shimbun* quoted both crew and relatives criticising the operation. One mid-career crew member was quoted, rather oddly, as saying, 'when I joined SDF, I never imagined I'd go anywhere near actual combat'.[14]

The fact was that for historic reasons it was more difficult for Koizumi to achieve a national consensus than for Prime Minister Atab Behari Vajpayee of India or Britain's Prime Minister, Tony Blair because they had historic role models on which they could fall back. Blair had simply to act as coordinator of the allied coalition, Vajpayee had to improve his country's position vis-à-vis Pakistan as his predecessors had tried to do in every Indo-Pakistan crisis since 1948. Japan had no such historical precedents to justify Koizumi's current behaviour. There had been analogous historical incidents, such as the rescue of the embassies in Beijing during the Boxer uprising in 1900, when Japan had played its full part as a Great Power, but Japan's relations with China were far too sensitive for them to form an effective historic reference point.

India and Pakistan

While Japan debated the constitutional impact of 9/11, Indian and Pakistani commentators often reacted with equal horror to events in the US. One

Indian writer perceptively suggested the level of sympathy with the US was so great because:

> America is in many ways so close to our hearts; much closer, if the truth be told, than Iraq or Libya. For many of us in India, America is the land of our golden futures. One can earn merit here, get rich, and lead a lifestyle free from the constraints of an encumbered past… It is the subscription, real and vicarious to the American dream that makes all the difference. It is this that explains, to a large extent, the widespread anger and grief that cut across classes when the towers of the World Trade Centre collapsed.[15]

The columnists of the stately, *Hindu*, based in Madras and claiming to be India's 'national' newspaper, generally followed this line, at least at first. According to one columnist, 'in all the talk of retribution [in the US], there is also the quiet and sober feeling that civilised nations think and act differently from uncivilised ones'. Kesava Menon advised the US to use the term jihad against 'a group filled with blind unreasoning hatred for anyone who does not subscribe to their lifestyles, world views or even dress and behavioural codes'. He argued that even if their views on Kashmir or Palestine were accepted, they would not change their fanatical hatred for everyone who failed to subscribe to their religion.[16]

An intense debate did, however, develop about the extent to which India should back the US. Some commentators argued that Indian opinion was too quick to support Washington and that it veered round again when the US began relying on Pakistan and when 'the rhetoric of the crusade was heard from Washington. Also the sporadic violence against Americans of South Asian descent dented support for the US president.'[17] Columnists in *The Hindu* deplored the level of destruction subsequently wreaked on Afghanistan, arguing that by January 2002 the 'collateral damage' exceeded the losses in 9/11 attacks. Critics pointed to the US mistakes, when, for example, it bombed a truck full of Afghan elders and, on another occasion, it attacked a village in Paktia province. US assaults on Afghanistan were creating growing ferment in Pakistan and increasing the threat of instability there.[18]

Looming behind all of this was the troubled Indo-Pakistani relationship and the way Pakistan had backed Muslim extremists in Afghanistan and Kashmir. Successive governments in Islamabad had also allowed them to flourish in Pakistan itself over the last decades. As one writer put it in *The Hindu*; 'the growing grip of Islamic extremism has defeated [President Perrez Musharraf's] attempts to limit the arbitrary application of the notorious blasphemy laws... President Musharraf must now choose. Supporting America could cost him his job; but failure to do will hasten the isolation and disintegration of Pakistan.'[19] For members of the Indian peace movement, such as Admiral Ramdass, the trauma of 9/11presented a golden opportunity to 'to take forward the peace process' between New Delhi and Islamabad.[20] But the great bulk of Indian writers were bitterly hostile to Islamabad and its policies. All the emphasis was on the hurts which had been done since independence and the terrible suffering which was being inflicted on Kashmir.[21]

The Hindu's commentators admitted that their leaders had initially believed they could use Bush's 'war on terrorism' to put pressure on Pakistan over Kashmir. As one columnist noted on 16 September,

> New Delhi and Washington find themselves on the same side of the global divide for a change, and the former's unconditional support for the war against terrorism is likely to transform the relationship between the two... Pakistan on the other hand is at a new fork in the road. It could either return to the civilised world by dismantling the infrastructure of international terrorism... Or it could go deeper into the embrace of the jehadis.[22]

However, by the middle of November it became clear that Pakistan had benefited more than India in the competition for US favour because Washington needed Islamabad's permission to overfly the country and to use some of its bases. India was on the same side as Washington, but it was not as important to the administration as New Delhi's historic enemy. The disappointment was as profound as the satisfaction across the border.

The Friday Times is a small, radical weekly journal written in the English language and proclaiming itself, 'Pakistan's first independent weekly newspaper'. Long before 11 September it had bemoaned the increasing domination of Pakistan by Muslim fundamentalism since the 1980s. Afterwards, it argued that the government should seize the moment, ignore the mullahs and turn its back on previous policies in Afghanistan and Kashmir.[23] It urged Musharraf forward as he began cautiously to follow this line. By the beginning of October it reported that the mainstream Pakistani parties had rallied round the country's leader, isolating the mullahs who were 'burning effigies and threatening jehad against the government'. This increased its complaints about the establishment who, in the past, had 'shirked.. responsibilities [and].. condoned the growth of violent militias'.[24] Its columnists quickly faced up to the economic costs of the US war in Afghanistan; textile and other exports were suffering to the tune of perhaps $1.25 billions, foreign companies were evacuating staff and thus threatening investments, consumption would be reduced and revenues would decline. Nevertheless, the paper's editor argued, 'it is in Pakistan's long-term national interest to stick with the international community and try to reap economic benefits rather than risk isolation and face economic meltdown'.[25]

By 7 December the journal's columnists were grumbling that the country had only received 'dribs and drabs of aid', $1,000 million from the US, $300 million from Japan and $100 million from Britain. It had taken the right course of action, but its allies had been less than generous.[26]

Meanwhile, the Indians believed Islamabad was receiving special treatment from the West. All their historic resentments against Pakistan boiled up when Muslim terrorists attacked the Indian Parliament on 13 December. Again the terrorists went beyond the culminating point of victory and encouraged the destruction of the forces which they had claimed to defend. Many Indians argued that the country was justified in attacking Pakistan, 'sustained consciously or unconsciously by the example of the US in recent years and particularly in Afghanistan' as one columnist put it in *The Hindu*.[27] Just as the Japanese looked back to the 1991 Gulf War and desperately wanted to avoid being accused of not helping the US enough, so the Indian opposition parties looked back to the Kargil incursion by militants based in Pakistan in 1999 and were afraid of again seeming insufficiently aggressive.

Prime Minister Vajpayee responded to public fury arguing ambiguously that the issue was 'under what circumstances there would be war... or whether there is even a need for war'.[28] He had to convince Musharraf and his own public that he was prepared to use force, without letting the crisis escalate out of control. According to a newspaper poll, some 85 per cent of the population wanted the guerrillas' training camps in Pakistani-occupied Kashmir attacked. Columnists maintained that India could weather a war economically far better than Pakistan, but that it would still have to depend on the expatriate community for financial support.[29] As the situation deteriorated through January, one *Hindu* columnist emphasised the irony that Western diplomats were scurrying to prevent a South Asian conflict 'even as the pounding of neighbouring Afghanistan was justified as a "war against terrorism"'. By contrast, his Western equivalents argued that a South Asian war would not only be a catastrophe for the Indians and Pakistanis, but a victory for the organiser of the Twin Towers disaster, Osama bin Laden.[30] The tension was so great by mid-January 2002 that most military equipment was deployed on the frontier and the 53rd Republic Day parade in New Delhi had little except the Agni-11 missile to display.[31]

Friday Times' columnists watched this process from the other side of the boundary, fearful that tension might actually lead to war but hopeful that the government would continue to repress the militants. Already by the middle of October they had, like their Indian equivalents, concluded that the Afghan struggle had improved Pakistan's status vis-à-vis India. 'The BJP-led government in New Delhi that was frantically wooing Washington found itself pushed back, while the alienated Islamabad suddenly regained its previous prominence and predominance.'[32]

However, after the Taliban's collapse and the attack on the Indian Parliament, Pakistani writers began to worry that their country had lost favour in the West. They noted that Blair had supported India's claim to a permanent seat on the Security Council and that President Bush had referred to Pakistanis as 'Pakis'. Instead of seeing this remark as a very unfortunate slip of the tongue, they believed it was intended to please India. As the crisis dragged on into February, without reductions in forces on the common frontier, they began to compare its severity with the Cuban missile crisis of 1962. They knew that the Indian government was keeping up the pressure to force Musharraf to continue to repress the Kashmiri extremists, but they also recognised the dangers inherent in the situation and pointed out that their own nuclear deterrent had failed to protect them from such pressure.[33]

The British Debate

From the start conservative British newspapers emphasised and revelled in the important part Britain was to play in the 'war against terrorism'. *The Times* headline on 22 September read: 'US banks on British troops'. On the other hand, commentators, in *The Guardian* and *Independent*, argued that, 'the worst thing about Mr Blair's missions-pretty-impossible is that they have come to be coated with a patina of national pride. They seek to blend past glories with present imperatives.'[34] Both British and South Asian media focused on Blair's role in the crisis. British commentators were satirical about his efforts to play Robin to Bush's Batman and about Foreign Secretary, Jack Straw's role as 'a little Sir Echo behind Colin Powell'.[35] On the other hand, *The Hindu*'s London correspondent concluded that Blair had 'a good war' because of his close identification with the US cause, despite criticisms in Britain that he was reducing the country to a rubber stamp. However, the view that Blair had been dominated throughout by Bush was widespread; 'there has been a distinct lack of American regard for British concerns'. Blair had, for example, stressed Muslim sensitivity; Bush had ignored the issue. The Pentagon had made the running and ignored many of Britain's offers of military assistance.[36]

Yet, if the British and South Asian media were often sceptical, the Japanese press sometimes praised Britain for not always agreeing with US policy. When Chancellor Gordon Brown went to Washington in December and called for massive aid to the Third World to combat the roots of terrorism, *The Nihon Keizai Shimbun* was sympathetic

> Japan tends to withdraw from any idea it thinks will not win US support. In contrast the UK, while willingly participating in the US-led military campaign, is bold enough to call attention to areas of

> disagreement. This is expert diplomacy that tends to weaken criticism when the US comes under a firestorm of criticism. Next year marks the 100th anniversary of what was once a partnership between Japan and the UK. Japan should mark the occasion by reconsidering working with Britain on initiatives in which the US has difficulty manoeuvring.[37]

The paper exaggerated the subtlety and efficacy of British diplomacy to emphasise what it saw as the shortcomings of its own government. Britain was hardly critical of US policies, at least by South Asian standards, but, compared with Japan, it was a model of independent action.

The British debate was unusual in the amount of space devoted to military tactics. There were two main historical images which influenced British thinking about the preparations for military operations in Afghanistan. One conjured up the allegedly invincible and ferociously brave Afghan tribesmen, who claimed to have defeated all those who invaded their country including the British in the nineteenth century and the Soviets in the 1980s. The second revived memories of bombing campaigns from the London Blitz to the Kosovo campaign in 1999.

Columnists used nineteenth century Afghan campaigns to exaggerate the strength of the Afghans and to warn of the dangers invaders would face. One columnist claimed in *The Times*, 'when Britain last retreated from Afghanistan in the nineteenth century, there was one British survivor out of 16,000 soldiers, camp followers, women and children'. A former editor of *The Times* claimed, equally erroneously, that 'marching on Kabul has the same record of historic success as marching on Moscow'. It was indeed the case that General Elphinstone's force had been destroyed in January 1842 after relying on an Afghan promise that it would be allowed to evacuate Kabul peacefully. However Afghan treachery was quickly avenged. New armies were sent to rescue British prisoners and to blow up the bazaar in Kabul. Again, three decades later, when the members of the British mission under Cavagnari were massacred in Kabul, a force under Lord Roberts was sent to occupy the Afghan capital.

It was hardly unreasonable that commentators should be cautious about encouraging military operations in such inhospitable zones, particularly after the Soviet failures there in the 1980s, but it was unwise for foreigners and for the Afghans themselves to exaggerate the difficulties involved. As the Consulting Editor of *The Friday Times* wisely observed,

> this untruth is the most unfortunate thing to happen to the Afghan nation. It did not stop people from invading Afghanistan and each time it was the Afghan who suffered. His pride was crushed by superior invading armies and his sovereignty was taken away by the deprivation of living in refugee camps.[38]

Some British commentators used other images to throw doubts on the efficacy of US military policy in Afghanistan. Here again history shaped their response. Those brought up during the Second World War had seen the indecisive impact of German bombs on Britain. Those who matured during the Vietnam War had often developed a profound scepticism about the ability of bombs to force an enemy to surrender and a loathing for their effects on civilians. Since the 1970s and 1980s civilian commentators in Britain have also been willing to take on the professional military and to dispute their judgements.

Thus, many were sceptical that US bombing of Afghanistan would destroy the Taliban's government. Simon Jenkins led the criticism in *The Times*. He admitted that attacks on bin Laden himself were justified but that 'accompanying such an operation with the now familiar allied bombing campaign would be worse than pointless, and would be harder to justify in international law.. the bombing would not contribute to the Taleban's fall, more likely hamper it by incurring anti-Americanism in the region'.

Jonathan Steele argued in *The Guardian* that the campaign in Afghanistan had been 'wrongly conceived from the start' and that images of civilian dead would destroy support for the air campaign.[39] Steele, Jenkins and others ignored the development of precision guided munitions and thus assumed that bombing had to be as indiscriminate as it had been 40 years before. Even when their decisiveness was clearly evident and when most of the civilian casualties in Afghanistan occurred because of intelligence errors rather than inaccuracy, they were reluctant to admit their mistakes. Memories of the blitz on North Vietnam in the 1960s had bitten very deep.

The British debate formed an interesting contrast to the one held in *The Friday Times* which actually proved a better guide to the march of events than the Western columnists quoted above. Here there were no references to the invincible Afghan warrior. There was deep concern about civilian casualties but no invincible conviction that aircraft were inherently inaccurate. Immediately after the 9/11 attack, *The Friday Times*' editorials predicted that the US would destroy the Taliban regime and that, 'after the Taliban has defeated, America will seek to establish a new, broad-based government in Kabul.' Columnists admitted that, 'Afghanistan has always been a difficult project. It is a rugged country, inhabited by hardy, largely nomadic peoples... all these factors combine to make it difficult for an invader to conquer in the sense of capturing territory and exploiting the gains.'[40]

Most claimed that the Taliban were weakened by their unpopularity, though one writer argued that it would take until the summer of 2002 for the US operations with the Northern Alliance to overthrow the government in Kabul. There was also a good deal of discussion of Pakistani volunteers for the Afghan cause and speculation on how many were in fact intelligence officers pretending to be Taliban. But in all this there was no effort to talk up the Taliban, no references to stupendous nineteenth century Afghan victories or to the invincibility of the Afghan warrior.[41]

The Japanese debate on the military prospect for US actions was curiously muted. If the British pattern had been followed, there would have been references to the impact of US bombs on Japan in 1944 and 1945, or even of Japanese bombs on Chinese cities in the 1930s. But such a debate was largely absent, so was any extended discussion of the Afghan warrior's ability to resist the US or of civilian support for the Taliban. Again Japan was atypical. The history of the 1930s and 1940s was just too painful to be useful to opinion-formers, seriously circumscribing the Japanese debate on the war.

Alongside the debate about military tactics and Britain's relationship with the US, there was a further major debate in Britain about the Muslims living there, some of whom not only failed to support the alliance with the US but actually volunteered to fight for the Taliban or joined Al Qaeda. Muslim alienation became obvious at a particularly sensitive time for Britain. Race riots in the previous summer in three northern former cotton towns had alerted the media to the extent of the problem. In October, the small, depressed Midlands town of Tipton became a focus of attention after a few of its Muslims left to join the Taliban. Some commentators saw this as a reason for British soul-searching. Mick Hume argued in *The Times* that 'it is a gradual loss of conviction at the centre of Western society that has made some see fundamentalism as more attractive than mainstream notions of what it means to be American or British'.[42]

Paradoxically, it was left to columnists in *The Friday Times* to rend the extremists living in Britain. Khaled Ahmed reported that 'some of the web-sites run by the author's friends in the UK are shocking in their conspiratorial content. The abuse hurled by these web-sites at the Western enemy is hair-raising. The host-hating expatriate Pakistani despises Pakistan for not being anti-West enough.' He went on to blame lax British immigration policies for allowing terrorist organisations, which encouraged attacks on Pakistan, to thrive in Britain.[43]

The extent of the problem was underlined in December 2001 when Robert Reid, a British Muslim attempted to blow up an American Airlines aircraft by lighting the explosives hidden in his shoes. In February another British Muslim, Ahmed Omar Saeed Sheikh was arrested in Pakistan for his alleged part in the plot to kidnap the US journalist, Daniel Pearl. Sheikh, a former student at the London School of Economics, had already been involved in terrorist incidents. The British link was also emphasised by suggestions that Pearl had been trying to track down the links between Reid and the Al Qaeda organisation.[44] Plainly, the British government was going to have to tighten its immigration proceedings and to work to improve race relations within the country while, at the same time, enhancing its surveillance of extremist Muslim groups.

The Causes of the Attacks

All the elite media surveyed pondered the causes of the attacks on the US. The fundamental issue was whether the US and its allies had inadvertently provoked the attack by their allegedly anti-Muslim policies on Israel, Iraq, Kashmir and Bosnia, and by basing US troops in Saudi Arabia. The alternative, and by no means mutually exclusive explanation, was that Muslim extremists were lashing out blindly against the forces of modernisation with which they were unable or unwilling to come to terms.[45] The issue was far from academic because it determined how the media advised governments to respond. If Western policies were primarily to blame, then their policies had to be changed. If Muslim conservatives were at fault, then they would have to be cajoled into adapting to the modern world.

The Hindu set out both sides of the debate. Rahul Mahajan and Robert Jensen wrote of 'the racism that lurks beneath a polite veneer' in Western societies. They complained that US citizens were unwilling to admit that their government had been responsible for atrocities such as Hiroshima and Nagasaki. 'To see India – long a staunch opponent of America's imperial adventures… reduced to among the most abject, craven supporters of this current military aggression is deeply saddening.'[46] On the other hand, the article stressed the intolerance and bigotry of many of the Muslim extremists. It printed a scathing denunciation of Taliban policy towards women when they were in power in Afghanistan, quoting one Afghani woman, now fled to India, who was given 20 lashes in public for showing her ankles and then gang raped.[47] Both the West and the Muslim world needed to adapt.

Similarly, *The Friday Times'* editorials emphasised the 'patently unjust American policies in certain situations' while excoriating Muslim failure to adapt to the modern world. Its consulting editor opined, 'most people think that extremism comes out of a misinterpretation of Islam. This is wrong. Extremism and violence occur when people do not accept what the Islamists regard as the irreducible crux of Islam, in the shape of the Shariah.'[48] While taking the Muslim side, Salman Tarik Kureshi also saw it as a moral and religious clash, which meant that, even if all the Muslim injustices were rectified,

> the Muslim rage would be in no whit abated. There is an instinctive revulsion. It is a deep-seated loathing, a stomach-wrenching hatred near the very centre of being, which is driving the Islamist attitude to the West… many of the most 'fundamentalist' Muslims are to be

> found among those who have migrated to Western countries, who share in that prosperity and social mobility while condemning everything they observe... It is disgust for hedonistic lifestyles, the sexual permissiveness, the anarchic family relationships, the imperialistic world presence.[49]

The same issue of the journal gave space to Hani Shukrallah, a columnist from the Egyptian *al-Ahram*, who devoted his article to an attack on the American writer, Francis Fukuyama and his view of democracy. Shukrallah argued that the clash between Muslims and the West was essentially economic and a reaction to the West's urge to establish neo-colonialist control over its former empire.[50]

The majority of British commentators avoided the issue perhaps fearing to exacerbate Muslim–Western relations and following their government's line that the war was being fought over terrorism not religion. A minority, like the historian, Jonathan Clark, dissented. Similarly, David Selbourne maintained that the struggle between the Muslim world and the West had been going on since the 1940s: 'all of them including the suicide bomber are apostles of the Islamic resurgence, as historians of Islam's modes of warfare (and conquest) know. In the past decade a cat's cradle of links has been woven across the Islamic world.'[51]

The Japanese press was even more cautious than the British about any suggestion that there was a clash of civilisations. Moreover, suggestions by Japanese commentators that the attacks were brought on by US policy or by poverty were denounced by Takeshi Kondo, a member of the Upper House. Kondo argued that the attack would have been planned whatever President Bush's policy in the Middle East and denied that poverty was the problem. Kondo feared that 'perverted arguments' had a wider audience in Japan than elsewhere.[52]

The Japanese press worried about the impact of US actions in Afghanistan but rarely criticised its responses, let alone the nature of Western civilisation or Western racism. This reflected not only the sensitivity of the Japanese themselves to outside criticism, but also their uncertainty about their place in the international order and their relationship with Washington. One exception was the *Nihon Keizai Shimbun* which produced a series of thoughtful editorials on relations between the West and the Muslim world. In October it complained that Japanese education did 'little more than gloss over Islamic culture'. A month later it pondered the way in which students in Japan and elsewhere could become caught up in radical movements, a tendency it thought accentuated by the population explosion in the Middle East and high levels of unemployment. Later it criticised the pro-Israeli bias in the US media and Congress. It went on, 'if the situation is considered only from the standpoint of peace and order, the underlying reasons for growth in Islamic fundamentalism will be missed, which will only invite a new round of attacks'. Finally, the article stressed the resentment building up in Saudi Arabia against Western criticisms of Islamic education.

Conclusion

Terrorists seek the maximum publicity for their attacks and no terrorist actions have achieved more publicity than those carried out on 11 September 2001. However, the response shows that terrorism is subject to the same strategic axioms as any other military initiative. Too great an impact can simply remove the constraints which usually limit governments' responses to terrorist incidents and evoke united resistance. Similarly, the attack on the Indian Parliament on 13 December 2001 empowered the Indian government to threaten Islamabad and reinforced the Pakistani government's determination to crush the religious extremists. In both cases, the terrorists knew that they were hitting national symbols and believed that their destruction would demonstrate the weakness of their enemies. Yet, neither the Twin Towers, nor the Pentagon, nor the Indian Parliament were centres of gravity or even of weakness. Their destruction or damage simply aroused national, and indeed international, outrage.

The extent of bin Laden's miscalculations was shown by the way in which, for five months, contrary to normal experience, journalists in the articles examined in Britain, Pakistan and Japan were often more critical of their own government's reaction to the crisis than they were of other governments. Japanese criticised their country's behaviour in 1941 and 1991 in language which no outsiders used, and they were much more impatient than the foreign press with Koizumi's hesitations in 2001. Pakistani journalists writing for *The Friday Times* were at least as hard on their country's previous policy in Kashmir as any Indian, and harder on the government's policy in Afghanistan than any Briton or American. British journalists were more satirical about Blair's posturing than most foreigners and concerned that the treachery of British Muslims was due to the failings of their own society rather than of Muslim ideology. They and the Japanese were far more cautious about ascribing the attacks on the US to the clash of civilisations than the columnists studied in India and Pakistan. Commentators in *The Hindu* debated the way that New Delhi responded to the attacks but rarely doubted that Washington had to react decisively.

Newspapers often refer to international opinion when they mean the opinion common in their own country or part of the world. But terrorist attacks, if sufficiently destructive, can unite large segments of elite opinion across the world. This empowers governments to respond in ways which have previously been regarded as impossible, removing the governments of other countries, using manpower and weapons on a scale normally undreamt of and policing financial transactions. A Pakistani columnist reacted to the transformation in his country's policy by arguing:

> The US war on Afghanistan has, at least for the foreseeable future, brought about a normative change in the way inter-state and intra-state relations are to be conducted. Violence perpetrated by non-state actors or sub-national groups, until now a necessary politico-military tool in the struggle for self-determination, is henceforth to be branded, rejected and suppressed as 'terrorism'.[54]

The continuing struggle between Palestinians and Israelis shows that, however violence may be branded, it will continue when passions are sufficiently aroused. However, the balance between state and non-state actors has changed. From now onwards weaker states will be much more cautious about harbouring or assisting terrorist groups which threaten the US and major regional powers such as India or China. They have no wish to share the fate of the Taliban or to be as constrained in their choice of policy as President Musharraf has been. Terrorists may attack the major powers' national or religious symbols but the response will be far more untrammelled than it has been in the past.

ACKNOWLEDGEMENT

I am grateful to Mr William Kirkman, Sir Nicholas Barrington, Professor N. M. Kosuge and Mr Tendayi Rwambiwa for their help locating material for this essay.

NOTES

1. 'Japan should join war against terrorism', *Asahi Shimbun* (13 Sept. 2001) (hereafter *AS*). 'Japanese emergency team on standby', *Japan Times* (13 Sept. 2001); 'Agency considers law', *AS* (17 Sept. 2001); 'Time for Japan to pull its weight', *Yomiuri Shimbun* (20 Sept. 2001). For a general overview regarding media and their reaction towards major international events see: Philip Towle, 'Ethics, Perception and Intervention', *Peace Forum,* Seoul, 15/27 (Winter 1999).
2. Ibid. See also 'Supporting the war on terrorism', *Japan Times* (22 Sept. 2001).
3. Masaru Honda, 'UN resolution necessary if Japan revises law', *AS* (28 Sept. 2001).
4. 'Japan involved as victim of terror attack', *AS* (20 Sept. 2001).
5. 'New law needed for effective anti-terror support', *Nihon Keizai Shimbun* (20 Sept. 2001).
6. 'Tokyo's imminent crisis is a quake, not terrorism', *AS* (10 Oct. 2001).
7. 'Never allow terror to throw world economy into turmoil', *AS* (14 Sept. 2001).
8. 'Japan's woes: Koizumi's leadership more critical than ever', *Nihon Keizai Shimbun* (19 Sept. 2001); 'Japan must fight terror resolutely', *Yomiuri Shimbun* (27 Sept. 2001) and 'Government must cover all bases', *Yomiuri Shimbun* (30 Oct. 2001).
9. 'Paradise lost: terror leaves travellers timid', *AS* (27 Oct. 2001) and 'Security can be acquired', *Yomiuri Shimbun* (8 Jan. 2002).

10. 'Japan may need to provide more than money', *Nihon Keizai Shimbun* (17 Sept. 2001); 'Koizumi says Government to mull ways to help Pakistan', *Dow Jones* (Tokyo 1 Nov. 2001); 'Japan-US co-chair Afghan recovery confab', *Kyodo* (Tokyo, 10 Nov. 2001).
11. Shunji Taoka, 'Are we seeing a new style of warfare ?', *AS* (13 Sept. 2001). For foreign comments on Pearl Harbor see W. Rees Mogg, 'Remember Pearl Harbor', *The Times* (1 Oct. 2001) and 'For the world's sake this has to be done', *The Times* (8 Oct. 2001).
12. 'Bush hails Japan's antiterrorism support on Pearl Harbor day', *Kyodo* (8 Dec. 2001).
13. 'Middle East trip should be Koizumi's priority', *AS* (24 Sept. 2001); Yoshibumi Wakamiya, 'Ambivalence may prevent true solidarity role', *AS* (9 Oct. 2001).
14. 'Mission baffles MSDF crew, kin', *AS* (10 Nov. 2001).
15. Dipankar Gupta, 'Bonded by threat' *The Hindu* (23 Sept. 2001).
16. Kesava Menon, 'Merchants of terror' and Sridhar Krishnaswami, 'A giant grievously wounded', *The Hindu* (16 Sept. 2001).
17. Harish Khare, 'A case to hasten slowly', *The Hindu* (23 Sept. 2002); Sevanti Menon, 'It was real', *The Hindu* (16 Sept. 2001).
18. 'Osama network disrupted', *The Hindu* (14 Oct. 2001).
19. Muralidhar Reddy, 'Sitting on a powder keg', *The Hindu* (14 Oct. 2001).
20. 'Golden chance for Indo-Pak dialogue', *The Hindu* (14 Oct. 2001).
21. Bhavat Verma, 'The brazen face of terror', *The Hindu* (23 Sept. 2001).
22. C.R. Mohan, 'Dealing with the enemy', *The Hindu* (16 Sept. 2001); Neena Vyas, 'Danger on the doorstep', *The Hindu* (23 Sept. 2002).
23. Ejas Haider, 'Musharraf's "sectarian" contradictions', *The Friday Times* (17–23 Aug.) 2001 (hereafter *FT*); 'Afghanistan is core issue', *FT* (7–13 Sept. 2001); 'Time to change tack', *FT* (14–20 Sept. 2001).
24. 'Demythologising Afghanistan', Iqbal Khattak, 'Religious parties fail to muster support for Taleban' and Khaled Ahmed, 'Limits of our pragmatism', *FT* (28 Sept.–4 Oct. 2001).
25. 'Think positively', *FT* (9–15 Nov. 2001).
26. Sherry Rehman, 'Does Musharraf have a plan and other questions?' *FT* (7–13 Dec. 2001).
27. Tabish Khair, 'Don't follow the leader', *The Hindu* (13 Jan. 2002).
28. 'The opposition does a balancing act', *The Hindu* (30 Dec. 2001).
29. Alok Mukherjee, 'War at what cost', *The Hindu* (6 Jan. 2002).
30. 'India a step away from Pakistan war', *The Times* (22 Dec. 2001); 'We'll survive nuclear war', *The Times* (31 Dec. 2001); 'Blair seeks to pacify nuclear rivals', *The Times* (2 Jan. 2001).
31. 'Security concerns overshadow R-Day parade in Delhi', *The Hindu* (27 Jan. 2002).
32. S.P. Udayakumar, 'Indian let-down and Pakistani gains', *FT* (19–25 Oct. 2001); 'Think positively' and Ejas Haider, 'Has India been upstaged ?' *FT* (9–15 Nov. 2001).
33. Hassan ali Shahzeb, 'The general and the limelight', *FT* (8–14 Feb. 2002); for Indian views of the changing balance of advantage been India and Pakistan see Muralidhar Reddy, 'Caught in the quicksand', *The Hindu* (18 Nov. 2001) and BMR, 'Testing times', *The Hindu* (25 Nov. 2001). See also M.V. Ramana, 'India-Pakistan standoff: recalling October 1962', *FT* (22–28 Feb. 2002); 'Diminishing returns from flexing muscle', *FT* (4–10 Jan. 2002); Ayesha Siddiqa-Agha, 'Credibility gap and threat of armed suasion', *FT* (1–7 March 2002).
34. 'US banks on British troops', *The Times* (22 Sept. 2002); 'Blair as Gladstone', *The Times* (3 Oct. 2001). John Pilger, 'Blair has made Britain a target', *The Guardian* (21 Sept. 2001) and Peter Preston, 'All domestic policy now has an international dimension', *The Guardian* (7 Jan. 2002).
35. Matthew Parris, 'No shades of grey on Tony's moral planet', *The Times* (3 Oct. 2001). But see also 'Britain has found its role in international affairs', *The Times* (1 Jan. 2001) and Anatole Kaletsky, 'A war that has served notice on all terrorists', *The Times* (15 Nov. 2001); Hywell Williams, ' Haunted by the ghosts of Suez', *The Guardian* (18 Oct. 2001) and Peter Preston, 'Bin Laden needs tackling but don't underestimate him', *The Guardian* (19 Nov. 2001).
36. 'Blair colleagues uneasy over pro-US line', *The Hindu* (23 Sept. 2001); 'Saddled with an ally's brashness', *The Hindu* (11 Nov. 2001); 'Riding roughshod', *The Hindu* (2 Dec. 2001); Sherry Rehman, 'Does Musharraf have a plan and other questions ?' *Friday Times* (7–13

Dec. 2001).See also Bronwin Maddox, 'Peacekeeping and saving face at Number 10', *The Times* (13 Dec. 2001); Anthony Howard, 'Blair pretending that there is no difference between Bush and himself', *The Times* (29 Jan. 2002).

37. 'UK proposes new Marshall plan for 21st Century', *Nihon Keizai Shimbun* (25 Dec. 2001).
38. Nick Danziger, 'Where war is a way of life', *The Times* (18 Sept. 2001); William Rees-Mogg, 'It's so bad you simply have to be an optimist', *The Times* (24 Sept. 2001). Charles Miller, *Khyber: The Story of the North West Frontier* (London: Macdonald and Jane's 1977) p.71ff; Lord Roberts of Kandahar, *Forty-one Years in India*, *Volume 2* (London: Richard Bentley 1897) p.121ff; Khaled Ahmed, 'The matter of pride and sovereignty', *FT* (1–7 March 2002).
39. Matthew Parris, 'The bigger they come the harder they fall', *The Times* (15 Sept. 2001); Simon Jenkins, 'Real hawks would not dispatch the bombers', *The Times* (3 Oct. 2001); idem, 'Fickle support for war leaves us all at risk', *The Times* (17 Oct. 2001); idem, 'These are landmines by any other name', *The Times* (26 Oct. 2001); Jonathan Steele, 'No parallel with Koso War', *The Guardian* (1 Nov. 2001). For casualties amongst civilians see 'An errant US bomb and a funeral instead of a wedding', *The Times* (20 Oct. 2001); 'Death falls from sky on village of innocents', *The Times* (2 Nov. 2001); 'War descends like a scythe on innocent Afghan village', *The Times* (25 Oct. 2001).
40. 'Support Musharraf !', *FT* (21–27 Sept. 2001); 'De-mythologising Afghanistan', *FT* (28 Sept.–4 Oct. 2001); Ejaz Haider, 'Taleban cannot withstand an Allied assault', *FT* (5–11 Oct. 2001); Hamid Mir, ' Error will produce more terror', *FT* (16 Oct.–1 Nov. 2001); Hassan A. Shahzeb, 'Washington hawks seize control', *FT* (9–15 Nov. 2001);
41. Ibid. See also 'Fundos boast thousands of Jehadis for Taleban cause', *FT* (19–26 Oct. 2001).
42. 'Young Moslems ready for Holy War', *The Times* (29 Sept. 20001); Mick Hume, 'If we must go in for nation-building, then let's start with ourselves', *The Times* (26 Nov. 2001); Moslem fanatics in a Midlands town', *Sunday Times* (27 Jan. 2002); 'Missing months of pals who vanished', *The Times* (28 Jan. 2002); 'Tapping discontent'. *The Hindu* (6 Jan. 2002).
43. Khaled Ahmed, 'The world view of the expat Pakistani', *FT* (16–22 Nov. 2001); See also Christopher Andrew, ' Websites that preach hatred', *The Times* (5 Dec. 2001).
44. 'Shoe bomber sparks travel alert', *The Times* (24 Dec. 2001); 'The bomber from Bromley', *The Times* (26 Dec. 2001); 'Two Britons held by US forces have violent past', *The Times* (20 Jan. 2002); 'British Muslim named as kidnap mastermind', *The Times* (6 Feb. 2002).
45. Jonathan Clark, 'Americans are blind to the barbarians at the gates', *The Times* (15 Sept. 2001); Kesava Menon,' Their anger is palpable', *The Hindu* (14 Oct. 2001); Khaled Ahmed, 'Pakistan's disenchantment with America', *FT* (26 Oct.–1 Nov. 2001); 'Questions Pakistanis ask', *FT* (9–15 Nov. 2001).
46. Rahul Mahajan and Robert Jensen, 'Never a good war or a bad peace', *The Hindu* (28 Oct. 2001); Kesava Menon, 'Suffering of the innocent', *The Hindu* (23 Sept. 2002).
47. Sudha Ramachandren, 'Behind the veil of oppression', *The Hindu* (4 Nov. 2001).
48. Khaled Ahmed, 'The myth of "misinterpreted Islam",' *FT* (11–17 Jan. 2002); Khaled Ahmed, 'Deconstructing the Islamic mythology ?', *FT* (18–24 Jan. 2002); Khaled Ahmed, 'What kind of Pakistan do we want ?', *FT* (25–31 Jan. 2002).
49. Salman Tarik Kureshi, 'Roots of terror', *FT* (9–16 Nov. 2001).
50. Hani Shukrallah, 'Capital strikes back', *FT* (9–16 Nov. 2001).
51. Jonathan Clark, 'Despite the denials this war is rooted in religion', *The Times* (6 Nov. 2001). David Shelbourne, 'This is a war that dare not speak its name', *The Times* (17 Nov. 2001); 'Interpretations of Islam', *The Times* (3 Oct. 2001).
52. 'Kondo: Japan involved as victim of terror attacks', *AS* (20 Sept. 2001); 'Frustration of ethnic mosaics calls for wider understanding', *AS* (11 Oct. 2001).
53. 'Greater understanding of Islamic culture needed', *Nihon Keizai Shimbun* (2 Oct. 2001); 'More than religion behind terrorism by Islamic extremists', *Nihon Keizai Shimbun* (2 Nov. 2001); 'Other issues need solving for war on terrorism to succeed', *Nihon Keizai Shimbun* (7 Dec. 2001); 'Religious misunderstandings plague war on terror', *Nihon Keizai Shimbun* (14 Dec. 2001).
54. Ejas Haider, 'Musharref changes ten-year Kashmir strategy', *FT* (11–17 Jan. 2002).

Bringing it All Back Home: Hollywood Returns to War

SUSAN L. CARRUTHERS

> Another and far more transcendant love came to us unbidden on the battlefields, as it does on every battlefield in every war man has ever fought. We discovered in that depressing, hellish place, where death was our constant companion, that we loved each other, we died for each other, and we wept for each other. And in time we came to love each other as brothers. In battle our world shrank to the man on our left and the man on our right and the enemy all around. We held each other's lives in our hands and we learned to share our fears, our hopes, our dreams as readily as we shared what little else good came our way. [1]

> Out there under the hot sun in their desert fatigues with their floppy camouflage sun hats on they were like a bunch of overgrown kids playing soldier… with real bullets and grenades. It was the sort of thing that made Rangering so cool. It was real soldiering. Hard core, heavy metal. It was way more fun than college. They were on an adventure, Sizemore and the rest of the guys bunked in that hangar. They were in Africa, not behind some desk or cash register or sitting in class staring out the window across a sleepy campus. They did things like jump out of airplanes, fast-rope out of helicopters, rappel down cliffs…. stuff like what they were doing over here, doing good, chasing around an exotic Third World capital after a murderous warlord.[2]

'Tell me I'm a good man', an octogenarian veteran beseechingly implores his wife. Stricken, he halts before the grave of an officer who, decades earlier, had rescued his recalcitrant younger self from the thick of battle in 1944 Normandy – dying along with several others in an extraction mission of questionable wisdom. Unconvinced that his subsequent years have vindicated the premature extinction of theirs, the aging former soldier seeks reassurance that he did indeed fulfil the officer's dying exhortation to 'earn it'. In Steven Spielberg's universe, the assuaging of moral ambiguity – the saving of Private Ryan – is wifely work.[3]

On a grander scale, national not connubial, the same balm has been administered by Hollywood in its recent re-workings of the combat genre. For all their discrepancies in style and sophistication, both Ridley Scott's *Black Hawk Down* (2002) and Randall Wallace's *We Were Soldiers* (2002) offer an ennobling, redemptive portrait of soldiers at war. More than merely 'good men', they are *heroes*.

The Good War

The valorization of men in uniform struck a particularly receptive chord in the US at their time of release. For all the hastily printed T-shirts that centered the crosshairs on a bin Laden branded 'America's Most Wanted', the designation properly belonged to an enlarged pantheon of uniformed Americans: the Fire Department of New York (icons of courage, self-sacrifice and, as scores of magazine articles attested, marital desirability) joining ranks with more traditional emblems of patriotic veneration. As heroes stepped forward, so was Hollywood requested for active service. Given loud calls from the White House that the industry reprise its 'Good War' role as provider of inspirational cinema, it is easy to read *Black Hawk Down* and *We Were Soldiers* as made-to-order mood music for the 'war on terror': perfectly synchronized responses to the call to arms.[4]

Of course, the degree of orchestration can be over-scored. Both movies were in production long before 9/11, requiring the deployment of multilateral coalitions as complex as anything assembled by the UN, and arguably more effective. Yet, for all their having been conceived in advance of the cataclysm, both read as reflective of a *Zeitgeist* peculiar to the weeks during which Ground Zero still smouldered and Afghanistan was purged of the Taliban. Revisiting past conflicts while America waged a new one, they appear as much *about* the US after 9/11 as Vietnam or Somalia, their historical and geographical locales.

Both films owe their genesis to bestselling accounts of battle. Journalist Mark Bowden's *Black Hawk Down: A Story of Modern War* offers a fast-paced, multi-perspectival account of the 'Battle of Mogadishu', during which Operation 'Restore Hope' collapsed into a furious fire-fight between US Rangers and Delta Force troops, and seemingly the entire population of the Somali capital. A relentless, 18-hour exchange of rockets, grenades, rifle and machine-gun rounds over the day and night of 3 October 1993, left 19 Americans and approximately 1,000 Somalis dead.

Despite these discrepant statistics, 'Mog' [Mogadishu] marked the point at which US confidence in 'Hope' expired. In the battle's immediate aftermath, the Clinton White House decided to call off a mission which had crept from feeding starving Somalis to hunting elusive 'warlords' vying for control over both food aid and Africa's most irremediably 'failed state'. Reducing Bowden's cast of characters to more manageable proportions – shrinking several US soldiers into composites, and abandoning the Somali eye-view almost altogether – Ridley Scott sets out to reconstruct the battle with as much verisimilitude as the most sophisticated technology, and the least salubrious locations in Morocco, would permit.

Randall Wallace's *We Were Soldiers* takes its retelling of the1965 battle of the Ia Drang from Lieutenant General Harold G. Moore's account, co-authored by journalist, Joseph L. Galloway (played in the film by Barry Pepper). Losing the second half of the book's title and its action alike, the movie reconstructs the fiercely contested three-day battle, substituting a location in central California for the Vietnamese valley. With similar emphasis on prosthetic body parts, shot in blood-spurting, stomach-churning close-up, *We Were Soldiers* viscerally conjures the confrontation of November 1965. Helicopters, the 'new war-horses' (and horsepower of Francis Ford Coppola's *Apocalypse Now*, 1979), cannot sufficiently sustain the rapidly outnumbered and isolated men of the 1st Battalion, 7th Cavalry – 'Custer's old regiment', as Mel Gibson in the lead role of Hal Moore, notes with appropriate foreboding. With 234 Americans killed in action, the 'dress rehearsal' at the Ia Drang was scarcely a propitious curtain-raiser for the war to come, despite both sides' attempts to claim victory.[5]

That both movies anticipated the event to which their cinematic release appeared a response suggests that the 'new militarism' was intensified, not instigated, by September's assault. Back in 1998, Steven Spielberg remobilized Hollywood with his effect-laden assault on Normandy: reaffirming the good war's enduring goodness along with Private Ryan's. However, of course World War II's moral status – and the stature of those Allied forces who won it – was never in question. Despite plenty of bad movies about the good war, Hollywood cinema had never assailed its rectitude in the way that the Great War's greatness was steadily eroded by a series of inter-war revisitations, from *The Big Parade* (1925) to *All Quiet on the Western Front* (1930).[6]

Since 1945, World War II's star had intermittently waned as a locus for action-adventure, but it was certainly in the ascendant by the time of the Twin Towers' attack. Documentary footage of a blighted Manhattan, shot on and in the days immediately after 9/11, reveals the ubiquity of billboards advertising the attractions of HBO's ten-part television serial, *Band of Brothers*, which continued the work of *Private Ryan*: a viewing nation mobilized to re-fight the indisputably good fight, oblivious to an impending surprise attack that was immediately, and inevitably, analogized with Pearl Harbor (the 2001 film subject of Randall Wallace's previous screenwriting sortie).

In the words of film scholar Thomas Doherty, Spielberg's war work is 'best understood as a kind of sacramental rite, the baby boomer sons kneeling before the World War II fathers in a final act of generational genuflection'.[7] Be that as it may, Hollywood's recent interest in military scenarios lacking the same serene 'closure' suggests something more at work than resurgent filial piety. *Black Hawk Down* and *We Were Soldiers* shift the register from veneration to atonement. Now Hollywood appears to crave the indulgence of those whose martial virtue its previous productions had seemingly impugned. For while the good war's stock remained unimpeachably high, respect for soldiering in wars of more questionable justness often appeared to go absent without leave. Cinematic representations of the war in Vietnam – John Wayne's aberrant *Green Berets* (1969) aside – are scarcely remembered for their favourable portrayals of Americans-at-arms. The combat genre's classic melding of cohesion from difference was more apt to dissolve – in Hollywood's Vietnam movies – into fratricidal strife between officers and men, racial antagonism between blacks and whites, and a vicious race war between Americans and Vietnamese. The martial melting pot vanished, with so much else, in the 'quagmire' of Vietnam.

A more protracted sojourn in Hollywood's Vietnam, or a more nuanced appreciation of its topography, might remind us that American GIs were apt to be treated as 'casualties of war', even (and perhaps especially) when raping, shooting, or unleashing napalm over Vietnamese civilians. Since the Vietnamese remained such spectral presences, rarely realized as characters, the balance of suffering often appeared highly asymmetric – weighted towards the American side. As in *Black Hawk Down*, for all that we may be told of the enemy's excessive losses, our spectatorial sympathies and attention remain so firmly fixed on the US forces that others' anguish barely registers. Hence while American soldiers were the sometime agents of atrocity, absolution lay at hand. They too were victims of the larger 'tragedy' of Vietnam – visited without discrimination upon those enveloped in a particularly hellish war. But that American soldiers were frequently redeemed from straightforward anti-heroism has generally been less well remembered than that Hollywood produced only one straightforwardly pro-Vietnam war film before dispatching Mel Gibson to the Ia Drang, California.

Hollywood's New Militarism

Those who mistrust the industry as a Trojan horse, smuggling perniciously 'liberal' values into the realm of Pepsi and popcorn, are wont to attribute a record of dishonorable wartime service to Hollywood. With such suspicions running high in the era of Bush the younger, it is tempting to conceive Hollywood's 'new militarism' as a concerted rearguard action to recuperate its own good name by reinvesting moral purpose, dignity and valor in those whose reputation it had hitherto tarnished. Certainly, the studios were quick to capitalize on the 'national mood' after 9/11. Both Paramount and Revolution Studios accelerated their release schedules so that *Black Hawk Down* and *We Were Soldiers* would provide timely embodiments of Americans' resurgent enthusiasm for military ventures, encouraging confidence in armed forces equipped to prosecute the 'war on terror' to a successful conclusion.

Sounding an alarmist note, one *New York Times* critic feared that the graphic combat realism of these movies, screened (apparently without precedent) during wartime, might undermine public morale at a time of acute national fragility.[8] However, both parts of this equation were misjudged. Not only have past wars commonly galvanized moral and martial rearmament for new ones, but these particular representations of men in battle – however realistic the flesh-wounds – were explicitly intended to reassure American audiences not alarm them. As one of the real-life Rangers, Sergeant Matt Eversmann, depicted in *Black Hawk Down* told the press:

> I think it's going to be good for people to see this movie in the wake of what has been happening. It's good for [the American public] to know that we have a capable military filled with guys willing to slide down the rope into the furnace if you'll pardon me using a cliché.[9]

A release originally scheduled for March 2002 (a 'thinking man's time', in Ridley Scott's estimation) was rapidly rearranged for Christmas.[10] In other circumstances, this might have been an unorthodox moment at which to unleash a war movie, but December 2001 was hardly an orthodox time. Leap-frogging the pre-release audience test stage, director Ridley Scott anticipated that any commercial risk was more than compensated by a level of 'world awareness' in the US higher than at any time since World War II.[11]

Vexed by Scott's pre-emptive strike that reversed the timeline – Paramount's Vietnam having been planned to precede Revolution Studios' Somalia – Paramount brought forward the release of *We Were Soldiers* from summer to March 2002. Sherry Lansing, chairwoman of the Paramount Motion Picture Group, spelt it out: 'It's about the sacrifices that soldiers make so the rest of us can be safe. I think we're ready for that at any time, but now it's particularly relevant.'[12]

For some critics, the movies' operative principle – in the wider strategic interest of Hollywood's patriotic regeneration – is essentially Orwellian.[13] War may not be peace, but with past defeats re-described as victories, dissonant legacies of Vietnam can be consigned to the 'memory holes' down which Winston Smith dispatched historical remnants no longer serviceable to present needs. By seamlessly stitching America back into the 'victory culture' of the immediate post-1945 era, the new war movies extinguish any vestigial doubts as to the beneficence of American power. Martial enterprises can once again animate pride rather than begging troublesome questions of principle and practice. Both films, of course, deny that the events they depict *were* defeats. (Indeed, Bowden has been quite insistent that 'Mog' [Mogadishu] *not* be seen as a debacle but as a military mission that, while tail-spinning out of control, nevertheless fulfilled its tactical objective of 'taking out' General Aideed's key henchmen.)[14]

But they make a bolder move, not fully captured by an insistence that their function is essentially that of historical revisionism. What both *Black Hawk Down* and *We Were Soldiers* imply is not so much that the battles of the Ia Drang and Mogadishu were actually victories, misconceived as defeats, but rather the superfluity of questioning military ventures, of weighing the proportionality of means against the justness of ends. All that matters is obeying orders; fighting courageously to save one's life and, more heroically, those of other men. War is reduced to a primal struggle to stay alive, to get back home, to 'leave no man behind'.[15] It is a duty. And while specific wars may not amount to sacred duties, nevertheless, by definition doing one's duty is *good*.

Pivotal characters in both films make this shrunken conception of 'why we fight' explicit. Training his recruits, Moore tells his men that he will teach them to take care of one another 'because when this starts, each other is all we're going to have'. As *We Were Soldiers* ends – with Moore's tear-jerking return to his adoring family – the journalist agonizes over his keyboard, pondering how to make the Ia Drang's losses meaningful. The screen fills with a panel of the Vietnam Memorial wall on which names of the Battalion's dead are etched, and Galloway delivers a blank summation: 'They went to war because their country ordered them to. But, in the end they fought not for their country or their flag, they fought for each other.' Nothing more. Indeed, we learn little more about the reasons why 'the country' sent them to such inhospitable terrain than the halting response Moore produces in answer to his four-year-old daughter's wide-eyed, bedtime enquiry: 'Daddy, what's a war?':

> It's something that shouldn't happen but it does…and, uh, it's when some people in another country – or any country – try to take the lives of other people… and then soldiers like your daddy have to go over there to try to stop them. It's called the 'white man's burden'.

In *Black Hawk Down*, repeated encounters between the 'idealist' Sergeant Eversmann (Josh Hartnett) and the 'realist' Delta Sergeant 'Hoot' Gibson (Eric Bana), reiterate the redundancy of politics to men of courage. 'Once the first bullet goes past your head, politics and all that shit goes out the window', is the sage, scatological counsel offered to the unbloodied young Sergeant. Sure enough, when the bullets come, the fire-fight is punctuated by similar utterances. As the casualties mount, Eversmann is entreated not to blame himself for these losses: 'It ain't up to you. It's just war.' Only know-nothing civilians would make the mistake of thinking that war must be *about* something. Safely returned to base, 'Hoot' delivers the *coup de grâce* to such home front ignorance: 'They won't understand why we do it. They won't understand it's about the man next to you. And that's it. That's all it is.'

Black Hawk Down belongs to a familiar combat sub-genre: the extraction movie. Initially the Delta Force objective is to snatch two of General Mohamed Farah Aideed's 'henchmen' while Ranger teams secure the area surrounding the 'target building'. When things go wrong – as they rapidly do – the mission shifts to extracting those beleaguered Rangers whose two Black Hawk helicopters have been shot down, leaving crew-members stranded in the path of advancing hoards of ululating, AK-47 equipped Somalis. As for Ridley Scott's extraction mission, its beneficiary is not only an operation to which virtue (if not Hope) is restored, but also the wider enterprise of militarized 'intervention'.

Evacuated from possibly mission-threatening scrutiny, such operations' intrinsic merits are airlifted to safety. Given that spectators are quartered cheek-by-jowl alongside the embattled soldiers – ducking under incoming fire, anxiously awaiting the arrival of reinforcements, or watching digitized images of battle from the increasingly helpless control room – the film's insistence that war requires the suspension of scruple becomes well nigh unarguable: not just a fact of combat experience but a civilian imperative.

Conflict viewed from this empathy-inducing vantage point squeezes space from which critical questions might be posed. It is hard enough to draw breath during the relentlessly-paced spectacle let alone find pause for thought. Only when the final crawl text announces the outcome – 'During the raid over 1,000 Somalis died, and 19 American soldiers lost their lives' – are we alerted to staggeringly lopsided losses. However, there is a difference between body counts and bodies that count: The very form of words lends greater gravity to 'losing life' than merely 'dying'.

The Estimation of the Enemy

Enemy losses are typically a depreciated currency in war movies' rate of exchange, so this deficit may be scarcely surprising. Where *We Were Soldiers* departs from generic convention is in according the Vietnamese not only speaking parts (subtitled in English) but respect as a worthy foe: highly motivated, professionally commanded, and strategically sophisticated. The officer who demeans the Vietnamese as a risible, rag-tag bunch in 'black pyjamas' exhibits hubris on a par with the Ranger who opines, during the longueurs before the mission's kick-off, that the 'Somalis can't shoot for shit'. Such underestimation – and the overconfidence of leaving water canteens and night vision goggles behind – will exact a heavy penalty before the final reel. Strikingly, the closing moments of *We Were Soldiers* reprise the opening dedication to 'the young men of the People's Army of Vietnam who died by our hand', cutting from Moore reverently inspecting the Vietnam Memorial to a young Vietnamese woman grieving over mementoes previously seen in the hands of an enemy soldier – her lover, now presumably dead.

This is a far cry from General William C. Westmoreland's claim that 'Orientals' did not mourn their dead in the same way. Indeed, commending the 'remarkable and admirable lengths' to which the film goes to 'make good on' its opening dedication to the People's Army of Vietnam, A. O. Scott in the *New York Times* proposes that *We Were Soldiers* might be the first Hollywood movie plausibly to suggest that the raw wounds of Vietnam 'have at least partly healed'.[16]

If psychic 'closure' is now at hand, allowing a more nuanced appreciation of the former enemy, what of the opponent in Somalia? *Black Hawk Down*'s treatment of the Somalis veers between archaic stereotypes and a somewhat subtler sensibility. The disjuncture, however, is projected as dualistic essence of Somalia and its people – whose Muslim identity is visually and aurally cued by the Islamic minarets of Mogadishu's skyline, a gun-slinging fighter at prayer, and a score that alternates between power rock for the Rangers and something more suitably Moorish for the militia. The post-apocalyptic landscape of Mogadishu appears simultaneously savage and spectacular: both heart of darkness and playground for heroes who hone their sharp-shooting skills in airborne game hunts. As one Ranger puts it while in flight over the white sand where Indian Ocean meets Horn of Africa, Somalia 'could almost be a beautiful place to visit'.

Instead it is a country in collapse, where guns have replaced butter in the market. The origins of this blight are firmly attributed to the actions of 'evil men'. *Black Hawk Down*'s opening titles inform us that in 1993 Somalia was afflicted by a famine of 'biblical proportions' – not the curse of divine disfavor (and certainly not of Cold War geopolitics) but 'years of warfare among rival clans'. Ruthlessly appropriated warlords' power hunger feeds on the denial of humanitarian relief to Somalia's starving, while their resistance to the UN cannibalizes usable elements of Western technology. Shepherds watching their flocks by day, in hills overlooking the UN base camp, send advance warning of military sorties by cellphone to militias in 'downtown Mogadishu'. The latter careen through the razed city on 'technicals' – open-backed vehicles with heavy weapons mounts – waging war on the UN, whose job is now to stop the natives from killing one another and their would-be rescuers. ('What's the alternative', asks Eversmann? 'We can either help or we can sit back and watch the country destroy itself on CNN', insists the young idealist, defending himself from the charge of 'liking the skinnies'.)

In a cast of multitudes, where the Rangers are so many – and so identikit – as to defy serious characterization, the 'skinnies' receive three significant speaking roles (all, in fact, played by British actors). In set-piece encounters with US officers these Somali characters contest the *utility* of America's mission, leaving its fundamentally benevolent intent uncontested. Their terms of disengagement invoke the familiar 'ancient hatreds' paradigm of Africa steeped in age-old animosities, impervious to outside intervention. In stopping considerably short of an indictment of the oxymoronic properties of humanitarianism-by-helicopter – a mission so swiftly transmogrified from restoring hope to engendering hatred – the film (unlike Bowden's book) leaves the Somalis' rage against the US presence inarticulate, inchoate, inexplicable: the work of mad mullahs and militias intent on plunging Somalia deeper into anarchy, and further back into antiquity.

Somalia's is a 'civil war, *our* war, not yours', insists Aideed's languidly urbane gunrunner. But with '300,000 dead and counting, that's not a war, that's genocide', Major General Garrison (Sam Shepard) reprimands. The language is striking since 'genocide' was never part of the legitimate vocabulary of the US-led intervention in Somalia (and all the more striking since it was wilfully withheld from 1994's slaughter in Rwanda, precisely so that a casualty-shy Washington could evade the clear obligation under international law to intervene in genocide's prevention.)

A second, less gentlemanly, disagreement elaborates the point. When downed pilot Mike Durant is captured by an angry mob intent on stripping him first of uniform and then of life, 'warlord' Firimbi intervenes –

recognizing his utility as a hostage and bargaining chip. 'My government will never negotiate for me', the brutalized American insists. The response, while contradicting the logic of having spared the pilot for ransom, is telling:

> In Somalia killing *is* negotiation…. Do you really think that if you get General Aidid we will simply put down our weapons and adopt American democracy? That the killing will stop? We know this: that without victory there can be no peace. There will *always* be killing. You see. This is how things are in *our* world.

Home and the Fighting Front

Black Hawk Down's clash of civilizations is paralleled in *We Were Soldiers* by the juxtaposition of two different worlds: the home and fighting fronts. Indeed, both films make considerable play with 'home' as the ultimate referent of war. But like Kansas in *The Wizard of Oz* (1939), home is a place of paradox. Revered from afar in idealized tones as the absentee's longed-for destination, home proves flat and colorless beside the attractions of Oz, Mog or Nam. Combat offers the allure of adventure, danger and comradeship with which familial tranquillity cannot possibly compete. Immersed in domesticity (or grinding coffee throughout the 1991 Gulf War, like Sergeant Grimes in *Black Hawk Down*) it is hard to 'Be All You Can Be' – the recruitment slogan intermittently invoked by Bowden's soldiers with varying degrees of ironic separation.

Home may, however, equip husbands and fathers with caring skills that will be vitally redeployed in combat. In *We Were Soldiers*, marital and martial prowess exist in symbiosis, and fortunately for Lt. Colonel Moore, his band of brothers comprises many brothers in wedding bands. The connections are heavy-handedly drawn early on, in a chapel-set encounter between the pious Moore and a young, untried officer who, as a new father, seeks reassurance that paternal and soldierly roles can be combined. 'Being good at one makes you better at the other', reassures the model father-of-five and loving husband. Sure enough, on the battlefield he dispenses not only tactical vision and courageous leadership-from-the-front but also words and gestures of affectionately fatherly encouragement.

Even the photo-journalist Galloway is welcomed into this fraternity, thus enabling *We Were Soldiers* to redeem another well-worn enemy in Hollywood's Vietnam: the media. As if in response to the taunt in *Hamburger Hill* (1987) that the North Vietnamese at least take sides while newsmen just take pictures, Galloway duly joins the battle, accepting the gun proffered as gauntlet. Firing it, he goes further than the *Green Berets*' journalist hate-figure who is ultimately salvaged by swapping liberal scepticism for an appreciative militarism, but who stops short of exchanging his typewriter for a rifle, claiming greater proficiency with the keyboard than a trigger.

War, then, is where men get to love one another and die for one another. This brotherly love – literally a blood brotherhood, in both *Black Hawk Down* and *We Were Soldiers* – renders war at once meaningful and purposeless. As Marilyn Young points out, 'The flat statement, that one kills and dies for the man next to you, never leads to the obvious question: what are both of you doing there?'[17] The closest approximation to an answer is offered by Moore: that you leave home in order to find a better one. Fort Benning, Georgia ('Home of the Infantry'), may be where the heart is, but the Ia Drang is where the action lies. For all its perils and privations, Vietnam offers certain improvements on the society his men will leave behind. Home is the last refuge of scoundrels: racists and politicians – war movies' familiar traitors, who bind military hands with impossible mandates (as in Somalia and Vietnam), and whose betrayals, impatience and ignorance ensures that men *do* get left behind.

Moore's stirring eve-of-deployment pep talk – to a battalion comprising Ukrainians and Puerto Ricans, Blacks and Hispanics, Jews and Gentiles – enunciates the superior 'home' found at war:

> Some men may experience discrimination, but all that is gone. We are moving into the valley of the shadow of death, where you will watch the back of the man next to you and he will watch yours, and you won't care what colour he is, or by what name he calls God. They say we're leaving home. We're going to what home was always supposed to be…

Where many previous Vietnam movies represented the military as pressure-cooker for ethnic strife, in *We Were Soldiers* war acts as the solvent to a racism still rampant back home. While Moore's men tend one another with exemplary disregard for ethnicity, back at base their fretfully waiting wives encounter the stubborn stains of Jim Crow. A GI bride (whose *näiveté* strikes as anachronistic note as Madeleine Stowe's collagen-swollen Julie Moore) puzzles over the laundrette window sign, 'WHITES ONLY', misreading it as an injunction against washing her coloreds.

In *Black Hawk Down*, by contrast, things are etched much more starkly in black and white. Confronting their African antagonists, the Rangers are an almost exclusively white brotherhood, though a somewhat more ethnically variegated bunch than in Bowden's account, which stresses the overwhelming whiteness of the burden-bearers. Less sentimentally sutured to home (a missed phone connection with a fiancée; a photo casually trampled into the dirt), the Rangers and Delta-boys relish the opportunity to experience the ultimate male adventure, whose attractions are not restricted to the affective homo-social bonds forged in and by combat. Where beauty queens typically aspire to 'travel and meet people', Rangers get to travel and kill people. As Bowden explains,

> The Rangers had taken all that fearless exuberance and pointless bravado [of adolescent street culture] and channelled it. That was the secret core of all the Hoo-ah discipline and esprit. You would be given permission, in battle, to break the biggest social taboo of all. You killed people. You were supposed to kill people. It wasn't often talked about that way, but there it was.[18]

And all this in the name of 'doing *good*'.

If *Black Hawk Down* offers a more explicit vision of combat's compensations, it shares a dim view of those who make 'home' an inferior place. Implicitly, the film contrasts the Rangers' creed ('Surrender is not a Ranger word') with Clinton's – to the latter's considerable disfavor. As the movie opened, Ridley Scott and Mark Bowden very publicly aired their private discussions as to whether or not the film's message should be spelt out in its closing crawl. And what *was* that message? That America's pusillanimity in October 1993 had directly emboldened Osama bin Laden, giving him a green light to unleash the attacks of 9/11 against a US that had proved its unwillingness to stomach a prolonged fight in Somalia, and then again in Rwanda, Bosnia, and Kosovo.

Bowden's afterword to *Black Hawk Down*, written in November 1999, had already made the point that America's retreat 'taught the world's terrorists and despots' that 'killing a few American soldiers, even at a cost of more than five hundred of your own fighters, is enough to spook Uncle Sam'. It is scarcely surprising that Bowden should have felt his conclusion vindicated: 'Routing Aidid would have, in the long run, saved American lives.' If only America's 'military credibility' had been firmly established, its enemies would have been 'less inclined to challenge America'.[19]

However, this moral of the sad Somali story was deemed self-evident (or perhaps a little too overtly 'political' for a movie that ostensibly sent 'politics and all that shit' out the window). 'In the end, I just felt it was obvious', Scott was reported in the *New York Times*. 'I felt that the questions posed were obvious, they were presented in the movie, and it really would have been too much to bring in Sept. 11 at the end.'[20] Only obvious, however, if the movie is accepted on its own insistent terms.

Conclusion

Reaching for a perspective attenuated from the eye of the storm, we might detect an alternative causal chain linking Mogadishu with Manhattan, October 1993 with September 2001. In Chalmers Johnson's appropriative coinage, these sinuous threads go by the name of 'blowback': the unexpected repercussions of US power deployed imperiously and unaccountably. Reconfiguring Bowden's logic, Johnson proposes that 'Terrorists attack innocent and undefended American targets precisely because American soldiers and sailors firing cruise missiles from ships at sea or sitting in B-52 bombers at extremely high altitudes or supporting brutal and repressive regimes from Washington seem invulnerable.'[21]

In other words, displays of high-handed might offer a better account of what opens America to enraged retaliation than isolationist pusillanimity. To the degree that 'spinelessness' *is* the provocation, as Bowden implies, it lies in the gulf between Washington's enthusiasm for imperial power-projection and its distaste for exposure to danger.

Following this reasoning, the Somali animus against the Rangers was less a product of clan warfare than a consequence of the chasm between Operation 'Restore Hope's' stated intent and its practical enactment – with the helicopter itself ('saver-destroyer, provider-waster', in Michael Herr's apt phraseology) symbolizing the mission's conflicted core. As food distribution turned to manhunt, the elusiveness of the quarry inspired escalating, and mutually reinforcing, levels of frustration and aggression. Hence at the very moment when the Rangers thought they had trapped their prey, the Somalis seized an uncommon opportunity to assail their hitherto elusive redeemer-harassers, whose intrusive over-flights and casual arrogance had aroused widespread animosity throughout the city.[22]

With this downwardly spiraling dynamic set in motion, remaining in Somalia (as Bowden and Scott would have had Clinton do) could only have made matters worse. Losing further lives to save face – the essence of maintaining 'credibility' – was, after all, a good part of the explanation for President Lyndon B. Johnson's escalation in Vietnam.

Have these films contributed to the kicking of that war's syndrome? They certainly insist that Americans feel proud of their uniformed representatives in combat, reclaiming war as a communal enterprise to which 'politics' are an irrelevance at best, a life-jeopardizing hindrance at worse. While courageous men struggle to leave no man behind, audiences are entreated to set larger questions of purpose aside. Since soldiers cannot be criticized because they are only discharging an onerous duty assigned off-screen, there is no higher authority to call to account.

But in conflating opposition to militarized interventions with criticism of men-in-uniform, both *Black Hawk Down* and *We Were Soldiers* follow an already well-entrenched trend. In the months that separated Saddam Hussein's invasion of Kuwait in August 1990 from the launching of war in January 1991, space in the US mainstream media for critical scrutiny of policy options dwindled steadily long before Operation 'Desert Shield' turned to 'Desert Storm'.[23]

In part this reflected the narrowing of opinion in Congress to which television network news has long calibrated its attention, but it was also reflective of media coverage that emphasized 'our boys in action' (even during long periods of desert-bound inaction). Insistently eliding anti-war opinion with anti-militarism, if not outright treachery, much television coverage suggested that to question policy was to impugn soldiers already sufficiently menaced by the enemy without the home front sniping.[24]

For all that Bush Senior proclaimed that the 1991 Gulf War had 'kicked the syndrome', it is hard to square subsequent events in Somalia with the President's premature obituary. As with the Vietnam war itself, many blamed media coverage: mobilizing an ill-conceived mission through pictures of starving Somalis, then demolishing US popular support by displaying images of a dead Ranger being dragged through Mogadishu. Although highly contestable, the notion that pictures got the US into Somalia, and out again, has become firmly entrenched.[25]

Given the astonishing, catalytic powers so often imputed to pictures, it is no surprise that one commentator should have suggested that another picture – of the collapsing Twin Towers – had mobilized Americans for the 'war on terror' that really *would* lay Vietnam to rest.[26]

To this end, motion pictures would also play their part. And certainly the US military appeared highly satisfied with Hollywood's contribution – an appreciation that extended from the loan of military men and materiel to Ridley Scott in Morocco, to the furnishing of post-production accolades. Images of brave men in mortal danger – a potent source of emotional energy – would prove just the tonic to overcome battle-shyness.

'When it comes down to it, it's still about somebody having to go down there and crawl inside that cave in Afghanistan', concluded Ridley Scott.[27] Quite so. However, at the end of the day, presumably we should not ask why British troops were left to do so much of the crawling?

NOTES

This essay deals primarily with the films *Black Hawk Down* (Dir. Ridley Scott, Revolution Studios 2001) and *We Were Soldiers* (Dir. Randall Wallace, Paramount Studios 2002).

1. Lt. Gen. Harold G. Moore (Ret.) and Joseph L. Galloway, *We Were Soldiers Once... and Young* (New York, NY: Harper Perennial 1993) pp.xviii–xix.
2. Mark Bowden, *Black Hawk Down: A Story of Modern War* (NY: Signet 2001), pp.186–7.
3. *Saving Private Ryan* (Dir. Steven Spielberg, Paramount Studios 1998).
4. Rick Lyman, 'White House Takes Steps to Renew Tie to Hollywood', *New York Times* (11 Nov. 2001).
5. Moore and Galloway (note 1) p.xviii. It is worth noting that the 'lost' second half of the book deals with what is unambiguously an American defeat, in which one of the companies withdrawing back to base camp from the fighting at the Ia Drang is decimated in an ambush, largely through sloppy march security.
6. On the cinema of World War I and its afterlife in interwar cinema, see Leslie Midkiff de Bauche, *Reel Patriotism: The Movies and World War I* (Madison: University of Wisconsin Press 1997).
7. Thomas Doherty, *Projections of War: Hollywood, American Culture, and World War II*, (NY: Columbia UP 2nd edn. 1999) p.301.
8. Kim Masters, 'Against the Tide, Two Movies Go to War', *New York Times* (4 Nov. 2001).
9. Rick Lyman, 'An Action Film Hits Close, But How Close?', *New York Times* (26 Dec. 2001).
10. Nancy Mills, 'Realism plays the lead in "Black Hawk" battle', *Daily News* (21 Dec. 2001).
11. Ibid.
12. *New York Times* (4 Nov. 2001) (note 8).
13. British critics tended to be quicker and louder with this interpretation, sometimes suggesting that historical revisionism was a trait unique to Americans', and America's, propensity for self- and national reinvention. See, for example, John Patterson, 'Do we get to win this time?', *The Guardian* (1 Feb. 2002).
14. Bowden (note 2) pp.408–9.
15. *Black Hawk Down* harkens back to the tagline for a Vietnam-based extraction movie, *Missing in Action* (1984), 'The War's Not Over Until the Last Man Comes Home'. And indeed both the recent films' insistence on the overwhelming imperative to bring everyone back, dead or alive, can hardly fail to read as a rebuke against those whose (unspoken) negligence, cowardice, or betrayal left the missing in action unaccounted for and abandoned in Vietnam.
16. A.O Scott, 'Early Vietnam, Mission Murky', *New York Times* (1 March 2002).
17. Marilyn Young, 'In the Combat Zone', *Radical History Review* (forthcoming).
18. Bowden (note 2) p.164.
19. Ibid. pp.428–9.
20. *New York Times* (26 Dec. 2001).
21. Chalmers Johnson, *Blowback: The Costs and Consequences of American Empire* (NY: Henry Holt 2000) p.9.
22. Alex de Waal, 'US War Crimes in Somalia', *New Left Review* 230 (July/Aug. 1998) pp.131–44.
23. Robert Entmann and Benjamin Page, 'The News Before the Storm: The Iraq War Debate and the Limits to Media Independence', in W. Lance Bennett and David L. Paletz (eds.) *Taken by Storm: The Media, Public Opinion, and US Foreign Policy in the Gulf War* (Chicago UP 1994) pp.82–101.
24. Dana L. Cloud, 'Operation Desert Comfort', in Susan Jeffords and Lauren Rabinovitz (eds.) *Seeing Through the Media: The Persian Gulf War* (New Brunswick, NJ: Rutgers UP 1994) pp.155–70.

25. For a critique of this notion and the surrounding debate (on the so-called 'CNN effect'), see Susan L. Carruthers, *The Media at War: Communication and Conflict in the Twentieth Century* (Basingstoke: Palgrave 2000) pp.197–224. For a more detailed discussion of the image of the dead Ranger – notably re-presented by Ridley Scott as the more Christ-like, semi-naked figure of Mike Durant, born aloft by the crowd of Somalis who capture him – see Cori Dauber, 'Image as Argument: The Impact of Mogadishu on US Military Intervention', *Armed Forces and Society* 27/2 (Winter 2001) pp.205–29.
26. Joe Roth, chief of Revolution Studios, reported in the *New York Times* (26 Dec. 2001).
27. Ibid.

Information Age, Terrorism and Warfare

KEVIN A. O'BRIEN

The advent of new technologies, advanced means of communication and ever-more sophisticated ways of moving money around have already influenced the way terrorists operate and will continue to do so. Terrorist organisers and fundraisers no longer have to be in the same country as their target or indeed as each other. Their communications to each other can be encrypted. And there is the potential, if the right targets are hit (such as strategic computer systems running banking or air traffic control operations), to affect thousands or even millions of people.

Jack Straw, UK Home Secretary,1998

Defining The Problem: Asymmetric Actors and Threats – The Place of Cyberwar

Since the end of the Cold War, much has been made regarding the changing security agenda and the emergence of new threats. In reality, most – if not all – of these threats to national and international security are evolutions of pre-existing threats, which have undergone modification brought about by numerous engines of change in today's world. The much vaunted globalisation, new liberalisation in formerly autocratic states, increasing privatisation of state functions, and, most importantly, the revolution in computing, telecommunications, and data transference capacities – commonly referred to as the Information Revolution – have all impacted strongly on the international security agenda and on the nature of the threat-actors in today's world.

This has given rise, in the threat-perceptions environment, to the introduction of the term 'asymmetric threat' to refer to those threats which have gained prevalence since 1990 and present non-traditional threat-postures to (generally) Western governments, defence and national security communities. Generally speaking, these threats do not present the danger of major conventional war to the developed world powers but do present equally (if not, in some cases, greater) dangers to the populations and governments of these states.

In essence, not much changed with the attacks on New York and Washington because the rise of increasingly lethal, unclaimed terrorist attacks designed to cause mass casualties has been evident for some time. Al Qaeda has long been an exemplar of the 'new terrorism' identified by RAND analysts. What has been striking recently has been the way in which terrorists have used the very infrastructures of modern, globalised society (air transportation, postal system) against the societies that rely on these infrastructures. This asymmetric strategy has enabled small groups with relatively limited resources to achieve disproportionate effect, always the goal of terrorists. However, this asymmetric approach is not surprising. Numerous studies and scenarios undertaken by Western security planners in recent years have identified this approach as the most likely one for the West's opponents.

The main change since 11 September 2001, of course, has been in public and political perceptions of the threat. The attacks have raised awareness of the degree of hostility felt towards the US by some communities and of the vulnerabilities of contemporary societies. Consequently, there is greater political willingness to address the risks posed by the combination of an increased, yet diffuse, threat and extensive, yet hard to quantify, vulnerabilities. In relation to information assurance and dependability, there are three main developments since 9/11 that influence efforts to protect the Information Society.

First, a recognition that protective efforts should focus not only on low-level, day to day threats such as hackers and criminals but that mass disruption attacks by 'high-end' terrorists also need to be taken seriously.

Second, a recognition that, while poor security does leave infrastructures wide open to attack, as in the US airline sector, good business continuity planning can mitigate risks, as in the New York financial sector.

Third, a recognition by governments and businesses that security and dependability need to be taken seriously and require concerted, international action.

Ultimately, however, terrorists will continue to prefer the very public means of destructive attacks in the real world, with the enhanced reaction that such attacks engender in the population; at the moment, carrying out similarly 'devastating' attacks in cyberspace (i.e. the destruction of a networked computer infrastructure, along the lines of the 'cyberwar' anti-Serbian government activities NATO conducted during the Kosovo War) results in little public reaction beyond a curious concern, certainly far short of the fearful emotional panic that loss-of-life terrorist attacks result in from threatened populations. For this reason, so-called 'cyber terrorism' remains an uncertain tool for real world terrorists to use; however, the use of cyber-means to enhance, distract from, or otherwise support a real world attack is becoming of increasing possibility and relevance to terrorist aims in today's world, as the 'target set' continues to evolve.

The proliferation of networked computers and telecommunications systems means that our physical infrastructure is now being overlaid by another layer: the National Information Infrastructure (NII). The NII has been defined as 'that system of advanced computer systems, databases and telecommunications networks ... that make electronic information widely available and accessible. This includes the Internet, the public switched network and cable, wireless and satellite communications.' Given the reliance of modern society on this NII, any major disruption could impact on the national economy as well as on individual government departments or businesses. And yet, the NII has not developed with security in mind. Specific portions of it are highly secure, notably some internal networks within government or in some financial institutions. However, overall the NII is extremely vulnerable to disruption from either physical attack (arson, bombs, etc.) or logical attack (such as malware and other software programs).

The US government has taken the lead in studying threats to its NII from hackers, terrorists or foreign governments. Its Department of Defense warned last year that the insecurity of the NII had created a 'tunnel of vulnerability previously unrealized in the history of conflict'. The CIA, meanwhile, has warned that it treats Information Warfare (IW) (a potential 'weapon of mass disruption') as one of the two main threats to American national security, the other being nuclear, biological and chemical weapons (all 'weapons of mass destruction'). Infrastructural attacks – or those perpetrated by 'mass casualty weapons' – are an off-shoot of both. Damage and destruction to infrastructures, and the concomitant loss of life that such can cause, as was clearly witnessed on 11 September 2001, can result from both.

This is asymmetric warfare – but it is not all that novel nor all that new: as US military analyst Colonel Charles J. Dunlap has stated, 'in a way, seeking asymmetries is fundamental to all war-fighting. But in the modern context, asymmetrical warfare emphasises what are popularly perceived as unconventional or non-traditional methodologies.'[1] In its most basic form, asymmetric warfare is an approach that tries to focus whatever may be one side's comparative advantages against its enemy's relative weaknesses.

Generally, an asymmetric threat implies that an opponent is incapable, due either to his own capabilities or the strength of the force opposed to him, of confronting an opponent (generally the developed world, although this could include multinational corporations, transnational financial communities, or an international organisation such as the UN) in a conventional manner using like means or weapons to his opponent. Therefore, he chooses an asymmetric approach, using means (including the element of surprise, weapons and tactics in ways that are unplanned or unexpected) that will foil, offset, reduce or circumvent the technological superiority of his opponent, or even give him the advantage over the opponent. As asymmetric attacks generally avoid strength and exploit vulnerabilities, an opponent could design a strategy that fundamentally alters the battlespace within which a conflict (generally low intensity but with high involvement) is fought. These threats can manifest themselves in different ways, forming part of both the ends to be achieved and the ways and means of achieving them. They can have tactical and strategic impacts.

At the strategic level, they work to exploit the fears of the civilian population in order to either weaken support for the democratic process, undermine the government, or to compromise its alliances and partnerships; in this sense, the threats have a strong psychological, as well as physical, impact (e.g., playing on the degree of comfort a population has with electronic commerce). In addition, the potential for attacks on international forces deployed regionally (witness the 1992–93 UN operations in Somalia) or on citizens, property or territory of the major powers itself increases the requirement for a flexible and, sometimes, unconventional response to the security of deployed forces, peace support operations, and Western interests abroad.

At the tactical level, they can force an actor to change course or tactics (e.g., by playing on the modern fear Western military forces have of casualties), or carry out attacks that are difficult for Western forces to confront and prevent (e.g. through terrorist activities or attacks, both physical and electronic, on critical national infrastructures). Threats deriving from terrorist activity, complex emergencies and peace support operations, economic disruption, civil disobedience and organised crime all represent an asymmetric approach to confronting a more powerful opponent.

Not only is it likely that many of the conflicts facing the West will be of an asymmetrical and devolving nature, it is also likely that these threats will come from diverse, differing and simultaneous vectors. For example, the possibility that transnational terrorism will be accompanied or compounded by cyber-/infrastructure-attacks damaging vital commercial, military, and government information and communications systems is of great concern. In this sense, a major Western country could suffer greatly at the hands of an educated, equipped, and committed group of fewer than 50 people; such an attack could cause an effect vastly disproportionate to the resources expended to undertake it.[2] It should be noted that one of the open questions regarding the attacks of September 2001 is why – as will be explored here later – did Al Qaeda not use the cyber-tools and knowledge at its disposal to cause additional destruction and chaos alongside its real world attacks.

All of these threats present the requirement for a massively improved intelligence capability to warn against and provide support to operations against these threats. While the traditional intelligence process may not present the best options for timely and cost-effective collection, processing, analysis, assessment and dissemination of intelligence relating to these threats, it is clear that traditional intelligence-collection means – very technologically-heavy and still driven by Cold War requirements – definitely do not present the best options for dealing with asymmetric threats. These threats present clear technologically- or technically-based profiles (such as through intercepted electronic and communications traffic, or the use of orbital assets to determine the location of transnational terrorist bases in Afghanistan or delivery-system testing in North Korea, Iran or Pakistan) will continue to be of use to the intelligence collection process. The best assets for intelligence-gathering on asymmetric threats will be human and open source.

Asymmetry and Informal Operations

One of the central pillars of asymmetry is the use of Informal Operations (IO) to counter an opponent; as will be noted throughout this essay, the linkages between this pillar and another – terrorism – lead to concerns about the ways in which today's terrorists can use cyber-space[3] to both plan and conduct their attacks. These 'information age terrorists' present potentially the single greatest threat (in terms of the potential to render mass destruction and death) to today's information-age societies.

The British Ministry of Defence recognises that 'our increasing dependence on high technology to provide our battle-winning edge – and the widening disparity between our military capabilities and those of potential adversaries – may lead potential aggressors to adopt alternative weapons or unconventional strategies [including] asymmetric warfare'; this is because 'integration of information systems into military operations offers significant advantages but also introduces new vulnerabilities'.[4]

Under such a scenario, information warfare could be used to disable critical national infrastructures throughout Western states through attacks on computer networks, paralysing communications, transportation, power systems, and industrial enterprises; other IO, including perception management operations and psychological warfare, would allow opponents to exploit the international news media to weaken the resolve of Western decision-makers (as happened during the Kosovo conflict).

The 1999 US *Quadrennial Defense Review* stated that a future adversary could 'employ asymmetric methods to delay or deny US access to critical facilities; disrupt our command, control, communications, and intelligence networks; or inflict higher than expected casualties in an attempt to weaken our national resolve'.[5]

Future asymmetric actors will have various tools at their disposal; these include the use of cyber- or cyber-based warfare and the acquisition of selected high-technology sensors, communications, and weapon systems. This could be called the 'strategy of the niche player', where cyber-weapons and -tools would be used to disrupt information technology (IT) military and civilian systems, as well as to launch attacks on NII and critical national infrastructures (CNI) in order to disrupt and destroy the information-based economies and infrastructures of Western states.[6]

The threat is compounded by the selected acquisition of high technology sensors, communications and weapons systems by rogue states and non-state actors such as Transnational Organized Crime (TOC). The exploitation of civilian sources such as the Internet and commercial satellite imagery, as well as the proliferation of advanced weapons, permit better operational planning, more accurate targeting and greater damage by the asymmetric actor.[7]

Most ironically, the developed world is making the asymmetric actor's job much easier through its over-reliance, increasing daily, on large volumes of information provided through a largely unregulated Internet. In most instances, the populations and governments of Western countries rely almost entirely on national critical information infrastructures (NCII) consisting of government and corporate computer servers, telecommunications facilities and Internet Service Providers. All of these present ready targets for any type of asymmetric attack discussed here; responding to a potentially-devastating cyber- or cyber-based attack has become one of the key priorities of most developed world governments today.[8]

The Relationship Between Cyber-Crime, Cyber-Terrorism and Cyber-War

Legal Considerations of Information Age Terrorism and Cyber-Terrorism

One of the starting-points for considering the growing threat from cyber-terrorism, as well as the use of cyberspace by transnational terrorist organisations, is the legal basis for considering such activities. This provides not only a comparative international framework for understanding the approach that governments are taking to combating cyber-terrorism and cyber-based terrorists, but also an appreciation of how governments perceive the threat.

As noted in the UK government's 1998 'Legislation Against Terrorism: A consultation paper', the threat from cyber-terrorism as well as the significant use of cyber-space continues to grow exponentially:

> The advent of new technologies, advanced means of communication and ever-more sophisticated ways of moving money around have already influenced the way terrorists operate and will continue to do so. Terrorist organisers and fundraisers no longer have to be in the same country as their target or indeed as each other. Their communications to each other can be encrypted. And there is the potential, if the right targets are hit (such as strategic computer systems running banking or air traffic control operations), to affect thousands or even millions of people. Such technologies could not have been envisaged when the existing counter-terrorist legislation was framed over 20 years ago, but the powers made available in future must be adequate – and flexible – enough to respond to the changing nature of the terrorist threat both now and in the years to come.[9]

The UK's Terrorism Act (2000) designates 'terrorism' as

> the use or threat of action where...(b) the use or threat is designed to influence the government or to intimidate the public or a section of the public, and (c) the use or threat is made for the purpose of advancing a political, religious or ideological cause [and the action] (e) is designed seriously to interfere with or seriously to disrupt an electronic system.

Significantly, the jurisdiction for such activities includes action 'outside the United Kingdom' and includes reference to any person or to property 'wherever situated'; reference to the public includes 'the public of a country other than the United Kingdom'; and reference to the government includes 'the government of the United Kingdom...or of a country other than the United Kingdom'. Finally, Section 5 states that 'a reference to action taken for the purposes of terrorism includes a reference to action taken for the benefit of a proscribed organisation'.[10]

Overall, for the purposes of cyber-terrorism, this means that any individual engaged in, for example, the e-Intifada that has been ongoing between supporters of the Israeli government and supporters of the Palestinian self-determination cause since 28 September 2000 when the real world Intifada kicked off again – regardless of where in the world they are based – are subject to prosecution under this Act, whether a member of a proscribed terrorism organisation or not. Significantly, at the moment, no cyber-based group (e.g., as known hacktivist groups such as the notable Pakistani cracker group G-Force Pakistan, a group active since February, 2000, which defaced 19 different sites within three days of the Intifada recommencing) has yet been added to any listing of proscribed (or even noted) international terrorist organisations.

In the US, the *Uniting and Strengthening America by Providing Appropriate Tools Required to Intercept and Obstruct Terrorism Act* – or

USA PATRIOT Act, passed on 24 October 2001 – includes an amendment to the Immigration and Nationality Act and US Code:

> (iv) ENGAGE IN TERRORIST ACTIVITY DEFINED: As used in this chapter, the term 'engage in terrorist activity' means, in an individual capacity or as a member of an organization – (I) to commit or to incite to commit, under circumstances indicating an intention to cause death or serious bodily injury, a terrorist activity; (II) to prepare or plan a terrorist activity; (III) to gather information on potential targets for terrorist activityy[11]

This – in conjunction with all of the points raised throughout USA PATRIOT relating to 'electronic crime' – obviously alludes to the mounting evidence that Al-Qaeda used the Internet to support its operations.

Canada defines terrorism as an action:

> taken or threatened for political, religious or ideological purposes and threatens the public or national security by killing, seriously harming or endangering a person, causing substantial property damage that is likely to seriously harm people or *by interfering with or disrupting an essential service, facility or system*. [emphasis added]

The act must:

> intentionally (C) cause a serious risk to the health or safety of the public or any segment of the public,… or (E) cause serious interference with or serious disruption of an essential service, facility or system, whether public or private, other than as a result of advocacy, protest, dissent or stoppage of work that is not intended to result in…harm...

Both statements clearly refer to cyber-terrorism.[12] They are applicable 'either within or outside of Canada' and are carefully circumscribed to make it clear that disrupting an essential service is not a terrorist activity if it occurs during a lawful protest or a work strike and is not intended to cause serious harm to persons. Canada will also sign the Council of Europe Convention on Cyber-Crime.

Finally, under Australia's *Security Legislation Amendment (Terrorism) Act 2002*, 'terrorism acts' are defined to include:

> an act, or threat of action, that is done or made with the intention of advancing a political, ideological or religious cause; and done or made with the intention of either coercing or influencing by intimidation the Government of Australia or of another country; or intimidating the public or a section of the public

Terrorism also includes an act that:

> (d) creates a serious risk to the health or safety of the public or a section of the public; or (e) seriously interferes with, seriously disrupts, or destroys, an electronic system including, but not limited to (i) an information system; (ii) a telecommunications system; (iii) a financial system; (iv) a system used for the delivery of essential government services; (v) a system used for, or by, an essential public utility; or (vi) a system used for, or by, a transport system.[13]

Thus, it is clear that cyber-terrorism and cyber-based terrorist organisations are regarded in the same light as real world terrorism; at the same time, national statutes and amendments to anti-terrorism laws are moving to confront the borderless nature of the cyber-terrorist threat – much in line with moves to deal with the transnational nature of the 'new terrorism'.

Threats and Actors: 'Information Age Terrorism'

The FBI defines terrorism as 'the unlawful use of force or violence against persons or property to intimidate or coerce a government, the civilian population, or any segments thereof, in furtherance of political or social objectives', while the US Department of Defense (DoD) outlines 'the unlawful use of – or threatened use of – force or violence against individuals or property to coerce or intimidate governments or societies, often to achieve political, religious, or ideological objectives'. Moving away from the DoD's emphasis on the act Bruce Hoffman, in his seminal work *Inside Terrorism,* defines terrorism as 'the deliberate creation and exploitation of fear through violence or the threat of violence in the pursuit of political change', thus emphasising the results (the 'fear') over the act itself. When considering the potential for cyber-based terrorism to exploit such fear – versus the capability of real world terrorism to do the same – this differentiation would be useful to keep in mind.

In the information age, terrorism has expanded its scope and found an increasingly-prominent use for instruments such as the Internet to facilitate these efforts. Tim Thomas has coined the term 'information terrorism' for this process of exploiting the Internet for terrorist purposes, defining it as (1) the nexus between criminal information system fraud or abuse, and the physical violence of terrorism and (2) the intentional abuse of a digital information system, network, or component toward an end that supports or facilitates a terrorist campaign or action. Computer attacks are the most often cited example of 'the use of force or violence' in the information age because they are the attacks with which everyone has some familiarity.[14]

Among both governments and businesses, there is increasing concern that information security breaches and cyber-crime will undermine trust in the new economy and threaten the development of the Information Society. In the UK, then-Foreign Secretary Robin Cook warned parliament on 29 March 2001 that 'a computer-based attack on the national infrastructure could cripple the nation more quickly than a military strike'.[15] In the same month, the European Commission pointed out that

> the information infrastructure has become a critical part of the backbone of our economies. Users should be able to rely on the availability of information services and have the confidence that their communications and data are safe from unauthorised access or modification. The take up of electronic commerce and the full realisation of Information Society depend on this.[16]

Information Warfare and Netwar

Information Dominance and Information Superiority

As the 'information spectrum' includes 'data', 'information' and 'knowledge', in a manner of speaking 'information warfare' can include threats, protection and activities along each of these paths.[17] Information itself exists in different forms:

- as ground truth
- as sensed
- as perceived by an individual (direct or indirect observation)
- as shared by two or more individuals

Deriving from information, awareness and understanding are the results of cognitive processes with these inputs. Thus, by attacking each of these points – or, indeed, defending each of them – one is engaging in the most basic form of IW. By defeating an opponent's awareness of the situation while maintaining yours, or by modifying his understanding of the facts and truth while enforcing one's own (or, indeed, the view which you want your opponent to have of a situation), one is succeeding in IW.

These concepts translate fluidly across the whole spectrum of IO (including elements such as computer network operations, Psychological Operations Forces (PSYOP) and propaganda, 'netwar' or cyberwar, etc): in any of these scenarios, one is attempting to change one's opponent's awareness and understanding of the situation; even in circumstances where attack and defence parameters are used in support of cyber-terrorism, the aim is to defeat the opponent's systems – often by 'taking them down', eliciting information from them, or modifying their contents in order to create a different impression or make a statement – and thereby change his understanding of reality.

Some terrorists, organised criminal groups or other sub-state malicious actors have the ability to use the date, information and knowledge resources available in the Information Society to plan and organise, finance and communicate, and ensure command and control (C2) over real world operations. This ability was clearly demonstrated over the past eight years by Al Qaeda and other pan-Islamist terrorist organisations, and not simply a realisation post-September 2001, as will be discussed later.

Even in these situations, however, the terrorists used the information and communications technology (ICT) resources both at their disposal and – most importantly – at the disposal of their opponents in both Western and Asian intelligence services to defeat that opponent through 'spoofing' his real intentions.

IO, Computer Network Operations and Netwar

With the West leading the world in information technologies and the Information Revolution sweeping large parts of the globe, the vulnerability of these states to cyber-based IO, as well as to the more 'traditional' aspects of IO such as psychological warfare and perception-management warfare, has increased markedly. Ironically, the more the world digitises, the more vulnerable it becomes. In the military and government fields, this is becoming all the more worrying: computerised weapons-systems are used for precision strikes, email is used for military communications, and logistics processes have become digitised; insiders, rogue hackers, and foreign military jammers can exploit all of these.[18]

In addition, the use of such non-technological IO means deployed against a much more capable and technologically-advanced conventional force was demonstrated more than adequately in the Kosovo campaign, where Belgrade easily 'won' the psychological and perception IO war against NATO.

However, in a more worrying sector – that of cyber-based IO – the West is becoming increasingly vulnerable as it becomes increasingly capable. This is not only in the military sector, but also in the civilian and commercial sectors, as was aptly demonstrated by both the Distributed Denial of Service (DDoS) attacks launched against the Internet-based companies Yahoo, Amazon and E-bay during 1999–2000, and by the ILOVEYOU email virus – estimated to have cost Western businesses US$7 billion (£4.7 billion) in damage[19] – launched seemingly as a practical joke from the Philippines by college students in 2000.[20]

IO are 'actions taken in support of objectives which influence decision makers by affecting other's information and/or information systems, while exploiting and protecting one's own information and/or information systems'.[21] Targets include the major elements of the national economy: the public telecommunications network, the financial and banking system, the electric power-grid, the oil and gas networks, and the national transportation system (including the air transportation system). The conduct of offensive IO poses a clear asymmetric threat to the West, with its increased reliance on information and information systems as a vital component of decision-making, presenting the possibility of organisations, or individuals, with hostile or malicious intent, taking action to deny, disrupt or destroy capabilities in this area. This could have devastating consequences combined with WMD or terrorist activities: for instance, taking down a city's emergency telephone system through a cyber attack while setting off terrorist bombs and interfering with the media could produce an asymmetric synergy, making the individual attacks much more effective than they would have been alone.[22]

IO has been used to infiltrate or disrupt military or civilian IT systems, including those used for command, control, communications and logistics, to modify or manipulate data, or to attack the national strategic infrastructure (i.e. by disrupting critical systems such as international air traffic control systems).[23] Offensive IO can be divided into three principle categories:

- *Attacks on Infrastructure*, 'activity that causes damage to information or information systems, or interferes with operations', involving a broad spectrum of operations – including activities such as computer network attack (CNA), electronic warfare and physical destruction – ranging from hacker vandalism of public Internet sites to coordinated reconnaissance, infiltration, data manipulations or DDoS on corporate or government information systems.
- *Deception*, 'designed to mislead an enemy by manipulation, distortion, or falsification of evidence to induce him to react in a manner prejudicial to his interests', including manipulation of the open media, such as propaganda operations through public communication channels including television, radio and the Internet, as well as misinformation and hoaxes, sometimes taking advantage of new video and audio manipulation technologies and computer animation.[24]
- *Psychological Operations*, 'ability to influence the will of another society', involving political or diplomatic positions, announcements, or communiqués, as well as the distribution of leaflets, radio or television broadcasts, and other means of transmitting information that promote fear or dissension, with its message reinforced through acts such as hostage taking or the threat of mass casualties.[25]

Interestingly, cyber-terrorism is not only about damaging systems but also about intelligence gathering. The intense focus on 'shut down' scenarios ignores other more potentially effective uses of IT in terrorist warfare: intelligence-gathering, counter-intelligence and disinformation. In addition, conflict in the form of cyber warfare that would blur conventional boundaries between crime and war might prove attractive to an opponent that sees no strategic benefit in a direct confrontation of the military of the West in a regional war.

Computer Network Operations & CyberWar

As outlined by Andrew Rathmell,[26] Computer Network Operations (CNO) are 'a subset of a broader set of malicious computer-mediated activities'. British military doctrine states that CNO comprises three key elements:

(a) Computer Network Exploitation (CNE), namely: 'the ability to gain access to information hosted on information systems and the ability to make use of the system itself';
(b) Computer Network Attack (CNA), namely: the 'use of novel approaches to enter computer networks and attack the data, the processes or the hardware'; and
(c) Computer Network Defence (CND), which is 'protection against the enemy's CNA and CNE and incorporates hardware and software approaches alongside people based approaches'.[27]

As outlined in a recent US Center for Strategic and International Studies (CSIS) study, there is currently a lack of clarity as to the nature of cyberwar and what it means for those defending against such attacks. The CSIS study concluded that, in order to be able to defeat cyberwar, we need a clear picture of current and projected cyberwar options for attackers:

- Effective defence and response requires a full-scale net technical assessment of what attackers can really do, key vulnerabilities, and requirements for defence and response
- Exercising responses to assumptions about such attacks is not analysis or adequate planning
- Cyber-war can occur at a number of levels and in conjunction with other means of attack
- A covert cyber-war may be possible where the attacker cannot be identified quickly or at all
- Largerscale cyber-war may involve clearly identifiable attackers.[28]

CNO are one element of IO; another is 'Netwar'.

Netwar

David Ronfeldt and John Arquilla first introduced the term 'netwar' several years ago to refer to 'an emerging mode of conflict at societal levels, short of traditional military warfare, in which the protagonists use network forms of organization and related doctrines, strategies, and technologies attuned to the information age'. The protagonists are likely to consist of dispersed small groups who communicate, coordinate, and conduct their campaigns in a networked manner, without a precise central command.[29]

Ronfeldt and Arquilla believe that a network's strength depends on five levels of functioning: organisational (design level), narrative (story being told), doctrinal (strategies and methods), technological (information systems in use), and social (personal ties to assure loyalty and trust). As an example of 'netwar', the Al Qaeda network functioned on all of these levels during the planning and execution of the attacks on the World Trade Center. The network also makes the group appear leaderless, and thus makes it harder to find those responsible.

During confrontations with Iraq – even as far back as Operation 'Desert Storm' – it is believed that CNO capabilities (such as computer viruses inserted into the Iraqi Command and Control computers) were used; in addition, during Operation 'Uphold Democracy' in Haiti (1994), the US used hacking to exploit knowledge about Haitian government intentions and capabilities.[30] By the time of the 1999 Kosovo conflict, NATO and its member-states were openly using CNO, distorting information perceived by Serbian air defence systems on their screens. Hackers disrupted and defaced Serb and NATO websites, and jammed computer messaging systems with 'email bombs'; US hackers based in the CIA and the National Security Agency – following a *Presidential Finding* – burrowed into Serb government email systems, while some infiltrated their way into the networked-systems of banks around the world in search of accounts held by the Serbian leadership.[31]

It is perhaps not surprising that the US military and government have advanced the furthest in developing concepts of netwar and IO for use in conflict. The US now includes IO as a key component of national security strategy and doctrine; this emphasis has only been heightened since September 2001. The US views Information Superiority (IS) as centring on three key areas: Intelligence; Command, Control, Communications and Computers (C^4); and IO, which builds on the traditionally narrower activities of Command and Control Warfare (C^2W) and IW. With components including Deception, Physical Destruction, Psychological Operations, Operational Security, and Electronic Warfare – underpinned and bound together by a foundation of Intelligence and Communications –

CNO (supported by the Joint Task Force-Computer Network Operations (JTF-CNO) under USSPACECOM) has recently been added as the ability to logically interfere with an information system and has become of increasing relevance.

Outside the US, IO is a relatively recent doctrinal construct not yet accepted by all NATO nations; even within the US Armed Forces it is viewed with scepticism by some. In the UK, for example, the MoD recently established the Land Information Assurance Group (Volunteers) comprising a 40-person-strong Territorial Army unit to develop effective countermeasures against cyber-attacks.

Transnational Terrorists and Cyberspace

In the wake of September 2001, it is clear that terrorists are using cyberspace for their own means. Indeed, terrorist organisations had already – before the rise of the Internet – begun to appreciate the opportunities that threats to infrastructure, as opposed to human beings, could cause. In the early 1990s, the Provisional IRA used this concept very effectively, sufficiently occupying the resources of the British government through infrastructural attacks (as opposed to direct attacks against people).

In the future, stock markets or other primary financial institutions might become high profile targets and the most effective means of accomplishing a terrorist's goal; indeed, more damage would be accomplished by taking the New York Stock Exchange offline for a few days than by actually bombing a building. According to February 2000 testimony to the US Congress by John A. Serabian, Jr (Information Operations Issue Manager of the CIA), 'Terrorists and other non-state actors have come to recognise that cyber weapons offer them new, low-cost, easily hidden tools to support their causes. The skills and resources of this threat group range from the merely troublesome to dangerous.' Groups such as Hizballah, Hamas, and Al Qaeda are using computerised files, email, and encryption to support their activities. While terrorists and extremists have long been using the Internet to communicate, raise funds, recruit, and gather intelligence, cyber-attacks offer terrorists the possibility of greater security and operational flexibility. Theoretically, they can launch a computer assault from almost anywhere in the world without exposing themselves.[32]

The Internet has changed terrorist communications networks from those of strong central control to ones with no clear centre of control due to its networked nature. Indeed, transnational terrorist organisations have begun to appreciate the full opportunities that cyberspace offers for their activities: the use of new/Internet-based technologies for coordinating, communicating and supporting the planning of terrorist (cyber-based and real-world) activities; the ability to develop and support so-called 'virtual sanctuaries' where the full C^3I of the terrorists is conducted solely in cyberspace; and other means outlined below with particular regard to Al Qaeda. In this same sense, the Internet can be used for clandestine communications through virtual private networks, posting messages on email and electronic bulletin boards, as well as steganography (hiding messages within pictures and objects) and encryption.

In June 2001, the CIA's top advisor on technology matters Lawrence Gershwin stated that, while terrorists still prefer bombs, 'We anticipate more substantial cyber-threats in the future as a more technically competent generation enters the terrorist ranks.'[33] The capabilities and opportunities offered to terrorists include such things as using the Internet to gather detailed targeting information; gathering and moving about money to support activities – or even manipulating stocks to benefit the terrorist organisations (as is suspected from September 2001); coordinating and planning activities from around the world; and using it as a platform for propaganda and publicity (e.g. terrorists leave messages of future or planned activities on web sites or email, while publicising accountability for acts of violence) – in a similar manner, the Internet can be used for psychological terrorism and rumour-mongering. It can also be used to conduct attacks against individuals, groups, or companies such as financial institutes, or to directly lobby decision-makers through extortion, brand-destruction, fraud and other means.

Leading terrorist organisations have made the migration to cyberspace, led by the LTTE (Tamil Tigers) and, oddly enough, the Scottish National Liberation Army. Other examples include a group calling themselves the Internet Black Tigers who took responsibility for attacks in August 1998 on the email systems of Sri Lankan diplomatic posts around the world, including those in the US; third-country sympathisers of the Mexican Zapatista rebels who crashed web pages belonging to Mexican financial institutions – generating propaganda and rallying supporters; and others such as Kurdish separatists in Greece and Turkey, Kashmiri separatists in India, and Zapatista rebels in Mexico, who have all also hacked official government websites and posted anti-government propaganda and pictures.

Perhaps the best known IT-advanced terrorist organisation is Aum Shinriyko/Aleph, which even owns its computer/IT firms – the M Group – which has served some of the giants of Japanese industry and government, and was only discovered in March 2000 to be linked to Aum/Aleph. According to a 2000 *Newsweek* report, 'Technology has always been Aum's secret weapon. In the 1980s its efforts to peddle bargain PCs through cult-owned electronics shops blossomed into a $1 billion empire.' The group's founder, Shoko Asahara, lured engineers, chemists and computer scientists from Japan's elite universities to work developing weapons of mass destruction.[34] There were also rumours that Aum's 1995 Tokyo subway attack was also supposed to have been supported by hacking into the subway ventilation and train-control systems in order to maximise the causalities caused by the sarin gas – a rumour that was later denied by officials in Japan.

Al Qaeda and Terrorism in Cyberspace

The Cyber-Trail of the Attacks

One of the ways in which officials world-wide will develop new methods for critical infrastructure protection (CIP) is through an understanding of how the terrorists carried out the 9/11 attack. Until as recently as last year, bin Laden used high-technology means (such as satellite telephones) to communicate with his followers. This stopped abruptly as bin Laden realised the potential threat this presented him. However, although bin Laden may only use the lowest technology means – such as in-person communication with his subordinates – these subordinates are believed to use encrypted Internet messages to correspond with each other.

Currently, it is believed that Al Qaeda uses both high and low technology means to coordinate its activities: in organising for the attacks, the terrorists used active cyber-means – booking airline tickets online, exchanging hundreds of emails, using the Internet to learn about the aerial application of pesticides – to plan their attacks; they also protected their communications by using public computer terminals, anonymous email services, and encryption or steganography on websites to relay information publicly. Much of this granted them the total anonymity that was essential to the preparations for these attacks. Yet, it also left, in the aftermath, an electronic trail for investigators to follow.

In 2000, former FBI Director Louis Freeh highlighted this issue to the Senate: 'Uncrackable encryption is allowing terrorists – Hamas, Hizbollah, Al Qaeda and others – to communicate about their criminal intentions without fear of outside intrusion.' Indeed, bin Laden may actually have used technological means to 'spoof' Western intelligence collection (such as Signals Intelligence and Imagery Intelligence) into believing that he was planning an attack 'overseas' and not on the continental US, turning the West's intelligence means against it, and using human couriers to carry the real messages: according to Congressional sources, US intelligence had intercepted communications discussing such attacks, and other warnings since May 2001 pointed towards an overseas attack on American interests, similar to the attack on the destroyer USS *Cole* in October 2000.

In the US, the powers granted by the Foreign Intelligence Surveillance Act (FISA) have allowed officials to develop a clear picture of the terrorists' activities prior to the attacks: for example, one FISA search authorised authorities to monitor the Internet communications of a particular user, which has yielded hundreds of emails linked to the hijackers in English, Arabic and Urdu. According to the FBI, some messages have included operational details of the attack. Other officials have seized library log-in sheets and computer equipment, and issued search-warrants to America On-Line, Microsoft, Earthlink, Yahoo, Google, NetZero, Travelocity and many smaller providers. It is hoped that lessons will be learned from this which will contribute to future detection and deterrence of attacks.

In December 2001, the Canadian Office for Critical Infrastructure Protection and Emergency Preparedness (OCIPEP) released a report on the potential for Al Qaeda to regroup in cyberspace, based upon its long-demonstrated use of the Internet and ICT to support its operations. Warning of 'a possible future cyberattack by agents or sympathizers of Osama bin Laden's al-Qaeda terrorist organization', the report stated that 'bin Laden's vast financial resources would enable him or his organization to purchase the equipment and expertise required for a cyberattack and mount such an attack in very short order'.

While bin Laden himself may no longer have (assuming he is even alive) the ICT resources to call on which he has used over the past decade, the study does not rule out the possibility of Al Qaeda agents or sympathisers in other countries carrying out sophisticated and co-ordinated cyber-attacks against critical infrastructure facilities, such as the US telecommunications grid, electric power facilities and oil and natural gas pipelines.[35]

Bin Laden demonstrated a sophisticated knowledge of ICT in the months between the August 1998 attacks in East Africa and the September 2001 attacks in the US. A report released the day after the US attacks stated that bin Laden may have deliberately used the West's intelligence capabilities against it by 'spoofing' these intelligence services – and particularly their signals Intelligence assets – into believing that an attack was going to take place in Africa and not the US. Since May 2001, there had been numerous warnings that bin Laden or another terrorist leader was preparing a major campaign against Americans, but all the intelligence suggested that any attacks would come overseas. Bin Laden appears to have used the communications he knew the US was monitoring to throw America's spies off his trail, instead using human couriers to carry his real messages and money.[36]

The Threat: The Rise of Non-Traditional Sub-State Actors

The spectrum of cyber-threats is commonly taken to range from recreational hackers at the bottom end to national intelligence services and armed forces at the top end. In between, in terms of capability, come sub-state entities such as semi-organised crackers, hacktivists, organised criminals and terrorists. Cyber-threats emanating from such groups can be defined as 'all forms of electronic attack as well as physical attacks and threats to system integrity'. The threats of concern surround both those that may cause observable disruption (e.g. direct action, terrorism) and those that may be clandestine (e.g. espionage and crime). Such threats are both to the functioning of information infrastructures and to the information carried on such infrastructures (i.e. to the confidentiality, integrity and availability of information and information systems).[37]

In the study of international and corporate security, it has become axiomatic that organised sub-state actors, including terrorists and insurgents, organised criminals and activist movements, have become increasingly powerful actors in international affairs as a result of social, political and technological changes. As the authors of a Norwegian government study put it: 'The coercive power of sub-state actors (i.e., the ability to influence state conduct through violence and sabotage or the threat to do so) is growing and will continue to grow in the future.'[38]

Several authors have championed the idea that evolutionary changes have led to the emergence of a 'new terrorism' in the 1990s.[39] Proponents of the 'new terrorism' thesis argue that political aims are being replaced by new motivations, ranging from the desire to alter society at a fundamental level (millennialism) to single issues like abortion, the environment or animal rights.

'New terrorism' is also defined by its adoption of novel organisational structures and new patterns of group membership. One of the most common themes regarding this facet of 'new terrorism' is that of flattened hierarchies. Traditional hierarchies have become increasingly unnecessary as advances information technology have made communications easier to arrange. Such leaderless resistance is the natural consequence of ever increasing levels of cellular disaggregation by sub-state actors. As Arquilla and Ronfeldt note, such organisations are a compromise between 'collective diversity' and 'co ordinated anarchy', with modern communications technologies allowing discreet and minimal communications for consultancy and mobilisation. Under this system, 'subversive networking' undermines state power through the utilisation of 'semi-autonomous cellular structures'. Examples of such activity include the networking of Mexican Zapatistas and US 'hacktivists' and the cellular organisation of London's J18 anti-capitalist protests.[40]

Cyber-terrorism is not only about damaging systems but also about intelligence gathering. The focus on 'shut down' scenarios and analogies to physically violent techniques ignore other more potentially effective uses of

IT in terrorist warfare: intelligence-gathering, counter-intelligence and disinformation. In addition, concomitant cyber-attacks with real-world terrorist incidents (as alluded to in the September 2001 attacks) could potentially multiply the disastrous consequences massively. Attacking an information system would be a good way to either distract the target or otherwise enable the terrorist to perform a physical attack. For example, had Aum Shinrikyo been able to crack the Tokyo power system and stop the subways, trapping passengers on the trains, the number of casualties caused by their 1995 sarin nerve gas attack might have been significantly larger.[41]

Competitor Governments and Cyberwar

Most interestingly, the perception that asymmetric threats are posed solely by those opponents of the West who possess little strength in any sector is quickly dismissed by the fact that the Chinese People's Liberation Army (PLA) has recently published studies in which asymmetric warfare and tactics are seen as key in any future conflict, whether military or otherwise, with the West (particularly the US). Stating that 'hacking into web-sites, targeting financial institutions, terrorism, assassinating US financiers, using the media and conducting urban warfare' are among the methods considered by the PLA, these studies are driven by the efforts of the PLA to modernise their IW/IO capabilities. Recognising that it cannot match the West in either conventional or nuclear weapons, the PLA has begun to emphasise the development of new information and cyberwar technologies, including viruses and similar cyber-threats, to neutralise or at least erode any enemy's political, economic and military information and command-and-control infrastructures.[42]

Designating this practice as 'unrestricted warfare', the PLA argue that China can outmanoeuvre Western high-tech sensors, electronic countermeasures and weaponry by employing different methods entirely. 'If [China] secretly musters large amounts of capital without the enemy nation being aware of this at all and launches a sneak attack against its financial markets,' they write,

> then after causing a financial crisis, buries a computer virus and hacker detachment in the opponent's computer system in advance, while at the same time carrying out a network attack against the enemy so that the civilian electricity network, traffic-dispatching network, financial-transaction network, telephone-communications network and mass-media network are completely paralysed, this will cause the enemy nation to fall into social panic, street riots and a political crisis.[43]

Indeed, the Chinese government and PLA may be behind the most sophisticated on-going cyberwar today. Known collectively as 'Solar Sunrise' (February 1998) and 'Moonlight Maze' (ongoing since mid-1999), this series of increasingly-sophisticated cyber-attacks and attempts at penetrating US government systems has been traced to sources in both China and Russia, but no clear perpetrators have come to light. While 'Solar Sunrise' exploited lax computer security in the DoD (and was ultimately traced to two California teenagers under the orders of an Israeli hacker), 'Moonlight Maze' was suspected of links to both the Chinese PLA and the Russian Academy of Sciences; the hackers accessed sensitive DoD science and technology information.[44]

Such concerns were enhanced when – following the 1 April 2001 downing of the US EP-3 surveillance aircraft by Chinese fighters – several US government websites were taken over and defaced by suspected Chinese hackers in the days following the incident. On one site at the Department of Labor, a hacker posted a tribute to Wang Wei, the Chinese pilot who was killed in a collision with the EP-3 on 1 April. By the end of the week, the so-called 'Honker Union of China' – an informal network of Chinese hackers – claimed that they had defaced more than 1,000 US websites. One message said: 'Don't sell weapons to Taiwan, which is a province of China.' American hackers responded with their own methods: for example, web-portal Sina.com was struck by a series of denial-of-service (DOS) attacks on the evening before 1 May.[45]

Thomas has also noted that, with regard to the Internet, a terrorist attempts to succeed by using the Internet's open promise of an integrated and cooperative world to discredit governments, degrade user confidence, and corrupt or disrupt key systems through the insertion of data errors or by causing intermittent shutdowns. This produces, in many cases, fear or alarm, and thus is a modern day supplement to traditional terrorism.[46]

One asymmetric response to military weakness is to seek to use international legal instruments to restrain vertical proliferation on the part of a rival, hence the Russian gambit at the UN. Russia's attempts to ban IO make strategic sense and mirror its efforts to restrict nuclear weapons in the early years of the Cold War. Russia recognises that, as it struggles to rebuild its economy, it is vulnerable to the advanced tools and doctrines of IO that its Western rivals are developing. Unable to counter in kind, or to afford comprehensive defensive measures, Russia is seeking to use international law to reduce America's military advantage. In this sense, the West will need to pay particular attention to this most pressing of new concerns.

Defending Against Cyber-Terrorism: Critical Infrastructure Protection and Information Assurance

By 2001, European and US policy makers at the highest levels were expressing their concerns that insecure information systems threatened economic growth and national security. President Bush's National Security Adviser Condoleezza Rice noted in March 2001 that: 'it is a paradox of our times that the very technology that makes our economy so dynamic and our military forces so dominating also makes us more vulnerable'. She warned: 'Corrupt [the information] networks, and you disrupt this nation.'[47] As a result of these concerns, a complex and overlapping web of national, regional and multilateral initiatives has emerged.[48] A common theme behind these initiatives is the recognition of the inadequacy of existing state-centric policing and legislative structures to police international networks and the importance of ensuring that private networks are secured against disruption. One way of grouping these initiatives is to use the standard information security paradigm of *deterrence; prevention; detection;* and *reaction*.

Deterrence: Multilateral initiatives to deter CNA include harmonising cyber-crime legislation to promote tougher criminal penalties and better e-commerce legislation (Council of Europe Convention, United Nations Commission on Trade).

Prevention: Multilateral initiatives to prevent CNA centring around promoting the design and use of more secure information systems (e.g. researched development initiatives between the US and EU; Common Criteria) and better information security management in both public and private sectors (e.g. International Organization for Standardization and Organization for Economic Cooperation and Development standards and guidelines initiatives). Other measures include legal and technological initiatives such as the promotion of security mechanisms (e.g. electronic signature legislation in Europe).

Detection: Multilateral initiatives to detect CNA include the creation of enhanced cooperative policing mechanisms (e.g. G-8 national points of contact for cyber-crime). Another important area is the effort to provide early warning of cyber-attack through exchanging information between the public and private sectors (e.g. US Information Sharing and Analysis Centres, FIRST, European Early Warning and Information System).

Reaction: Multilateral initiatives to react to CNA include efforts to design robust and survivable information infrastructures; development of crisis management systems; and improvement in coordination of policing and criminal justice efforts.

Overall, these initiatives involve significant investments of time and effort from a variety of government departments in many nations, from numerous international organisations and from numerous companies, large and small.

Many initiatives are pre-existing, many are being pursued in isolation. Nonetheless, there has emerged a coherent and effective set of initiatives involving states and businesses, not to mention some non-governmental organizations, that is focused upon improving the security of the emerging global information environment.

ACKNOWLEDGEMENT

The author would like to thank Dr Andrew Rathmell particularly, for his thought contribution to this study; he would thank colleagues in RAND and RAND Europe – including Dr Lorenzo Valeri, Prof. Bruce Hoffman, Dr John Arquilla and Dr Greg Treverton – for their support of many of the ideas contained here, as well as Joseph Nusbaum and Allison Van Lare for assistance with research which contributed to this essay.

NOTES

1. Michael Evans, 'Conventional Deterrence in the Australian Strategic Context', Land Warfare Studies Centre Working Paper 103 (May 1999): <www.defence.gov.au/lwsc/wp103.html>.
2. <www.emergency.com/asymetrc.htm>.
3. The term 'cyberspace' is used here to refer to any and all aspects of the Internet and World Wide Web (including communications and informational means), as well as any networked system or systems which are connected to other systems outside of themselves.
4. <www.dti.gov.uk/ost/forwardlook99/states/mod/text.htm#section02>.
5. <http://forum.ra.utk.edu/summer99/asymmetric.htm >.
6. Robert H. Allen, *Asymmetric Warfare: Is The Army Ready?*, Army Management Staff College, Seminar 14, Class 97-3 (1997): <www.amsc.belvoir.army.mil/asymmetric _warfare.htm>.
7. Government of Canada – Department of National Defence, *Threat Definition: Asymmetric Threats And Weapons Of Mass Destruction* (3000-1 (DNB CD) April 2000) p.17.
8. Ibid. p.18.
9. Presented to Parliament by the Secretary of State for the Home Department and the Secretary of State for Northern Ireland by Command of Her Majesty (Dec. 1998): <www.archive.official-documents.co.uk/document/cm41/4178/4178.htm>.
10. Government of the United Kingdom and Northern Ireland, *Terrorism Act* (2000) s1(1–5) 'Terrorism: Interpretation': <www.hmso.gov.uk/acts/acts2000/00011--b.htm#1>.
11. Government of the United States, *Uniting and Strengthening America by Providing Appropriate Tools Required to Intercept and Obstruct Terrorism Act* (25 Oct. 2001) HR 3162 RDS (107th CONGRESS, 1st Session): SEC. 411. "DEFINITIONS RELATING TO TERRORISM – Amendment to Section 212(a)(3) of the Immigration and Nationality Act (8 U.S.C. 1182(a)(3))": <http://frwebgate.access.gpo.gov/cgi-bin/getdoc.cgi?dbname=107_cong_public_laws&docid=f:pub1056.107>.
12. Government of Canada, *Anti-terrorism Act.* Bill C-36 (18 Dec. 2001): s83.01 (1)(b)(ii).
13. Government of Australia, *Security Legislation Amendment (Terrorism) Bill 2002* (13 March 2002) Part 5.3:100.1(2) 'Definitions': <http://search.aph.gov.au/search/ParlInfo.ASP?action=view&item=0&from=browse&path=Legislation/Current+Bills+byTitle/Security+Legislation+Amendment+(Terrorism)+Bill+2002+[No.+2]/Text+of+bill&items=1> – updated as the *Security Legislation Amendment (Terrorism) Act No. 65 2002 <http://scaletext.law.gov.nau/html/comact/11/6499/top.htm>.*
14. Timothy L. Thomas, *Deterring Asymmetric Terrorist Threats to Society in the Information Age* (Carlisle, PA: US Army War College Strategic Studies Inst. Oct. 2001).
15. Hansard, 29 March 2001:Column 1125.
16. Commission Of The European Communities, *Creating a Safer Information Society by Improving the Security of Information Infrastructures and Combating Computer-related Crime.* COM(2000) 890 final (26 Jan. 2001).
17. David S. Alberts, *Information Superiority and Network-Centric Warfare.* Presentation for Research and Strategic Planning, OASD (C3I), 19 June 2000.
18. <www.amsc.belvoir.army.mil/ecampus/pme/research/Prof_Articles/1997/asymmetric_warfare.htm>.

19. <www.zdnet.com/zdnn/stories/news/0,4586,2570175,00.html>.
20. This essay will not – except in passing and where it relates directly to 'terrorism' or 'war' – discuss cyber-crimes or criminal activities perpetrated using new technologies, whether in the form of old crimes (i.e. fraud) or new crimes (i.e. criminal threats to the information infrastructures themselves).
21. Canada (note 7) p. 12.
22. Joseph C. Cyrulik, 'Asymmetric Warfare and the Threat to the American Homeland', *Landpower Essay Series* 99–8 (Nov. 1999) – Institute of Land Warfare, Association of the US Army.
23. Canada (note 7) p. 12.
24. Cyrulik (note 22)
25. Canada (note 7)p. 12.
26. Andrew Rathmell, 'Controlling Computer Network Operations', *Information & Security Journal:* Special Issue on *The Internet and the Changing Face of International Relations and Security*: <www.nato.int/acad/fellow/99-01/rathmell.pdf>.
27. Government of the UK – Ministry of Defence, *Draft Doctrine for Information Operations; Joint Doctrine Pamphlet XX-01*. Joint Doctrine and Concepts Centre, Shrivenham (1 March 2001), p.8.
28. Center for Strategic and International Studies, *Asymmetric Warfare and Homeland Defense* (8 Dec. 2000), p.39.
29. John Arquilla, David Ronfeldt and Michele Zanini, 'Networks, Netwar and Information-Age Terrorism', in Ian O. Lesser, Bruce Hoffman, John Arquilla, Brian Jenkins, David Ronfeldt and Michele Zanini (eds.), *Countering the New Terrorism* (Santa Monica, CA: RAND 1999) p.47.
30. Wiliam M. Arkin, 'The Cyberbomb in Yugoslavia', *The Washington Post* (25 Oct. 1999).
31. 'Pentagon Sets Up New Center for Waging Cyberwarfare', *Military and C4I:* <www.infowar.com/MIL_C41/99/mil_c41_10000999a_j.shtml>, accessed 9 March 2000.
32. John A. Serabian, Jr, *Statement for the Record before the Joint Economic Committee on Cyber Threats and the U.S. Economy,* Central Intelligence Agency (23 Feb. 2000), Washington DC: <www.cia.gov/cia/public_affairs/speeches/archives/2000/cyberthreats_022300.html>.
33. Tim McDonald, 'CIA to Congress: We're Vulnerable to Cyber-Warfare', *NewsFactor Network* (22 June 2001):< www.osopinion.com/perl/story/11478.html>.
34. 'A doomsday cult's secret weapon: high tech', *Newsweek* (13 March 2000): <www.newsweek.com/nw-srv/printed/us/in/a17040-2000mar5.htm>.
35. Dan Verton, 'Report warns of al-Qaeda's potential cybercapabilities', *The New York Times* (4 Jan. 2002).
36. 'How al-Qaeda Spoofed the West – Bin Laden may have tricked spies: Officials say their intelligence pointed to an attack overseas', *Seattle Times* (12 Sept. 2001).
37. Cyber threats as defined by the Information Assurance Advisory Council (IAAC) Threat Assessment Working Group – see: <www.iaac.org.uk>.
38. Lia Brynjar, and Annika S Hansen, *An Analytical Framework for the Study of Terrorism and Asymmetric Warfare* (Kjeller: Norwegian Defence Research Establishment 1999) p.10.
39. Bruce Hoffman, *Inside Terrorism* (NY: Columbia UP 1998); and Ian O. Lesser *et al. Countering the New Terrorism* (note 29). Also see Walter Laqueur, *The New Terrorism: Fanaticism and the Arms of Mass Destruction* (Oxford and NY: OUP 1999).
40. John Arquilla and David Ronfeldt, *The Advent of Netwar* (National Defense Research Institute, Santa Monica: RAND 1996): 67–75; Richard Reeves, Nicole Veash and John Arlidge, 'Virtual Chaos Baffles Police', *The Observer* (20 June 1999).
41. Johan J Ingles-le Nobel, 'Cyberterrorism hype', *Jane's Intelligence Review* 11/12 (Dec. 1999).
42. <www.insightmag.com/archive/200002063.shtml>.
43. Ibid.
44. 'DOD Official Says Hackers Are More Sophisticated Since Solar Sunrise', *Hacker Sitings and News* (25 Oct. 1999): <www.infowar.com/hacker/99/hack_102599b_j.shtml>.
45. 'Chinese Hackers Invade 2 Official U.S. Web Sites', *The New York Time* (28 April 2001); 'Hackers Report a Truce', *Reuters* (10 May 2001).
46. Thomas (note 14).
47. 'National Security Adviser sees cyberterrorist threat', Associated Press (26 March 2001).
48. An overview of such activities is included in Andrew Rathmell and Kevin O'Brien (eds.), *Information Operations: A Global Perspective* (Coulsden, UK: Jane's Information Group 2000).

Conclusion: The Future of Terrorism Studies

THOMAS R. MOCKAITIS

No event since the collapse of Communism has prompted such intense scrutiny of the expert analyses that many felt should have predicted 9/11. How could the largest, most sophisticated and high-tech intelligence apparatus in the world have failed to predict the attack? Why was the US so unprepared to meet this manifestation of such a pervasive threat? Most of the finger pointing and claims of 'I told you so' have occurred within the intelligence community. The academy has not, however, been without its critics. Surely some of the many scholars ensconced in think-tanks, terrorism centers, and universities across the country might have seen the attack coming.

Beyond the recriminations, there has been little serious reassessment of the vast body of terrorist works pre- and post-9/11 to determine what insights remain useful and what new lessons have been learned (or at least identified). An anthology on terrorism such as this should fittingly end with a review of the literature that highlights recurrent themes, identifies significant works, and suggests possible directions for future research.

The devastating conventional attacks of 9/11 notwithstanding, weapons of mass destruction (WMD) continue to pose the greatest threat to states plagued by terrorism. For the past several years, researchers have focused on this threat, and nothing in the recent attacks has caused them to change their minds. Judith Miller, Stephen Engelberg, and William Broad had nearly completed *Germs: Biological Weapons and America's Secret War* (New York: Touchstone Books 2002) when the airplanes slammed into the Twin Towers. Published soon after the attack, their book made number one on the *New York Times* bestsellers' list. This disturbing account chronicles the origins and development of America's own biological weapons program. Ironically, the strains of anthrax and other pathogens now in the hands of rogue sates and possibly terrorist as well were grown in American laboratories. Baghdad purchased its strains from the US in what must be one of the best examples of 'blow back' in history.

More worrisome by far than the American program, Soviet germ warfare development actually effected a mass killing. Anthrax accidentally released into the air killed thousands in the Russian town of Sverdlovsk in the 1950s. Much of the old Soviet arsenal remains poorly guarded and perhaps has gone missing. Miller, Engelberg, and Broad conclude their chilling tale with an 'Afterward' on the 2001 anthrax incident. This very limited attack produced few casualties, but revealed the unpreparedness of the country to deal with such an outbreak.

Even before 9/11 analysts spoke of a 'new' terrorist threat when discussing WMD. Their works remain all too relevant. Nadine Gurr and Benjamin Cole, *The New Face of Terrorism: Threats from Weapons of Mass Destruction* (London: I.B. Tauris 2000) also concluded that the West is extremely vulnerable to biological as well as to chemical and nuclear attack, although the latter seems least likely of the three. Following discussion of the terrorism trends and the technical aspects of acquiring and using WMD, the authors provide a detailed analysis of the incentives and disincentives terrorists face in considering whether or not to use such weapons. Unfortunately, religious terrorists have shown the least restraint in using conventional means and can be expected to use the same abandon with nuclear, chemical, or biological weapons should they acquire them. The authors maintain that since the government cannot prevent all unconventional attacks, it should concentrate on mitigating their impact. The October 2001 anthrax incident demonstrated the wisdom of this recommendation and the failure of the US to heed it.

Noted security analyst Walter Laqueur, *The New Terrorism: Fanaticism and the Arms of Mass Destruction* (New York: Oxford University Press 1999) has also weighed in on the subject of terrorism and WMD. He shares the conclusions of Gurr and Cole that religiously motivated terrorism has become the most prevalent and the most dangerous threat to international peace and security. Written before 9/11, Laqueur's study points out that no great world religion is without fanatics willing to distort its theology to justify anything. The White supremacist Christian patriot movement and Jewish vigilantes in the occupied territories as well as Muslim extremists share a maniacal hatred of the 'other' and a ruthlessness uncharacteristic of leftist terrorists during the 1970s and 1980s. This willingness to inflict mass casualties on a demonized population and the ability to actually perpetrate such a holocaust will be a cause of grave concern for the years to come.

Current trends and future threats also worry Max Taylor and John Morgan, *The Future of Terrorism* (London and Portland, OR: Frank Cass 2000). This eclectic collection of articles and essays developed from a 1999 terrorism conference held at University College Cork, Ireland. Not surprisingly, WMD and the chaotic landscape of contemporary terrorism dominated discussion. This anthology contains articles on Romanian organized crime, European political extremism, and animal rights terrorism.

The authors maintain that discerning terrorists' motives remains the key to combating them, but they also assert that the nature of many organizations makes comprehending them particularly difficult. The various writers also tackle the 'newness' debate, with some stressing continuity and others the uniqueness of the contemporary security environment.

Discerning historical trends and persistent patterns in terrorist organizations and operations is crucial to combating them. Bruce Hoffman, *Inside Terrorism* (New York: Columbia 1998) remains one of the best comprehensive studies. Hoffman traces the evolution of terrorism throughout the twentieth century, recognizing a decided shift from locally based to international terrorism during the last few decades. He also provides a detailed analysis of terrorist organization and tactics. Christopher Harmon, *Terrorism Today* (London and Portland, OR: Frank Cass 2000) echoes many of Hoffman's conclusion. He also includes one thought-provoking chapter on popular misconceptions about terrorists and terrorism and another very useful chapter on countering terrorism.

How to effectively counter terrorism is, of course, what most practitioners hope to learn from the experts. Unfortunately, few really good works on the subject exist, and those must struggle to distill useful lessons from past, not wholly analogous examples. Yonah Alexander (ed.) *Combating Terrorism: Strategies of Ten Countries* (Ann Arbor: University of Michigan Press 2002) examines the successes and failures of states threatened by terrorism. The contributors examine counter-terrorism in the US, Argentina, Peru, Colombia, the UK, Japan, India, Israel, and Turkey. Unfortunately, since most of the counter-terrorism campaigns are on-going, the jury is still out on whether the methods of countries such as Turkey, India, or Israel can truly be deemed 'successful'. Only Peru can claim a clear-cut victory over a terrorist organization, Shining Path. Britain has enjoyed considerable success against the Provisional Irish Republican Army, but peace has come through compromise and the insurgents' realization that their goals may be better achieved through legitimate politics than through armed conflict. Still this volume contains a wealth of very useful information on the nature of terrorism and the variety of ways states can respond to it.

The September 11 attack has, not surprisingly, prompted a deluge of books, most of which offer little insight into the events. As with any crisis, journalist flock to the publishers with accounts based largely if not exclusively on secondary sources supplemented by their own reporting. Because these authors on the whole write much better than most academics, the public finds their works accessible and persuasive. Such works can be recognized by the grandiloquence of their titles and the weakness or absence of their documentation. The terrorist attack will, of course, take years to digest, and the veil of secrecy shrouding most documents hampers this generation of scholars. Despite this limitation, a few good books have already been written.

James F. Hoge Jr and Gideon Rose, editors of *Foreign Affairs,* pulled together a very useful anthology in short order. *How Did this Happen? Terrorism and the New War* (New York: Public Affairs 2001), contains 22 articles by former White House Officials, a Secretary of Defense, a retired general, and numerous scholars. Such an eclectic collection will undoubtedly contain essays of very uneven quality. However, many of the articles on homeland security, the Muslim world, and American foreign policy will remain timely and relevant for some time after 9/11. The sheer breadth of topics covered reveals the complexity of the 'war on terror' and serves as a sobering reminder that glib political rhetoric and facile journalism need to be corrected with serious scholarship.

Rohan Gunaratna, *Inside Al Qaeda: Global Network of Terror* (New York: Columbia University Press 2002) is easily the best of the post 9/11 works, no doubt because the author began his research well before the attacks. The author documents his work with an impressive array of evidence, including numerous interviews. In 1996 he had the unique privilege (or dubious honor) of interviewing Osama bin Laden himself. What emerges from such meticulous research is a detailed and revealing analysis of the Al Qaeda organization and its operations. Bin Laden also takes on flesh and blood in this account of his journey from wealthy Saudi engineering student to international terrorist. Gunaratna is perhaps the foremost authority on Al Qaeda. While the books discussed here represent but a sample of what has been published, they do reveal consistent themes and current gaps in the literature.

Virtually all of the authors consulted discerned a marked shift from the left wing, ideologically driven terrorism of the 1960s and 1970s to the right wing religiously motivated terrorism of the 1990s and beyond. They also noticed a disturbing increase in the lethality of terrorist attacks over the past two decades. Religious fanaticism tends to remove the restraints that have mitigated violence in the past. The desire for symbolic, high profile targets has not changed over the last century. The media revolution, particularly the Internet and satellite television, has, however, given terrorists a global audience and, as a result, magnified the impact of each incident. Everyone who studies this phenomenon, of course, worries about WMD, particularly biological ones. Germ warfare has the potential to be the deadliest form of terrorism. The virtual impossibility of defending countries as complex, vulnerable, and open as the US and its European allies intensifies this anxiety.

As prophets, the academics have proven no better than the intelligence community. Many of the pre-9/11 works knew of Osama bin Laden, but none commented on the Al Qaeda organization in depth, and some do not appear to have been aware of it at all. The terrorist organization succeeded in remaining below virtually everyone's radar for the first decade of its existence.

Since scholars lack the classified information available to the CIA and FBI, they may merit greater forgiveness than these organizations for failing to predict 9/11. Indeed, many analysts have criticized the shift from human intelligence to technological surveillance in the 1980s and 1990s. Satellites and spy planes did well enough locating Soviet missile batteries and tank divisions, but they have little use in tracking terrorist cells. Rebuilding a network of informers and agents around the world remains the most urgent, albeit the most sordid, of counter-terrorism tasks. Most experts remain silent on how precisely to develop such contacts.

The terrorism literature also says little about how to mount an effective hearts-and-minds campaign, a strategy which alone promises to develop at least some intelligence leads. Scholars of Islam and regional specialists (Middle East, South Asia) do not talk to each other enough. As a result persistent stereotypes, glib generalizations, and inaccurate assumptions about Islam and the Arab world underlie even the best terrorism research. The Al Qaeda attacks have produced no serious reassessment of US foreign policy nor even the recognition that the soft core of support surrounding bin Laden's extremists might have roots in legitimate grievances. Calls for change have been easily brushed aside with the cliché that any alteration of US goals amounts to 'giving in to terrorism?' Unfortunately, no counter-terrorism campaign has ever been won by military means alone.

Homeland Security, whatever that vague term means, also needs to be studied. Analysts have just begun to define the parameters of what promises to become a subfield of terrorism studies. Striking the balance between security and freedom is without a doubt the most urgent area of concern. Since 9/11 American has witnessed the most serious erosion of civil liberties since the internment of Japanese Americans during World War II. No compelling case has yet been made that the extraordinary powers of search, surveillance, and detention without trial will make any one safer. Considerable historical evidence suggests that such methods could prove counter-productive. Internment in Northern Ireland, for example, actually increased support for the IRA. Once again the human rights activists have weighed in on the ethical issues of the Patriot Act without being joined by the terrorism experts who might raise practical concerns about extra-legal methods.

The fragmentation of research is perhaps the most serious issue facing terrorist studies. Devising a strategy to counter this complex and pervasive threat will require a mustering of experts from a variety of fields. This need runs counter to the pervasive academic tendency to refine discourse into ever-narrower specialties. Also, research on terrorism must not be confined to the pages of esoteric journals. If ever there were a need for public scholars, it is now. Expert testimony in a variety of public forums can help dispel the exaggerated fear that stampedes an ill-informed electorate into supporting extreme measures that hurt only themselves.

Finally, good terrorism research requires breaking down the walls of rhetoric that have caused soldiers and scholars to view each other with suspicion if not disdain. The two have much to say to each other if they can only find a common language. In any event, there is plenty of work for all of us to do. In considering the challenge posed to the field of terrorism studies by the events of 9/11, I am reminded of the old Chinese curse: 'May you live in interesting times.' Indeed we do.

Abstracts

Winning Hearts and Minds in the 'War on Terrorism'

Thomas R. Mockaitis

Ten days after the attacks on the World Trade Center and Pentagon US President George W. Bush addressed a joint session of Congress. In an emotional speech he declared war on terrorism and vowed that the US would not rest until all of the perpetrators were brought to justice and Al Qaeda destroyed. In virtually the next breath he hastened to add that the US-led campaign would not be a war on Islam, a promise Muslims might have found more reassuring had the President not sounded so much like a Baptist preacher. Whatever its propaganda value, the speech distorted the reality of the struggle facing the West while tacitly acknowledging an important truth. Since terror is merely a weapon in a larger struggle, there can be no war on terrorism per se. The West faces a counterinsurgency campaign on a global scale. Winning the hearts and minds of disaffected people in lands where terrorism thrives must be central to conducting this campaign.

Al Qaeda and the Radical Islamic Challenge to Western Strategy

Paul Rich

The September 11 global crisis prompted by the attacks on the World Trade Center and the Pentagon raises major questions concerning the nature and trajectory of terrorism in the post-Cold War global order. Hitherto, terrorism has been largely debated by analysts at the level of nation states. Terrorist and insurgent movements have also been largely anchored in nationalist and ethnic power bases even when they have sought to mobilise a transnational ideological appeal on religious or class grounds. There have been a few exceptions to this pattern such as the alliance between the German Baader-Meinhof group and the Japanese Red Army Faction, but even such international alliances as this did not, until at least the 1980s, presage anything like a global terrorist network necessitating a global strategic response. This study examines terrorism and global strategic responses.

Operation 'Enduring Freedom': A Victory for a Conventional Force Fighting an Unconventional War

Warren Chin

The track record of the US military in unconventional wars has not been good and there were fears that Operation 'Enduring Freedom' might suffer the same fate as previous campaigns. This contribution explores why the Taliban were defeated so easily by the US in 2001. It challenges the view that America's victory was due solely to changes in its modus operandi or that the outcome heralds a change in the fortunes of the US when fighting unconventional war. It also questions the idea that America's victory was a consequence of Taliban incompetence. Instead, it explains the defeat of the Taliban in terms of the prevailing political conditions within Afghanistan, which made them vulnerable to attack. The essay concludes that current political circumstances could, in the long run, permit the resurrection of the Taliban and undermine the US-led coalition's victory.

United States Special Operations Forces and the War on Terrorism

Anna Simons and David Tucker

Those leading the war on terrorism have emphasized from the beginning that this war would be unlike other wars. Special Operations Forces (SOF) are military forces unlike other military forces. The implication is that SOF and the war on terrorism are thus made for each other. This contribution examines this assumption, the war on terrorism and SOF in greater detail.

Warfare by Other Means: Special Forces, Terrorism and Grand Strategy

Alastair Finlan

This contribution looks at the role of Special Forces in anti-terrorist operations with particular emphasis on the British Special Air Service. It argues that Special Forces have played a pivotal role in such operations since the era of Palestinian terrorism in the early 1970s. The essay looks at the operations in Afghanistan leading to the overthrow of the Taliban in 2001 and shows that the seven Special Forces involved there proved crucial to the success of the limited ground forces. In particular they served a valuable force multiplier by acting as a nexus between the regional warlords and the use of air power as well as mobile strike units against fortified Al Qaeda and Taliban positions. In the latter instance their success was mixed, involving attacks on difficult cave hideouts, though overall it can be concluded that Special Forces have demonstrated their capacity in fighting unconventional warfare against mobile and transnational terrorist groupings.

Muslims, Islamists, and the Cold War
Ghada Hashem Talhami

A new devil has emerged to challenge Western values and public virtue, and ever so conveniently, the devil masqueraded in religious garb. Terrorism has become synonymous with Islamic fundamentalism if not with Islam itself, and a new iron wall has descended on the world, as Churchill said, separating East from West, Christendom from Islam. This study examines the question why US policy makers feel a persistent urge to draw foreign policy in moralistic terms and religious metaphor, often to their own detriment.

An Ambivalent War: Russia's War on Terrorism
Stephen Blank

Since 9/11 the Russian Federation has professed strong support for the US war on terrorism and claimed to be Washington's most reliable ally in its victory over Afghanistan. Closer examination of Russian actions, however, reveals a consistently ambivalent approach to combating international terrorism. Russian actions in Chechnya and elsewhere are better understood in terms of traditional interests unchanged since Soviet times. Domestic considerations too have sometimes dictated Russian actions. Moscow will use the conflict in Chechnya to divert attention from problems at home. Even were the Russian Federation willing to pursue a more consistent and aggressive policy toward terrorism, its security forces lack the capability to do so effectively. The current reorganization of Russian armed forces does not promise to improve this situation.

11 September 2001 and the Media
Philip Towle

The attacks on the Twin Towers and the Pentagon on 11 September 2001 went beyond the culminating point of victory, pushed the US into declaring war on its enemies, and immediately united sections of the elite media across the world in horrified denunciation of the terrorists. The various national media usually react very differently to major international events, interpreting them according to their national interests and dispositions. However, until President Bush's State of the Union address at the end of January 2002 criticised the so-called axis of evil, condemnation of the attacks and sympathy for the US largely united those sections of the elite media in Japan, Britain, Pakistan and India, which are the subject of this essay.

Bringing It All Back Home: Hollywood Returns To War

Susan L. Carruthers

This essay looks at two Hollywood films *Black Hawk Down* and *We Were Soldiers* as reflective of a more general popular mood in the US that accompanied Operation 'Enduring Freedom' and the removal of the Taliban regime in Afghanistan. In part this mood was a militaristic one, though this can also be seen as a rather belated response by Hollywood to invest moral purpose in the US military following an earlier spate of hostile Vietnam war films. The two films examined are different in form: *Black Hawk Down* is a combat film about extraction while *We Were Soldiers* is unusual for a US Vietnam war film for investing moral purpose in both the US combat troops as well as the Vietnamese enemy. Overall it is possible to conclude that both films contribute to a kicking by Hollywood of its earlier Vietnam war 'syndrome' which is likely to have wider cultural and political repercussions.

Information Age, Terrorism and Warfare

Kevin A. O'Brien

This essay will discuss two of the key pillars of asymmetry: notably Information Operations and terrorism, including the links between the two. While a great deal changed on 11 September 2001, one thing that has not changed in substance is the challenge of protecting the Information Society, notably from cyber-threats. Although the immediate threat to Western societies is from the physical and possibly bio-weapons favoured by Al Qaeda and its associates, it is time now to prepare for future threats to the information society, including cyber-threats.

About the Contributors

Stephen Blank has served as the US Army War College's Strategic Studies Institute's expert on the Soviet bloc and the post-Soviet world since 1989. Prior to that he was Associate Professor of Soviet Studies at the Center for Aerospace Doctrine, Research, and Education, Maxwell Air Force Base, and taught at the University of Texas, San Antonio, and at the University of California, Riverside. Dr Blank is the editor of *Imperial Decline: Russia's Changing Position in Asia*, co-editor of *Soviet Military and the Future*, and author of *The Sorcerer as Apprentice: Stalin's Commissariat of Nationalities, 1917–1924*. He has also written numerous articles on the Russian CIS and Eastern European security issues.

Susan L. Carruthers is an Associate Professor of History at Rutgers University, New Jersey, specialising in the United States and the World. Her research concentrates on the intersection of culture and international politics. She has published widely in this field, including two books, *Winning Hearts and Minds: British Governments, the Media and Colonial Counterinsurgency* (1995) and, most recently, *The Media at War* (2000).

Warren Chin currently lectures in Defence Studies at the Joint Services Command and Staff College and the Royal College of Defence Studies. He was also a lecturer in War Studies at the Royal Military Academy Sandhurst. He specialises in the study of war and in particular military theory and the revolution in military affairs.

Alastair Finlan teaches at the American University in Cairo. Prior to this, he was a Senior Lecturer in the Department of Strategic Studies and International Affairs at Britannia Royal Naval College, of which he is now an Associate Senior Lecturer. He also has lectured at the Universities of Keele and Plymouth.

Thomas R. Mockaitis is Professor of European History at DePaul University. He has written three books and numerous articles on insurgency, peace operations, and terrorism. His most recent book, *Peace Operations and Intrastate Conflict: the Sword or the Olive Branch?* (1999) examines the challenges of intervention in civil wars. He has given presentations at military colleges in the US, Britain,

Canada, and Austria. Professor Mockaitis has spoken to numerous and diverse audiences since 9/11 and is a frequent terrorism commentator on television and radio. He is book reviews editor for *Small Wars and Insurgencies.*

Kevin A. O'Brien is a Senior Policy Analyst with RAND Europe, based in Cambridge, UK; previously, he served as the Deputy Director of the International Centre for Security Analysis and a Visiting Fellow – teaching and researching in intelligence studies – in the Department of War Studies, King's College London. He has published widely on intelligence and security issues, as well as on the continuing transformation of national security structures and operations in the post-Soviet era, especially with regard to information operations and asymmetric warfare strategies – including terrorism.

Paul B. Rich is currently a Visiting Research Fellow at the Centre of International Studies, University of Cambridge. He is the joint editor of *Small Wars and Insurgencies* and is the author of studies on terrorism, sub-state conflict and warlordism including *The Counter Insurgent State* and *Warlords and International Relations.* He is currently working on a longer term research project on the strategic aspects of contemporary terrorism.

Anna Simons is an Associate Professor of Defense Analysis at the US Naval Postgraduate School, where she specialises in ethnic conflict, military anthropology, and special operations. She has written three books and several articles, including, *The Company They Keep: Life Inside the U.S. Army Special Forces* (1998). Before coming to the NPS, Dr Simons taught at the University of California, Los Angeles.

Ghada Hashem Talhami, is D. K. Pearsons Professor of Politics at Lake Forest College, Illinois, where she teaches courses on the Middle East, Third World Development and Women in the Third World. She is the past editor of *Arab Studies Quarterly*, and is on the board of editors of *Muslim World.* She has recently been named to the editorial board of *Alternatives: Turkish Journal of International Relations* and to the board of the Center for American and European Studies in Amman, Jordan. She has written four books and over 40 articles on the Middle East. Her fifth book, *The Palestinian Refugees: Pawns to Political Actors* is forthcoming.

Philip Towle is Reader in International Relations at the Centre of

International Studies, University of Cambridge, where he has taught for the last 20 years. His most recent publications are *Enforced Disarmament from the Napoleonic Campaigns to the Gulf War* (1997), *Democracy and Peacemaking* (2000) and (co-edited with Margaret Kosuge and Yoichi Kibata) *Prisoners of War* (2000).

David C. Tucker is Associate Professor, Department of Defense Analysis, US Naval Postgraduate School. He has written two books and several articles on terrorism and unconventional war, including *Skirmishes at the Edge of Empire, the United States and International Terrorism* (1997). Prior to joining the faculty of the NPS, Dr Tucker served as Deputy Director, Special Operations, Office of the Assistant Secretary of Defense, Special Operations and Low-Intensity Conflict.

Index